PROPORTIONALITY AND JUDICIAL ACTIVISM

The principle of proportionality is currently one of the most discussed topics in the field of comparative constitutional law. Many critics claim that courts use the proportionality test as an instrument of judicial self-empowerment. *Proportionality and Judicial Activism* tests this hypothesis empirically; it systematically and comparatively analyses the fundamental rights jurisprudence of the Canadian Supreme Court, the German Federal Constitutional Court and the South African Constitutional Court. The book shows that the proportionality test does give judges a considerable amount of discretion. However, this analytical openness does not necessarily lead to judicial activism. Instead, judges are faced with significant institutional constraints, as a result of which, all three examined courts refrain from using proportionality for purposes of judicial activism.

NIELS PETERSEN is Professor of Public Law, International Law and EU Law at the University of Münster, Germany. He is the author of a number of articles published in leading comparative constitutional law journals.

PROPORTIONALITY AND JUDICIAL ACTIVISM

Fundamental Rights Adjudication in Canada, Germany and South Africa

NIELS PETERSEN
University of Münster, Germany

CAMBRIDGE
UNIVERSITY PRESS

CAMBRIDGE
UNIVERSITY PRESS

University Printing House, Cambridge CB2 8BS, United Kingdom
One Liberty Plaza, 20th Floor, New York, NY 10006, USA
477 Williamstown Road, Port Melbourne, VIC 3207, Australia
4843/24, 2nd Floor, Ansari Road, Daryaganj, Delhi – 110002, India
79 Anson Road, #06-04/06, Singapore 079906

Cambridge University Press is part of the University of Cambridge.

It furthers the University's mission by disseminating knowledge in the pursuit of education, learning, and research at the highest international levels of excellence.

www.cambridge.org
Information on this title: www.cambridge.org/9781107177987

10.1017/9781316823330

First published 2017

A catalogue record for this publication is available from the British Library.

Library of Congress Cataloging-in-Publication Data
Names: Petersen, Niels, author.
Title: Proportionality and judicial activism: fundamental rights adjudication in Canada, Germany and South Africa / Niels Petersen, Professor of Public Law, International Law and EU Law, University of Münster – Faculty of Law.
Description: Cambridge, United Kingdom; New York, NY, USA: Cambridge University Press, 2017. | Based on author's thesis (Habilitation – Universität, Bonn, 2012) issued under title: Verhältnismässigkeit als Rationalitätskontrolle: eine rechtsempirische Studie verfassungsrechtlicher Rechtsprechung zu den Freiheitsgrundrechten. | Includes bibliographical references and index.
Identifiers: LCCN 2016058544 | ISBN 9781107177987 (hardback)
Subjects: LCSH: Political questions and judicial power – Canada. | Political questions and judicial power – Germany. | Political questions and judicial power – South Africa. | Proportionality in law – Canada. | Proportionality in law – Germany. | Proportionality in law – South Africa. | Court of last resort – Canada. | Court of last resort – Germany. | Court of last resort – South Africa.
Classification: LCC K3367.P48 2017 | DDC 342.08/5–dc23
LC record available at https://lccn.loc.gov/2016058544

ISBN 978-1-107-17798-7 Hardback

For Salwa

CONTENTS

ACKNOWLEDGEMENTS

The book is the result of my postdoctoral research, which was formally approved as a postdoctoral thesis (*Habilitation*) by the law faculty of the University of Bonn. For this reason, the main thesis of my research was first published in German under the title *Verhältnismäßigkeit als Rationalitätskontrolle* (2015). However, this book is not a mere translation of the German manuscript. Instead, the presentation of the argument was changed and condensed considerably.

The work on this book was an intellectual journey. When I embarked on the journey, I did not know where it would take me. The book looks now very different than I imagined it when I first started to think about the topic in 2008. Many people showed me directions and shaped my thinking. Christoph Engel gave me an intellectual home at the Max Planck Institute for Research on Collective Goods. He showed me that legal research is not just a normative enterprise and introduced me to empirical perspectives on the law, which fundamentally shaped the research question of this book. I could not have found a better place for my postdoctoral research than the Max Planck Institute because it provided me both intellectual freedom and stimulation.

Samuel Issacharoff originally gave me the idea for this research project and was a wonderful mentor during the time that I worked on the book. His remarks and suggestions always showed my ideas the right direction. Joseph Weiler's advice to take advantage of the opportunity of postdoctoral research to seek an intellectual transformation was very significant for the route that the journey took. Moreover, I could always count on his support and guidance. Emanuel Towfigh accompanied me for most of the journey not just as a close colleague but also as an invaluable friend.

I had wonderful and stimulating discussions with many people about different aspects of the book. Among them are Or Bassok, Jochen von Bernstorff, David Bilchitz, Armin von Bogdandy, Gráinne de Búrca, Bruce Cain, Sujit Choudhry, Paul Craig, Barry Friedman, Stephen Gardbaum,

Dieter Grimm, Christian Hillgruber, Pascal Langenbach, Valéria Guimarães de Lima e Silva, Koos Malan, Jud Mathews, Gianluca Parolin, Pasquale Pasquino, Lourens du Plessis, Catherine O'Regan, Arie Rosen, Wojciech Sadurski, Re'em Segev, Indra Spiecker gen. Döhmann, François Venter, and Erika de Wet.

Although the main thesis of this book is presented for the first time in English, some of the ideas expressed in this book have previously been developed in individual articles. The main argument of Chapter 2 was based on my article 'How to Compare the Length of Lines to the Weight of Stones – Balancing and the Resolution of Value Conflicts in Constitutional Law', 14 *German Law Journal* 1387–1408 (2013). The conceptual framework developed in Chapter 3 and the findings related to the German Constitutional Court in Chapter 4 have previously been published in my article, 'Balancing and Judicial Self-Empowerment: A Case Study on the Rise of Balancing in the Jurisprudence of the German Federal Constitutional Court', 4 *Global Constitutionalism* 49–80 (2015). Finally, some of the results regarding the South African Constitutional Court in Chapters 4 and 5 can already be found in 'Proportionality and the Incommensurability Challenge in the Jurisprudence of the South African Constitutional Court', 30 *South African Journal on Human Rights* 405–429 (2014).

This book is dedicated to my wife Salwa, the most precious gift that life could have made me.

Introduction

The Catholic Church has always played a pivotal role in the cultural life of Bavaria. Bavaria is the German state with the second-highest percentage of Catholics, and the influence of the church becomes visible in various public institutions. For a long time, an ordinance of the Bavarian government instructed all schools to display a crucifix on a wall of each classroom. These crucifixes were, collectively, the centrepiece of one of the most controversial judgments that the German Federal Constitutional Court has ever issued. The complaint of the parents of two Bavarian schoolchildren gave rise to the dispute. The applicants adhered to an anthroposophical conviction and argued that the display of crucifixes had a religious influence on their children that ran counter to their own conviction.

In its judgment, the Federal Constitutional Court affirmed the position of the applicants.[1] The judges held that the obligation to display crucifixes in classrooms violated the negative freedom of religion of the applicants. Consequently, they overturned the challenged Bavarian ordinance. The judges thought that they had taken a routine decision that was, in their eyes, a logical consequence of their jurisprudence on the separation of state and church that the court had developed previously.[2] They were all the more taken aback by what followed. The decision caused huge public outrage.[3] Some politicians openly advocated disregarding the judgment,[4]

1 Entscheidungen des Bundesverfassungsgerichts [BVerfGE] vol. 93, p. 1.

2 See Georg Vanberg, *The Politics of Constitutional Review in Germany* (Cambridge: Cambridge University Press, 2005), p. 126; Uwe Kranenpohl, 'Die Bedeutung von Interpretationsmethoden und Dogmatik in der Entscheidungspraxis des Bundesverfassungsgerichts' (2009) 49 *Der Staat* 387–409 at 406.

3 Vanberg, *Politics of Constitutional Review*, p. 3; Justin Collings, *Democracy's Guardians: A History of the German Federal Constitutional Court 1951–2001* (Oxford: Oxford University Press, 2015), pp. 262–6.

4 Gary S. Schaal, 'Crisis! What Crisis? Der "Kruzifix-Beschluss" und seine Folgen', in Robert Christian van Ooyen and Martin H.W. Möllers (eds.), *Das Bundesverfassungsgericht im politischen System* (Wiesbaden: V. S. Verlag für Sozialwissenschaften, 2006), pp. 175–86 at 175.

and Bavaria only made half-hearted efforts to implement the decision.[5] Furthermore, the decision induced an intensive debate in the legal and political-science scholarship on a potential legitimacy crisis of the German Constitutional Court.[6]

At a different level, the judgment was also grist for the mill of some prominent critics of the German Constitutional Court. The individual rights jurisprudence of the court has a two-step structure. At the first step, the court determines whether an individual right has been restricted and, at the second step, whether such a restriction can be justified. The core of the justification analysis is the proportionality test. According to this test, a measure restricting an individual right is proportionate if it pursues a legitimate purpose, if the measure is rationally connected to the purpose, if it is the least restrictive of all equally effective means, and if it is not disproportionate in the strict sense.

The most important step in the practice of the court is the last one.[7] In principle, this balancing test amounts to a cost–benefit analysis, in

[5] Neue Zürcher Zeitung, 16 December 1995 (cited in Vanberg, *Politics of Constitutional Review*, p. 4).

[6] See Josef Isensee, 'Bundesverfassungsgericht – quo vadis?' (1996) 51 *Juristenzeitung* 1085–93; Ulrich Haltern, 'Demokratische Verantwortlichkeit und Verfassungsgerichtsbarkeit' (1996) 35 *Der Staat* 551–80 at 552–3; Helmuth Schulze-Fielitz, 'Das Bundesverfassungsgericht in der Krise des Zeitgeists – Zur Metadogmatik der Verfassungsinterpretation' (1997) 122 *Archiv des öffentlichen Rechts* 1–31 at 2–3; Wolfgang Knies, 'Auf dem Weg in den "verfassungsgerichtlichen Jurisdiktionsstaat"?', in Joachim Burmeister (ed.), *Verfassungsstaatlich keit: Festschrift für Klaus Stern* (München: C. H. Beck, 1997), pp. 1155–82 at 1156–7; Udo Di Fabio, *Das Recht offener Staaten* (Tübingen: J. C. B. Mohr, 1998), p. 66; Otfried Höffe, 'Wieviel Politik ist dem Verfassungsgericht erlaubt?' (1999) 38 *Der Staat* 171–93 at 171.

[7] Fritz Ossenbühl, 'Abwägung im Verfassungsrecht' (1995) 110 *Deutsches Verwaltungsblatt* 904–12 at 906; Isensee, 'Bundesverfassungsgericht', 1090; Hartmut Schiedermair, 'Das Bundesverfassungsgericht auf der Grenze zwischen Recht und Politik', in Michael Brenner, Peter Michael Huber and Markus Möstl (eds.), *Der Staat des Grundgesetzes – Kontinuität und Wandel: Festschrift für Peter Badura* (Tübingen: Mohr Siebeck, 2004), pp. 477–89 at 483; Franz Josef Lindner, *Theorie der Grundrechtsdogmatik* (Tübingen: Mohr Siebeck, 2005), p. 217; Donald P. Kommers, 'Germany: Balancing Rights and Duties', in Jeffrey Goldsworthy (ed.), *Interpreting Constitutions* (Oxford: Oxford University Press, 2006), pp. 161–214 at 202; Dieter Grimm, 'Proportionality in Canadian and German Jurisprudence' (2007) 57 *University of Toronto Law Journal* 383–97 at 393; Moshe Cohen-Eliya and Iddo Porat, 'The Hidden Foreign Law Debate in *Heller*: The Proportionality Approach in American Constitutional Law' (2009) 46 *San Diego Law Review* 367–413 at 399; Matthias Jestaedt, 'Phänomen Bundesverfassungsgericht: Was das Gericht zu dem macht, was es ist', in Matthias Jestaedt et al. (eds.), *Das entgrenzte Gericht: Eine kritische Bilanz nach sechzig Jahren Bundesverfassungsgericht* (Berlin: Suhrkamp, 2011), pp. 77–157 at 146; Oliver Lepsius, 'Die maßstabsetzende Gewalt', in Matthias Jestaedt et al. (eds.), *Das entgrenzte Gericht: Eine kritische Bilanz nach sechzig Jahren Bundesverfassungsgericht* (Berlin: Suhrkamp, 2011), pp. 159–279 at 206–7; Claus Dieter Classen, 'Das Prinzip der

which the court balances the benefits for the public purpose against the costs for the restricted individual right.[8] However, this last step has also been subject to severe criticism by legal scholars across national borders.[9]

Verhältnismäßigkeit im Spiegel europäischer Rechtsentwicklungen', in Michael Sachs and Helmut Siekmann (eds.), *Der grundrechtsgeprägte Verfassungsstaat: Festschrift für Klaus Stern* (Berlin: Duncker & Humblot, 2012), pp. 651–67 at 652; Gertrude Lübbe-Wolff, 'The Principle of Proportionality in the Case-Law of the German Federal Constitutional Court' (2014) 34 *Human Rights Law Journal* 12–7 at 15; Niels Petersen, 'Balancing and Judicial Self-Empowerment: A Case Study on the Rise of Balancing in the Jurisprudence of the German Constitutional Court' (2015) 4 *Global Constitutionalism* 49–80 at 65; Michaela Hailbronner, *Traditions and Transformations: The Rise of German Constitutionalism* (Oxford: Oxford University Press, 2015), p. 118.

8 Anne van Aaken, *'Rational Choice' in der Rechtswissenschaft: Zum Stellenwert der ökonomischen Theorie im Recht* (Baden-Baden: Nomos, 2003), p. 330; Christoph Knill and Florian Becker, 'Divergenz trotz Diffusion? – Rechtsvergleichende Aspekte des Verhältnismäßigkeitsprinzips in Deutschland, Großbritannien und der Europäischen Union' (2003) 36 *Die Verwaltung* 447–81 at 458; Julian Rivers, 'Proportionality and Variable Intensity of Review' (2006) 65 *Cambridge Law Journal* 174–207 at 180; Christoph Engel, 'Öffentliches Wirtschaftsrecht aus Sicht der ökonomischen Theorie', in Dirk Ehlers, Michael Fehling and Hermann Pünder (eds.), *Besonderes Verwaltungsrecht. Band I: Öffentliches Wirtschaftsrecht* (Heidelberg: C.F. Müller, 3rd edn, 2012), pp. 40–62 at para. 52; Patricia Popelier, 'Preliminary Comments on the Role of Courts as Regulatory Watchdogs' (2012) 6 *Legisprudence* 257–70 at 262; Aurelien Portuese, 'Principle of Proportionality as Principle of Economic Efficiency' (2013) 19 *European Law Journal* 612–35 at 620.

9 See, e.g., Ernst Forsthoff, *Der Staat in der Industriegesellschaft* (München: C. H. Beck, 2nd edn, 1971), pp. 137–42; Bernhard Schlink, *Abwägung im Verfassungsrecht* (Berlin: Duncker & Humblot, 1976); Karl August Bettermann, *Hypertrophie der Grundrechte* (Hamburg: Hamburgischer Anwaltverein, 1984), p. 4; T. Alexander Aleinikoff, 'Constitutional Law in the Age of Balancing' (1987) 96 *Yale Law Journal* 943–1005; Peter W. Hogg, 'Section 1 Revisited' (1991) 1 *National Journal of Constitutional Law* 1–24 at 23–4; Jürgen Habermas, *Between Facts and Norms: Contributions to a Discourse Theory of Law and Democracy* (William Rehg trl., Cambridge: Polity Press, 1996), pp. 253–61; Stuart Woolman, 'Out of Order? Out of Balance? The Limitation Clause of the Final Constitution' (1997) 13 *South African Journal on Human Rights* 102–34 at 114–21; Walter Leisner, *Der Abwägungsstaat – Verhältnismäßigkeit als Gerechtigkeit?* (Berlin: Duncker & Humblot, 1997); Matthias Jestaedt, *Grundrechtsentfaltung im Gesetz: Studien zur Interdependenz von Grundrechtsdogmatik und Rechtsgewinnungstheorie* (Tübingen: Mohr Siebeck, 1999), p. 206–60; Loammi Blaauw-Wolf, 'The 'Balancing of Interests' with Reference to the Principle of Proportionality and the Doctrine of *Güterabwägung* – A Comparative Analysis' (1999) 14 *SA Public Law* 178–214 at 210; Bernhard Schlink, 'Der Grundsatz der Verhältnismäßigkeit', in Peter Badura and Horst Dreier (eds.), *Festschrift 50 Jahre Bundesverfassungsgericht. Zweiter Band: Klärung und Fortbildung des Verfassungsrechts* (Tübingen: Mohr Siebeck, 2001), pp. 445–65; Henk Botha, 'Rights, Limitations, and the (Im)possibility of Self-Government', in Henk Botha, André van der Walt and Johan van der Walt (eds.), *Rights and Democracy in a Transformative Constitution* (Stellenbosch: Sun Press, 2003), pp. 13–31 at 21–3; Ernst-Wolfgang Böckenförde, 'Schutzbereich, Eingriff, verfassungsimmanente Schranken: Zur Kritik gegenwärtiger Grundrechtsdogmatik' (2003) 42 *Der Staat* 165–92 at 190; Karl-Heinz Ladeur, *Kritik der Abwägung in der Grundrechtsdogmatik* (Tübingen: Mohr Siebeck, 2004);

Critics argue that the balancing test required the comparison of incommensurable values and thus lacked a 'rational' standard of comparison.[10] For this reason, balancing is considered an instrument of political rather than of legal decision-making.[11] Some authors even claim that courts use

Jeremy T. Gunn, 'Deconstructing Proportionality in Limitations Analysis' (2005) 19 *Emory International Law Review* 465–98; Frank Raue, 'Müssen Grundrechtsbeschränkungen wirklich verhältnismäßig sein?' (2006) 131 *Archiv des öffentlichen Rechts* 79–116; Basak Çali, 'Balancing Human Rights? Methodological Problems with Weights, Scales and Proportions' (2007) 29 *Human Rights Quarterly* 251–70; Matthias Jestaedt, 'Die Abwägungslehre – ihre Stärken und ihre Schwächen', in Otto Depenheuer et al. (eds.), *Staat im Wort – Festschrift für Josef Isensee* (Heidelberg: C. F. Müller, 2007), pp. 253–75 at 260–75; Stuart Woolman and Henk Botha, 'Limitations: Shared Constitutional Interpretation, an Appropriate Normative Framework & Hard Choices', in Stu Woolman and Michael Bishop (eds.), *Constitutional Conversations* (Pretoria: Pretoria University Law Press, 2008), pp. 149–86 at 157–60; Ralph Christensen and Kent D. Lerch, 'Dass das Ganze das Wahre ist, ist nicht ganz unwahr' (2007) 62 *Juristenzeitung* 438–44; Andreas Fischer-Lescano, 'Kritik der praktischen Konkordanz' (2008) 41 *Kritische Justiz* 166–77; Iddo Porat, 'Some Critical Thoughts on Proportionality', in Giorgio Bongiovanni, Giovanni Sartor and Chiara Valentini (eds.), *Reasonableness and Law* (Dordrecht: Springer, 2009), pp. 243–50; Stavros Tsakyrakis, 'Proportionality: An Assault on Human Rights?' (2009) 7 *International Journal of Constitutional Law* 468–93; Grégoire C.N. Webber, *The Negotiable Constitution* (Cambridge: Cambridge University Press, 2009), pp. 87–115; Benjamin Rusteberg, *Der grundrechtliche Gewährleistungsgehalt* (Tübingen: Mohr Siebeck, 2009), pp. 64–76; Davor Susnjar, *Proportionality, Fundamental Rights, and Balance of Powers* (Leiden: Martinus Nijhoff, 2010); Grégoire C. N. Webber, 'Proportionality, Balancing, and the Cult of Constitutional Rights Scholarship' (2010) 23 *Canadian Journal of Law and Jurisprudence* 179–202 at 194–8; Juliano Zaiden Benvindo, *On the Limits of Constitutional Adjudication. Deconstructing Balancing and Judicial Activism* (Berlin: Springer, 2010); Jochen von Bernstorff, 'Kerngehaltsschutz durch den UN-Menschenrechtsausschuss und den EGMR: Vom Wert kategorialer Argumentationsformen' (2011) 50 *Der Staat* 165–90 at 184–90; Christian Hillgruber, 'Ohne rechtes Maß? Eine Kritik der Rechtsprechung des Bundesverfassungsgerichts nach 60 Jahren' (2011) 66 *Juristenzeitung* 861–71 at 862–3; José Juan Moreso, 'Ways of Solving Conflicts of Constitutional Rights: Proportionalism and Specificationism' (2012) 25 *Ratio Juris* 31–46; Philip Sales, 'Rationality, Proportionality and the Development of the Law' (2013) 129 *Law Quarterly Review* 223–41; Renata Camilo de Oliveira, *Zur Kritik der Abwägung in der Grundrechtsdogmatik* (Berlin: Duncker & Humblot, 2013); Jochen von Bernstorff, 'Proportionality without Balancing – Why Judicial *Ad Hoc*-Balancing Is Unnecessary and Potentially Detrimental to the Realization of Individual and Collective Self-determination', in Liora Lazarus, Christopher McCrudden and Nigel Bowles (eds.), *Reasoning Rights: Comparative Judicial Engagement* (Oxford: Hart, 2014), pp. 63–86; Philipp Reimer, 'Verhältnismäßigkeit im Verfassungsrecht, ein heterogenes Konzept', in Matthias Jestaedt and Oliver Lepsius (eds.), *Verhältnismäßigkeit: Zur Tragfähigkeit eines verfassungsrechtlichen Schlüsselkonzepts* (Tübingen: Mohr Siebeck, 2015), pp. 60–76 at 68–70.

10 See, in particular, Habermas, *Facts and Norms*, p. 259.

11 Schlink, *Abwägung*, p. 190; Ernst-Wolfgang Böckenförde, *Zur Lage der Grundrechtsdogmatik nach 40 Jahren Grundgesetz* (München: Carl Friedrich von Siemens Stiftung, 1989), p. 54; Schlink, 'Grundsatz der Verhältnismäßigkeit', p. 461; Webber, *Negotiable Constitution*, pp. 147–8; Hillgruber, 'Ohne rechtes Maß? Eine Kritik der Rechtsprechung des

balancing as a tool to acquire political power.[12] It thus becomes a Trojan horse for judicial activism in legal decision-making.

The crucifix decision of the Federal Constitutional Court seems to affirm this position. The court had based its reasoning on a balancing of the competing values at stake.[13] It argued that the display of crucifixes in classrooms restricted the negative religious freedom of the applicants. In the justification analysis, it balanced this negative religious freedom against the positive religious freedom of the majority of Bavarians and the educational mandate of the state.[14] On the one hand, the court found that the negative freedom of the applicants was severely impaired because displaying a crucifix in the classroom 'represses the sentiments of believers of a different faith'.[15] On the other hand, it argued that the right to display crucifixes in classrooms affected the positive religious freedom of the majority only marginally: 'The idea of tolerance for believers of a different faith is a central part of Christianity as a cultural factor.'[16]

With this evaluation of the competing rights, the result of the balancing test was quasi-automatic: Only the negative religious freedom of the applicants could prevail. However, this conclusion is not imperative. The cross is not just a religious symbol, but also an expression of the cultural self-perception of a community.[17] Consequently, the assumption that the display of a crucifix in a classroom constitutes a severe impairment of the religious freedom of believers of a different faith can be challenged with good reasons. Had the court made a different evaluation of the competing positions, it may well have come to a different result in its balancing test.

Bundesverfassungsgerichts nach 60 Jahren', 862; Sales, 'Rationality', 225; Camilo de Oliveira, *Kritik der Abwägung*, pp. 223–31; von Bernstorff, 'Proportionality without balancing', p. 66.

[12] Ulrich Haltern, 'Integration als Mythos. Zur Überforderung des Bundesverfassungsgerichts' (1997) 45 *Jahrbuch des öffentlichen Rechts der Gegenwart* 31–88 at 69; Leisner, *Abwägungsstaat*, pp. 170–3; Christensen and Lerch, 'Dass das Ganze das Wahre ist', 440; Classen, 'Verhältnismäßigkeit', p. 653; Benvindo, *Limits of Constitutional Adjudication*, pp. 31–81; Grant Huscroft, 'Proportionality and Pretense' (2014) 29 *Constitutional Commentary* 229–55 at 255. See also Duncan Kennedy, 'A Transnational Genealogy of Proportionality in Private Law', in Roger Brownsword et al. (eds.), *The Foundations of European Private Law* (Oxford: Hart, 2011), pp. 185–220 at 187 (arguing that proportionality leads to a 'politicisation of legal technique').

[13] BVerfGE 93, 1 at 21–24.

[14] Id.

[15] Id. at 24.

[16] Id. at 23.

[17] Martin Heckel, 'Das Kreuz im öffentlichen Raum – Zum 'Kruzifix-Beschluß' des Bundesverfassungsgerichts' (1996) 111 *Deutsches Verwaltungsblatt* 453–82 at 482; Höffe, 'Wieviel Politik?', 191. See also *Lautsi v. Italy* [2011] ECHR 2412

Even though proportionality has initially been developed as a doctrinal instrument for fundamental rights review by the German Constitutional Court,[18] some form of proportionality test is used by most courts exercising judicial review outside of the United States today.[19] As much as proportionality is a global phenomenon, criticism of balancing as a tool of judicial activism is not limited to Germany. We find similar criticism in South Africa[20] or Canada,[21] where the courts equally adopted the proportionality test as the central doctrinal instrument of fundamental rights review.

One of the most controversial decisions of the Canadian Supreme Court was the *Chaoulli* judgment.[22] In *Chaoulli*, the court decided that a statute prohibiting private health insurances from offering services that were covered by the public health insurance scheme was unconstitutional. The judgment was severely criticised in the legal literature.[23] Several authors

[18] Alec Stone Sweet and Jud Mathews, 'Proportionality Balancing and Global Constitutionalism' (2008) 47 *Columbia Journal of Transnational Law* 73–165 at 98–112.

[19] Id. at 75; Stylianos-Ioannis G. Koutnatzis, 'Verfassungsvergleichende Überlegungen zur Rezeption des Grundsatzes der Verhältnismäßigkeit in Übersee' (2011) 44 *Verfassung und Recht in Übersee* 32–59; Aharon Barak, *Proportionality – Constitutional Rights and Their Limitations* (Cambridge: Cambridge University Press, 2012), pp. 181–210; Johannes Saurer, 'Die Globalisierung des Verhältnismäßigkeitsgrundsatzes' (2012) 51 *Der Staat* 3–33; Kai Möller, *The Global Model of Constitutional Rights* (Oxford: Oxford University Press, 2012), p. 178; Vlad Perju, 'Proportionality and Freedom – An Essay on Methods in Constitutional Law' (2012) 1 *Global Constitutionalism* 334–67 at 334; Moshe Cohen-Eliya and Iddo Porat, *Proportionality and Constitutional Culture* (Cambridge: Cambridge University Press, 2013), pp. 10–4; Florian Becker, 'Verhältnismäßigkeit', in Hanno Kube et al. (eds.), *Leitgedanken des Rechts: Paul Kirchhof zum 70. Geburtstag. Band I: Staat und Verfassung* (Heidelberg: C.F. Müller, 2013), pp. 225–36 at paras. 12–27; Grant Huscroft, Bradley W. Miller and Grégoire C.N. Webber, 'Introduction', in Grant Huscroft, Bradley W. Miller and Grégoire Webber (eds.), *Proportionality and the Rule of Law: Rights, Justification, Reasoning* (New York: Cambridge University Press, 2014), pp. 1–17 at 1; Moshe Cohen-Eliya and Iddo Porat, 'Proportionality and Justification' (2014) 64 *University of Toronto Law Journal* 458–77 at 459. But see also Jacco Bomhoff, *Balancing Constitutional Rights: The Origins and Meanings of Postwar Legal Discourse* (Cambridge: Cambridge University Press, 2013) (arguing that there is not a single concept but, in fact, there are different local concepts of balancing).

[20] See Woolman, 'Out of Order?', 114–21; Blaauw-Wolf, 'Balancing of interests', 210; Botha, 'Rights, Limitations', pp. 21–3; Woolman and Botha, 'Limitations', pp. 157–60.

[21] See Hogg, 'Section 1 Revisited', 23–4; Webber, *Negotiable Constitution*, pp. 87–115; Webber, 'Proportionality', 194–8.

[22] *Chaoulli v. Quebec (Attorney General)* [2005] 1 S.C.R. 791.

[23] See Sujit Choudhry, 'Worse than Lochner?', in Colleen M. Flood, Kent Roach and Lorne Sossin (eds.), *Access to Care, Access to Justice: The Legal Debate Over Private Health Insurance in Canada* (Toronto: University of Toronto Press, 2005), pp. 75–100; Robert E. Charney and S. Zachary Green, 'Auton and Chaoulli: Who Decides the Future of Health Care in Canada?' (2005) 19 *National Journal of Constitutional Law* 263–83 at 274–82;

even likened the decision to the infamous *Lochner* decision of the US Supreme Court,[24] which is often regarded as one of the main illustrations of judicial activism.[25]

Like the German Constitutional Court in its crucifix decision, the Canadian Supreme Court also relied on proportionality considerations. However, there is one central difference between both decisions. Whereas the German Court resorted to the balancing stage of the proportionality test, the Canadian Court argued that the public monopoly in the health-insurance sector was not necessary to ensure the effectiveness of the public-health-insurance scheme.[26] The central argument was, therefore, an empirical one. However, the framing of the empirical inquiry entailed significant normative valuations. The judges asked whether a public and a private health-insurance scheme could co-exist. But even if such co-existence is possible, a parallel system may lead to a situation in which individuals who are privately insured are treated more favourably than individuals who are enrolled in the public scheme. Health services would then be allocated according to financial means and not according to medical necessity. This example shows that the balancing stage is not the only problematic stage of the proportionality test. Instead, all stages of the proportionality test may entail difficult normative valuations.

The pivotal question is not whether the courts should have reached different conclusions in these two decisions. Rather, it is whether the proportionality test is the right methodological instrument to decide these kinds of cases. There is a controversial and extensive normative discussion on this question across different jurisdictions.[27] This book does not primarily try to add another dimension to this already rich debate. Instead, it has

Theodore R. Marmor, 'Canada's Supreme Court and Its National Health Insurance Program: Evaluating the Landmark Chaoulli Decision from a Comparative Perspective' (2006) 44 *Osgoode Hall Law Journal* 311–25; Martha Jackman, '"The Last Line of Defence for [Which?] Citizens": Accountability, Equality, and the Right to Health in Chaoulli' (2006) 44 *Osgoode Hall Law Journal* 349–75; Marie-Claude Prémont, 'L'affaire Chaoulli et le système de santé du Québec: cherchez l'erreur, cherchez la raison' (2006) 51 *McGill Law Journal* 167–95; Colleen M. Flood, 'Chaoulli's Legacy for the Future of Canadian Health Care Policy' (2006) 44 *Osgoode Hall Law Journal* 273–310 at 275–93; Joan M. Gilmour, 'Fallout from Chaoulli: Is It Time to Find Cover?' (2006) 44 *Osgoode Hall Law Journal* 327–47 at 328; Geneviève Tremblay McCaig, 'L'affaire Chaoulli c. Procureur général du Québec: appartient-il aux tribunaux de remettre en question les objectifs politiques qui modèlent le système de santé?' (2007) 41 *Revue juridique Thémis* 157–204.

[24] *Lochner v. New York* 198 U.S. 45 (1905).

[25] Choudhry, 'Worse than Lochner?'; Charney and Green, 'Auton and Chaoulli', 275.

[26] *Chaoulli v. Quebec* [2005] 1 S.C.R. 791 at 827–36.

[27] For a reconstruction of this debate, see, Chapter 2.

an empirical approach. The main research question that will be addressed on the following pages is whether courts use balancing as an instrument of judicial self-empowerment. Is balancing indeed the Trojan horse that enables judicial activism, as some critics claim?[28]

During the course of the book, we will see that the crucifix and the *Chaoulli* decisions are clear outliers in the proportionality jurisprudence. Courts usually use the proportionality test to review the rationality of legislative decision-making. This book will show that the normative discussion on proportionality neglects one important dimension. Even if one comes to the conclusion that the proportionality test grants judges considerable discretion, one should be careful not to throw out the baby with the bathwater. Judicial methodology is not the only factor that constrains judicial decision-making. Judges also face institutional constraints. They cannot implement their decisions themselves, so that legitimacy is their main source of power. However, courts jeopardise their legitimacy if they use balancing extensively, thus appearing to be political.

The argument will be developed in six steps. Even though the main research question of the book is an empirical one, the book will set off by elaborating a normative framework. Every empirical study depends on a specific choice of the perspective, which is often guided by normative considerations.[29] The first two chapters are supposed to make these normative considerations explicit. The main research question of the book is whether courts use the proportionality test as an instrument for judicial activism. This requires a definition of the concept of judicial activism. The term is usually used with a negative connotation: Activist courts are thought to be too political. However, decisions of apex courts are never exclusively determined by legal texts. Instead, judicial review necessarily has a political element. But it is difficult to draw a clear line between the degree of political influence that is still acceptable and the degree that marks judicial activism. For this reason, I shall take a different approach. In the first chapter, I will determine the function of judicial review. This function will serve as a guideline for the subsequent empirical analysis.

The core of the normative debate on balancing centres on different normative conceptions of constitutional courts in a democratic society.[30]

[28] See earlier note 12.

[29] See Niels Petersen, 'Avoiding the Common Wisdom Fallacy: The Role of Social Sciences in Constitutional Adjudication' (2013) 11 *International Journal of Constitutional Law* 294–318 at 316–17.

[30] Niels Petersen, 'How to Compare the Length of Lines to the Weight of Stones – Balancing and the resolution of value conflicts in constitutional law' (2013) 14 *German Law Journal*

When critics argue that the balancing test is irrational, they express an underlying fear that it does not place sufficient constraints on judicial decision-making.[31] The evaluation of the principle of proportionality thus depends to a certain extent on the function that is attributed to constitutional courts in the political system. I will argue that constitutional courts are supposed to correct systematic malfunctions of the democratic process. For the purpose of this study, two failures are particularly relevant: the disregard of the interests of discrete minorities, and the capture of the political process by well-organised lobby groups. To the extent that judgments are in line with the role of constitutional courts in liberal democracies, they are not considered to be activist. Activism starts wherever courts go beyond the correction of the identified representation biases. To be sure, there may also be debates about the precise limits of this conception. However, social sciences are never just a mechanical exercise, but always involve a certain amount of discretion on the part of the researcher.

The second chapter reconstructs the normative discussion on proportionality and balancing. It addresses two strands of criticism that are directed against balancing. On the one hand, critics argue that balancing presupposes a comparison of incommensurable values and that it was impossible to make such a comparison in a rational way. On the other hand, some authors point out that *ad hoc* balancing, which focuses on the circumstances of each individual case, jeopardises legal certainty. I will show that this critique is based on specific assumptions on the role of courts in the political process and the fundamental importance of legal certainty. There is no 'theoretically pure' solution for the challenges that balancing poses.[32] Instead, we are facing a trade-off: on the one hand, balancing gives courts considerable discretion and thus opens the door for a potential abuse of power; on the other hand, it provides judges with an effective instrument to review and control the political process in order to correct its pathologies.

The third chapter develops an empirical theory of the use of balancing in the judicial review of legislation. It will be shown that balancing is a rather unsuitable instrument to hide judicial activism. The legitimacy

1387–408; similarly Jud Mathews and Alec Stone Sweet, 'All Things in Proportion? American Rights Review and the Problem of Balancing' (2011) 60 *Emory Law Journal* 102–79 at 122.

[31] Frederick Schauer, 'Balancing, Subsumption, and the Constraining Role of Legal Text', in Matthias Klatt (ed.), *Institutionalized Reason: The Jurisprudence of Robert Alexy* (Oxford: Oxford University Press, 2012), pp. 307–16 at 310.

[32] See Christoph Engel, 'Offene Gemeinwohldefinitionen' (2001) 32 *Rechtstheorie* 23–52 at 49.

of constitutional and supreme courts depends on the general perception that they are neutral actors deciding according to legal – and not political – considerations. The fierce methodological critique of balancing suggests that the potential for 'political' decision-making is more obvious when courts balance than when they base their decisions on other arguments. For this reason, we can expect courts to refrain from using balancing as an instrument for judicial activism. Chapter 4 turns to the empirical analysis. The subject of the analysis is the jurisprudence of three different apex courts that have used the proportionality test as a central instrument of judicial review: the Canadian Supreme Court, the German Federal Constitutional Court and the South African Constitutional Court. The chapter presents the results of a quantitative analysis of the fundamental rights jurisprudence of these three courts. The main emphasis is on cases in which the courts overturned legislation, because the conflict between the judicial and the legislative branch is particularly pronounced in this situation.

The analysis shows significant differences between the courts and their approach to the last step of the proportionality test. The data on the German case law shows a historical trend. In the first decades, the Federal Constitutional Court was extremely reluctant to rely on balancing in judgments in which it overturned legislation. In contrast, the court used balancing frequently when it corrected decisions of lower courts or when it confirmed legislation. This changed in the late 1970s. From 1978 onwards, the constitutional court based about one-third of the decisions in which it declared a law as unconstitutional on balancing. Balancing thus becomes the key methodological framework of the fundamental rights jurisprudence. The Canadian Supreme Court was in general very reluctant to rely on balancing when overturning legislation. However, a possible recent turning point could suggest that the Canadian Court might use balancing more extensively in the future. Finally, the South African Constitutional Court almost never relies on the balancing stage. I will argue that these observations are in line with the hypotheses developed in Chapter 3. The stronger their institutional positions are and the more balancing is accepted as a doctrinal test in legal scholarship, the more likely the courts are to use balancing.

Chapter 5 then takes a closer look at what the courts do when they avoid balancing. The classification underlying the empirical analysis in Chapter 4 relied on the labels that the courts themselves gave their arguments. The disadvantage of this approach is that the courts may not be doing what they are saying. They may classify an argument as a less-restrictive-means argument, but in fact they rely on implicit balancing. The *Chaoulli* decision illustrates that the other elements of the proportionality test may also contain significant normative valuations. For this reason, the chapter analyses the non-balancing arguments and examines the extent to which they are driven by implicit balancing. I argue that implicit balancing often occurs in the context of non-balancing arguments. In most cases, however, the extent of this implicit balancing is limited. It predominantly concerns the lacking fit between measure and purpose of a norm, which usually indicates that the legislature either was not sufficiently diligent in the drafting process or had secondary aims that it did not reveal explicitly. In the vast majority of cases, moreover, the courts do not challenge the central purpose of the norm, but only require corrections at the margins.

Chapter 6 takes a closer look at the content and the argumentation strategy in the judgments in which legislation is overturned on the basis of balancing. It shows that the courts do not primarily use balancing to second-guess or correct policy decisions of the legislature. All three courts use balancing in order to correct disproportionate legislation in the area of criminal or criminal procedure law. In this area, politicians have incentives to be too tough, rather than too lenient on crime, so that courts have an important corrective function. Outside the field of criminal law, the Canadian Supreme Court and the South African Constitutional Court rely on balancing only very exceptionally. The German Constitutional Court uses balancing more often. However, almost all the remaining decisions fit into one of the following four categories: first, the court corrects the assignment of financial burdens. It basically accepts the purpose of the individual rights restriction. However, it shifts its costs from the individual- rights bearers to either the state or the primary beneficiaries of the measure. Second, it analyses the fit of the measure and the purpose. In many cases, this includes a comparison of the adopted measure with alternative, less restrictive measures. Often, these alternative measures are not quite as effective as the adopted measure. However, the court does not deem the difference in effectiveness sufficiently important to justify the more severe restriction of the individual right. Third, the court combines the balancing test with a consistency test. It holds that a measure is disproportionate because it is inconsistent. Finally, the court uses balancing to correct cases of individual hardship. In these cases, the court does not second-guess the legislative policy choice either. However, it requires an exception for groups that are affected by the measure in a particularly severe way. For this reason, I argue that balancing can be characterised as a means of reviewing the rationality of the legislative process, rather than as a tool for judicial self-empowerment.

The conclusion merges the different strands of analysis of the book. The main argument of the book is that methodological constraints can only partly explain judicial decisions. Even if doctrinal argumentation frameworks grant them a considerable amount of discretion, this does not mean that judges use this discretion for judicial activism. Instead, judges also face considerable institutional constraints. Chapters 4–6 have shown that this hypothesis holds with regard to the analysed courts. The observation is constant across all three courts. This suggests that it is not due to a particular integrity and professional ethos of the constitutional judges. Instead, it is well-understood self-interest that keeps judges from using balancing as a tool of self-empowerment. This does not mean that the courts refrain from judicial activism. But if they engage in it, they usually rely on other methodological instruments, rather than proportionality.

1

Judicial Review and the Correction of Political Market Failures

On the last day of his term in office in March 1801, President John Adams appointed several new justices. With this move, he intended to restrict the room for manoeuvre of the incoming president, Thomas Jefferson. One of the newly appointed justices was the Justice of the Peace William Marbury. However, Marbury did not receive his letter of appointment in time, so that Jefferson refused to appoint him. Marbury turned to the US Supreme Court and demanded to be handed his letter of appointment. The ensuing judgment was the birth of modern judicial review of legislation. In *Marbury v. Madison*, the Supreme Court assumed the competency to review the constitutionality of legislative acts.[1] The Supreme Court acknowledged that Marbury, in principle, had a right to be appointed. However, the court held that the statute on which the applicant had based the jurisdiction of the court violated the constitution and thus denied Marbury his appointment.

The judgment was of fundamental importance because the US Constitution of 1787 did not explicitly confer any power to exercise judicial review of legislation to the Supreme Court. After *Marbury v. Madison*, it took more than fifty years until the Supreme Court made use of its power to overturn legislation a second time.[2] Since then, however, there is no doubt about the Supreme Court's power of judicial review in practice.[3] Nevertheless, there is still a heated theoretical debate in US legal scholarship about the legitimacy of judicial review.[4]

[1] *Marbury v. Madison* 5 U.S. (1 Cranch) 137 (1803).

[2] *Dred Scott v. Sandford* 60 U.S. 393 (1857).

[3] Erwin Chemerinsky, *Constitutional Law: Principles and Policies*, 4 edn. (New York: Wolters Kluwer, 2011), p. 45.

[4] See Jeremy Waldron, 'A Right-Based Critique of Constitutional Rights' (1993) 13 *Oxford Journal of Legal Studies* 18–51; Jeremy Waldron, *Law and Disagreement* (New York: Oxford University Press, 1999); Jeremy Waldron, 'The Core of the Case Against Judicial Review' (2006) 115 *Yale Law Journal* 1346–406; Richard Bellamy, *Political Constitutionalism: A Republican Defense of the Constitutionality of Democracy* (Cambridge: Cambridge University Press, 2007) (denying the legitimacy of judicial review); Mark Tushnet, *Taking the Constitution*

In the three jurisdictions analysed in this book, the controversy concerning judicial review is less pronounced. In each case, the power of judicial review is explicitly contained in the constitution. In Germany, the competence of the Federal Constitutional Court to review legislation is expressly confirmed in Articles 93 and 100 of the German Constitution. Article 167 of the South African Constitution authorises the Constitutional Court to "decide on the constitutionality of any parliamentary or provincial Bill". In Canada, the Canadian Charter of Rights and Freedoms grants the Supreme Court the power to review whether legislation is in conformity with the individual rights of the Charter. However, according to Article 33 of the Canadian Charter, the Canadian Parliament has the power to decide that a statute should be operational notwithstanding its incompatibility with certain individual rights.

Away from the Courts (Princeton: Princeton University Press, 1999); Larry D. Kramer, *The People Themselves: Popular Constitutionalism and Judicial Review* (Cambridge, MA: Harvard University Press, 2004) (denying the supremacy of the US Supreme Court to interpret the constitution); Robert H. Bork, 'Neutral Principles and Some First Amendment Problems' (1971) 47 *Indiana Law Journal* 1–35; William H. Rehnquist, 'The Notion of a Living Constitution' (1976) 54 *Texas Law Review* 693–706; Antonin Scalia, 'Originalism: The Lesser Evil' (1989) 57 *University of Cincinnati Law Review* 849–65; Robert H. Bork, *The Tempting of America: The Political Seduction of the Law* (New York: Free Press, 1990); Michael J. Perry, *Constitutional Rights, Moral Controversy, and the Supreme Court* (New York: Cambridge University Press, 2009) (arguing that judicial review can only be justified with an originalist understanding of the constitution); Alexander M. Bickel, *The Least Dangerous Branch. The Supreme Court at the Bar of Politics* (New Haven: Yale University Press, 1962); Bruce Ackerman, 'The Storrs Lectures: Discovering the Constitution' (1984) 93 *Yale Law Journal* 1013–72; Bruce Ackerman, 'Constitutional Politics/Constitutional Law' (1989) 99 *Yale Law Journal* 453–547; Bruce Ackerman, *We the People: Foundations* (Cambridge, MA: Harvard University Press, 1991) (according to whom the Supreme Court is supposed to protect the fundamental values or the historical identity of society); John Hart Ely, *Democracy and Distrust: A Theory of Judicial Review* (Cambridge, MA: Harvard University Press, 1980) (proposing a procedural model of constitutional review); Ronald Dworkin, *Freedom's Law: The Moral Reading of the American Constitution* (Cambridge, MA: Harvard University Press, 1996) (advocating a moral interpretation of the constitution); Stephen Gardbaum, 'The New Commonwealth Model of Constitutionalism' (2001) 49 *American Journal of Comparative Law* 707–60; Mark Tushnet, *Weak Courts, Strong Rights: Judicial Review and Social Welfare Rights in Comparative Constitutional Law* (Princeton: Princeton University Press, 2008); Stephen Gardbaum, *The New Commonwealth Model of Constitutionalism* (Cambridge: Cambridge University Press, 2013); Stephen Gardbaum, 'Are Strong Constitutional Courts always a Good Thing for New Democracies?' (2015) 53 *Columbia Journal of Transnational Law* 285–320 (favouring a model of "weak-form" judicial review, in which parliament has the power to correct decisions of apex courts); Dimitris Kyritsis, *Shared Authority: Courts and Legislatures in Legal Theory* (Oxford: Hart, 2015) (arguing that courts and legislature should exercise shared authority and that judicial interpretation should be guided by the separation of powers doctrine).

Even though there is no legal uncertainty regarding the fundamental power of judicial review of the three analysed courts, the debate on the legitimacy of judicial review is nevertheless important. The discussion on judicial activism is a debate on the scope of judicial review. In this context, determining the legitimacy of judicial review provides us with an external standard to evaluate the proportionality jurisprudence of the analysed courts. The question of whether courts acted in an activist manner depends on whether they were in line with the role that they are supposed to play in a liberal democratic political system.

The underlying assumption of this chapter is that legal decisions of constitutional courts are not exclusively guided by legal texts.[5] Language is indeterminate, and there is often no clear hierarchy between competing legal norms, so that courts have a considerable margin of discretion in their decision-making. These considerations are largely confirmed by empirical studies on the US Supreme Court, according to which the Justices are influenced by ideological or political considerations in their decision-making.[6] That does not mean that their decisions are exclusively political. Instead, there are some studies that see an influence of legal doctrine.[7] However, both positions are not mutually exclusive.[8] Rather, it is

[5] See Martin Shapiro, *Courts: A Comparative and Political Analysis* (Chicago: University of Chicago Press, 1981), p. 28 (stating that "[n]early all contemporary students of courts agree [on this point]").

[6] Jeffrey A. Segal and Albert D. Cover, 'Ideological Values and the Votes of U.S. Supreme Court Justices' (1989) 83 *American Political Science Review* 557–65; Jeffrey A. Segal *et al.*, 'Ideological Values and the Votes of U.S. Supreme Court Justices Revisited' (1995) 57 *Journal of Politics* 812–23; Jeffrey A. Segal and Harold J. Spaeth, *The Supreme Court and the Attitudinal Model Revisited* (New York: Cambridge University Press, 2002). See also Thomas Brennan, Lee Epstein and Nancy Staudt, 'The Political Economy of Judging' (2009) 93 *Minnesota Law Review* 1503–34 (claiming the economic factors also play an important role) and Thomas M. Keck, 'Party, Policy, or Duty: Why Does the Supreme Court Invalidate Federal Statutes?' (2007) 101 *American Political Science Review* 321–38 (pointing out that the division among judges often does not follow partisan lines). See Susumu Shikano and Verena Mack, 'Judges' behaviour and relationship with political parties in a non-common-law country: The Case of the German Federal Constitutional Court', Working Paper, University of Konstanz (2014) (arguing that judges of the German Constitutional Court are also influenced by their political background).

[7] See Saul Brenner and Marc Stier, 'Retesting Segal and Spaeth's Stare Decisis Model' (1996) 40 *American Journal of Political Science* 1036–48; Stefanie A. Lindquist and David E. Klein, 'The Influence of Jurisprudential Considerations on Supreme Court Decision Making: A Study of Conflict Cases' (2006) 40 *Law & Society Review* 135–61; Michael A. Bailey and Forrest Maltzman, 'Does Legal Doctrine Matter? Unpacking Law and Policy Preferences on the U.S. Supreme Court' (2008) 102 *American Political Science Review* 369–84.

[8] Barry Evan Friedman, 'The Politics of Judicial Review' (2005) 84 *Texas Law Review* 257–337 at 276.

likely that judges are influenced by different factors: Their decisions are based on legal as well as non-legal factors.[9]

If decisions of constitutional courts are not primarily motivated by legal considerations, they are in need of an external justification. In this chapter, I will argue that judicial review serves the function of correcting political market failures. The argument will be developed in four steps. In the first section, I will outline the conception of democracy upon which the argument is based. Determining the function of a constitutional court requires a sense of how to divide powers between the different branches of government. This seems impossible without discussing the function of the remaining branches – that is, parliament and government.

The second section will develop the main argument: judicial review is supposed to correct political market failures. This conceptualisation of judicial review is not entirely new. Instead, it is largely based on *John Hart Ely*'s account on the legitimacy of the US Supreme Court.[10] However, I will extend Ely's model in several respects. For this purpose, I will identify different cases of political market failures and show how courts can react to them. The third section then asks why courts are in a better position than legislatures to take such decisions. Finally, the fourth section concludes.

1. Democracy and Judicial Review

In the current discussion on democratic theory, there are two main strands. On the one hand, we have the theory of competitive democracy. The central element of this theory is that political parties compete for votes of the electorate. The theory can be traced back to the work of Joseph Schumpeter,[11] but it has been developed significantly since then.[12] On the other hand, there is the theory of deliberative democracy.[13] Adherents of

[9] See Tracey E. George and Lee Epstein, 'On the Nature of Supreme Court Decision Making' (1992) 86 *American Political Science Review* 323–37; Mark J. Richards and Herbert M. Kritzer, 'Jurisprudential Regimes in Supreme Court Decision Making' (2002) 96 *American Political Science Review* 305–20.

[10] Ely, *Democracy and Distrust*.

[11] Joseph Alois Schumpeter, *Capitalism, Socialism and Democracy* (Abingdon: Routledge, 2010), pp. 241–51.

[12] See Philippe C. Schmitter and Terry Lynn Karl, 'What Democracy Is . . . and Is Not' (1991) 2.3 *Journal of Democracy* 75–88; Adam Przeworski, 'Minimalist Conception of Democracy: A Defense', in Ian Shapiro and Casiano Hacker-Cordón (eds.), *Democracy's Value* (Cambridge: Cambridge University Press, 1999), pp. 23–55; Ian Shapiro, *The State of Democratic Theory* (Princeton: Princeton University Press, 2006).

[13] Seminally, Habermas, *Facts and Norms*, pp. 287–328. See also James S. Fishkin, *Democracy and Deliberation: New Directions for Democratic Reform* (New Haven: Yale University Press,

deliberative theories of democracy argue that deliberation improves the quality of collective decision-making.

Both theories have their virtues and their vices. Nevertheless, the argument developed in this chapter will be based on a competitive conception of democracy. Democratic theory always has a normative and a descriptive dimension.[14] The normative dimension focuses on what democracy ought to be, on how we could ameliorate the system in order to achieve better results. By contrast, the descriptive dimension describes the democratic system that we currently have. Both dimensions cannot be neatly separated from each other. However, for our purposes, the descriptive dimension is more important. When we want to analyse the role that constitutional courts should play in a democracy, we have to look at the current institutional setting, not at an idealised political system. If the institutional framework of the political process changes, we might have to re-evaluate the role of constitutional courts. However, I will try to analyse the role of judicial review under present circumstances.

For this purpose, the theory of competitive democracy seems to be more useful. Although deliberative democracy is normatively attractive, its goal is to change the current political setting, not to explain it. By contrast, the theory of competitive democracy is probably the best explanation of the functioning of democracy as we observe it today.[15] According to this theory, democracy is the response to a representation problem. Representative decision-making contains two major risks: On the one hand, representatives can abuse their power; on the other, they

1991); Rainer Schmalz-Bruns, *Reflexive Demokratie. Die demokratische Transformation moderner Politik* (Baden-Baden: Nomos, 1995); Amy Gutman and Dennis Thompson, *Democracy and Disagreement* (Cambridge (Mass.): Belknap Press, 1996); Joshua Cohen and Charles Sabel, 'Direct-Deliberative Polyarchy' (1997) 3 *European Law Journal* 313–42; John Ferejohn, 'Instituting Deliberative Democracy', in Ian Shapiro and Stephen Macedo (eds.), *Designing Democratic Institutions* (New York: New York University Press, 2000), pp. 75–104; Cass R. Sunstein, *Designing Democracy: What Constitutions Do* (Oxford: Oxford University Press, 2001). However, those who adhere to the theory of deliberative democracy comprise no coherent school. Instead, there are several sub-strands that either stress the participatory or the rationalist element of deliberation; see Rainer Forst, 'The Rule of Reasons. Three Models of Deliberative Democracy' (2001) 14 *Ratio Juris* 345–78; Erik Oddvar Eriksen, 'Deliberation und demokratische Legitimität in der EU – Zwischen Konsens und Kompromiss', in Peter Niesen and Benjamin Herborth (eds.), *Anarchie der kommunikativen Freiheit* (Frankfurt a.M.: Suhrkamp, 2007), pp. 294–320 at 296.

14 *See* Giovanni Sartori, *The Theory of Democracy Revisited. Part I: The Contemporary Debate* (Chatham: Chatham House, 1987), pp. 182–5.

15 Emanuel Towfigh, *Das Parteien-Paradox* (Tübingen: Mohr Siebeck, 2015), p. 61.

can harm the interests of the represented citizens if they lack a proper level of expertise.[16] Democracy tries to mitigate these dangers by giving citizens an opportunity to react to political decision-making through regular elections. If a government is incompetent, it can be replaced through elections. The citizens have an exit option.[17] Furthermore, elections give representatives incentives to act in the public interest. If they do not, they have to fear not being re-elected. In a democracy system, majority decisions in parliament should thus, in theory, usually reflect the preferences of the majority of the citizens.

However, representative democracy does not guarantee that decisions are taken in the public interest. Sometimes, there are information asymmetries because of which citizens are not completely informed about the circumstances of political decision-making. Without adequate information, citizens are not able to sanction decision-making through elections. Furthermore, many decisions are highly complex. They involve bargains between different political groups, or their consequences are difficult to observe. These two considerations show that democracy cannot completely solve the representation problem. The following section will thus argue that constitutional courts have the function to correct some of the political market failures and thus to reduce the risks of representative decision-making.

2. Correcting Political Market Failures

If the political process worked perfectly and if it took all relevant societal interests into account in the decision-making process, we would not need constitutional courts. However, the political process is prone to certain market failures, as a result of which specific societal groups are systematically favoured over others. It is the task of judicial review to correct these market failures and to create a counterbalance for those groups that are usually disfavoured by political decision-making.

This function of correcting political market failures is no alien element in the design of democratic institutions. *Mattias Kumm* has recently pointed

[16] Sartori, *Theory of Democracy*, p. 217. See also Fritz W. Scharpf, *Governing in Europe: Effective and Democratic?* (Oxford: Oxford University Press, 1999), p. 188 (according to whom representative decision making needs to fulfil two criteria: "capacity for effective problem-solving" and "institutional safeguards against the abuse of public power").

[17] Albert O. Hirschman, *Exit, Voice, and Loyalty* (Cambridge, Mass.: Harvard University Press, 1970), p. 28.

out that questions of democratic design always entail compromises.[18] The choice of representative democracy is already such a compromise. If democracy aimed at reflecting precisely the preferences of the electorate, direct democracy would be the superior mode of decision-making. By contrast, representative democracy promises efficiency gains.[19] Only very few citizens have sufficient time to inform themselves about all relevant political issues. Consequently, the delegation of political decisions to representatives is supposed to increase their quality. These considerations can also be applied to judicial review. To the extent that judicial review is able to correct political market failures, it can increase the quality of collective decision-making.[20]

In this section, I will discuss five constellations in which judicial review plays an important role of counterbalancing the political process. The oldest function of constitutional courts is their role as arbitrators in competency disputes between different institutions on a horizontal level or between states and the federation on a vertical level. The other four cases deal with the prevention of elite dominance. The most prominent function in this regard is the protection of minorities against the "tyranny of the majority".[21] However, sometimes the problem is reverse when influential minorities dominate the political process and the public has to be protected against legislative capture. Furthermore, the constitutional court serves as a competition agency preventing collusions of the political elites that try to manipulate the political process in their favour. Finally, the court may intervene if certain decisions have external effects and disfavour groups that could not participate in the decision-making process.

2.1 Competency Disputes

The oldest function of constitutional courts is their role as arbitrators in competency disputes.[22] The distribution of competencies often resembles an incomplete contract. Norms that attribute competencies to a specific institution or a specific level in a federal state are often open-textured in

[18] Mattias Kumm, 'The Idea of Socratic Contestation and the Right to Justification: The Point of Rights-Based Proportionality Review' (2010) 4 *Law & Ethics of Human Rights* 141–75 at 166.

[19] Sartori, *Theory of Democracy*, p. 122.

[20] Kumm, 'Socratic Contestation', 166.

[21] Alexis de Tocqueville, *De la démocratie en Amérique* (Paris: Pagnerre, 1835).

[22] Höffe, 'Wieviel Politik?', 172.

order to be able to take new developments into account. Furthermore, there are often interconnections between different matters that the drafters of the constitution were not aware of. Consequently, it is necessary to have a neutral arbiter who can resolve competency conflicts between states and the federal state or different institutions on a horizontal level.

2.2 *Protection of Minorities*

The protection of minorities is often seen to be the fundamental function of constitutional courts.[23] The constitution is supposed to protect minorities against exploitation by the majority. However, why should minorities be protected in the first place if majority decision-making is one of the primary characteristics of democracy? If we look at its philosophical justification, democracy cannot be reduced to majority decision-making.[24] According to the political philosophy of the enlightenment, individual liberty was the most fundamental value.[25] This is expressed by the famous Kantian dictum that liberty is "the sole original, inborn right belonging to every man in virtue of his humanity".[26]

However, if we assume that liberty should be the foundation of every societal order, then every exercise of sovereign power that restrains individual liberty needs to be justified.[27] The most prominent attempt to justify political power is the social contract. Certainly, the social contract does not refer to an actual contract of all citizens in the state of nature. It is rather a fiction that does not depend on actual consent, but rather on being designed in such a way that all citizens could consent to it. This idea is expressed most elegantly through the Rawlsian "veil of ignorance", according to which a social order has to be designed in such a way that all citizens would accept it if they did not know their position in society.[28] The social contract is thus a means to evaluate the legitimacy of a constitutional order.[29] In this context, majority decision-making

23 Friedman, 'Politics of Judicial Review', 309.
24 Dworkin, *Freedom's Law*, pp. 6–7.
25 Wolfgang Kersting, *Die politische Philosophie des Gesellschaftsvertrags* (Darmstadt: Wissenschaftliche Buchgesellschaft, 1994), p. 11.
26 Immanuel Kant, *The Metaphysics of Morals* (Mary Gregor trl., Cambridge: Cambridge University Press, 1996), p. 30.
27 Mattias Kumm, 'Alexy's Theory of Constitutional Rights and the Problem of Judicial Review', in Matthias Klatt (ed.), *Institutionalized Reason: The Jurisprudence of Robert Alexy* (Oxford: Oxford University Press, 2012), pp. 201–17 at 214.
28 John Rawls, *A Theory of Justice* (Oxford: Oxford University Press, 1999).
29 Kersting, *Gesellschaftsvertrag*, p. 199.

is an important element. However, it is not the only one. The aim of the social contract is to guarantee the liberty of every citizen, not merely the liberty of the majority. Consequently, it is incomplete if the constitutional order does not contain effective guarantees for the protection of the minority.

There are two arguments that can be raised against the necessity of minority protection. First, the social contract only refers to the acceptability of the basic order, not of each collective decision. Individuals are part of a political community with a common identity. They accept majority decisions, in which they sided with the minority, because of their commonalities with the other members of the political community.[30] If the others are like me, I respect their values even if our political opinions and interests differ.[31] If this argument is right, then common identity already guarantees sufficient protection of minority rights.

However, a society in which mutual respect is based on commonality requires rather strong homogeneity.[32] However, the requirement of strong homogeneity does not reflect the composition of modern societies in many democracies.[33] Even formerly homogenous nations become more and more heterogeneous. Certainly, identity is a social construction that is not necessarily rooted in ethnicity or religion, but can be based on ideas and ideals. Furthermore, identity is malleable. At the same time, however, it cannot simply be imposed. Moreover, it is sometimes precisely in the interest of political actors to stress social, ethnic or religious divisions in society. In such situations, a common national identity is not sufficient protection of minority rights, because this identity can be superseded by other identities, such as the belonging to a specific social, religious or ethnic group.

[30] Cf. Joseph H. H. Weiler, *The Constitution of Europe* (Cambridge: Cambridge University Press, 1999), p. 328 (pointing out that 'identity' and 'identical' have common semantic roots).

[31] This is one of the fundamental assumptions of Waldron's critique of judicial review; see Waldron, 'Case Against Judicial Review', 1365.

[32] For this reason, some German authors consider homogeneity to be a fundamental societal premise. See Josef Isensee, 'Abschied der Demokratie vom Demos: Ausländerwahlrecht als Identitätsfrage für Volk, Demokratie und Verfassung', in Dieter Schwab, Dieter Giesen and Joseph Listl (eds.), *Staat, Kirche, Wissenschaft in einer pluralistischen Gesellschaft: Festschrift für Paul Mikat* (Berlin: Duncker & Humblot, 1989), pp. 705–40 at 708.

[33] See Samuel Issacharoff, *Fragile Democracies. Contested Power in the Era of Constitutional Courts* (New York: Cambridge University Press, 2015), pp. 5–6.

Second, it is often argued that minorities are protected by the dynamics of the political process.[34] Today's majority can be tomorrow's minority. Consequently, the majority has incentives to take the interests of the minority into account and not to impair the latter more than necessary if they expect comparable respect in the future when the majority has shifted. However, the protection through the dynamics of the political process is limited. Jeremy Waldron has made the differentiation between decisional and topical minorities.[35] Decisional majorities and minorities are dynamic to the extent that societal values change.

By contrast, topical majorities and minorities are structurally related to certain questions. The political decision in these cases is predetermined by the social, religious or ethnic identity of the voters. Here, the dynamics of the political process do not help the minority to turn into a majority as long as the composition of society does not change. Furthermore, mere majority decision-making lacks legitimacy in such situations because it might be pure chance that certain social groups are stronger than others.[36] If two wolves and a sheep decide on what to have for dinner, there is no normative reason that the majority of votes should be the decisive decision-making criterion.[37]

Sometimes, it is argued that topical minorities can organise decisional majorities by building coalitions with other societal groups.[38] However, coalition building is only possible if there are no prejudices and no social stigma attached to the respective group. The history of the black minority in the United States demonstrates how difficult and ineffective coalition building can sometimes be as a means to protect minority rights.[39] It is certainly possible that the appreciation of topical minorities by the social majority changes. However, until such a change is achieved, minorities need institutional protection of their rights and interests.

[34] Ernst-Wolfgang Böckenförde, 'Demokratie als Verfassungsprinzip', in Josef Isensee and Paul Kirchhof (eds.), *Handbuch des Staatsrechts der Bundesrepublik Deutschland. Band II: Verfassungsstaat* (Heidelberg: C. F. Müller, 3 edn. 2004), ch. 24 at para. 54; Oliver Lepsius, 'Der Hüter der Verfassung – Demokratietheoretisch betrachtet', in Olivier Beaud and Pasquale Pasquino (eds.), *La controverse sur le "gardien de la constitution" et la justice constitutionnelle. Kelsen contre Schmitt* (Paris: Editions Panthéon-Assas, 2007), pp. 103–26 at 120–1.

[35] Waldron, 'Case Against Judicial Review', 1397.

[36] Sartori, *Theory of Democracy*, pp. 137–41; Issacharoff, *Fragile Democracies*, p. 4.

[37] The example is taken from an intervention of Anthony D'Amato at a conference on 'Legitimacy in International Law' that was held in Heidelberg in June 2006. The discussion is reprinted in Rüdiger Wolfrum and Volker Röben (eds.), *Legitimacy in International Law* (Berlin: Springer 2008), p. 106.

[38] Tushnet, *Taking the Constitution*, p. 159.

[39] Ely, *Democracy & Distrust*, p. 135.

In principle, there are two conceptual possibilities to protect minorities. The first option would be to protect minorities by granting them group rights. Then minority protection would not primarily be an expression of individual rights but would protect the collective autonomy of specific social groups.[40] However, such an approach requires that we clearly determine which minorities are worthy of protection. The discussion in US legal scholarship on minority protection often takes an *obiter dictum* of the US Supreme Court in its *Carolene Products* decision as a starting point:

> [P]rejudice against *discrete and insular minorities* may be a special condition, which tends seriously to cur-tail the operation of those political processes ordinarily to be relied upon to protect minorities, and which may call for a correspondingly more searching judicial inquiry.[41]

The obiter dictum thus stresses the structural disadvantages that a minority faces as a reason for protection. However, we can imagine a group of citizens who believe that our society would best be organised along socialist values. To express such an opinion is certainly protected by the freedom of expression. However, the implementation of such an idea is an integral part of the political process. As long as our socialists are not able to organise a political majority, it is not the role of a constitutional or supreme court to exercise minority protection in order to support them. Yet, arguably, our socialists are a discrete and insular minority.

Sometimes, it has been proposed that only those minorities that are defined by unchangeable characteristics are worthy of protection. Minorities based on race, ethnicity or sex should be protected, whereas political minorities would not enjoy protection. However, this criterion of distinction has significant problems.[42] Certainly, changeability is basically a binary criterion. However, it also has a gradual component. Some characteristics might be more easily changeable than others. Furthermore, some changeable characteristics are nevertheless deemed worthy of protection. In principle, every individual can easily change religion. However, the freedom of religion, which is part of every liberal society, is supposed to protect individuals precisely against being forced to change their religion.

[40] On this distinction, see Christoph Engel, 'Freiheit und Autonomie', in Detlef Merten and Hans-Jürgen Papier (eds.), *Handbuch der Grundrechte. Band II: Grundrechte in Deutschland: Allgemeine Lehren I* (Heidelberg: C.F. Müller, 2006), ch. 33 at para. 15.

[41] *United States v. Carolene Products Co.* 304 U.S. 144 at 152 (note 4) (1938).

[42] See Ely, *Democracy & Distrust*, pp. 150–5.

For these reasons, it seems impossible to determine in the abstract which minorities are worthy of protection. Consequently, the conception of minority protection as a protection of specific social groups cannot be realised. The alternative option would be to conceptualise minority protection as a reflection of individual fundamental-rights protection. The concept of minority has a justificatory role in this context. However, the notion of minority is not static but dynamic. Whether an individual belongs to a minority worthy of protection depends on the circumstances of each individual case and our normative predetermination.

In order to make this solution more concrete, we have to turn to the specific dangers that minorities face in the political process. In principle, there are three types of dangers. First, the political majority may intentionally disregard the costs that are imposed on a minority by a specific measure because minority interests are not sufficiently represented in the political process.[43] If the majority prohibits the construction of minarets, then the costs for the affected Muslim population are usually higher than the utility for the majority that considers Islamic religious symbols as a danger for their cultural hegemony.

Second, measures that affect minorities may be due to false stereotypes.[44] If the majority in a society believes that people with red hair have a significantly higher criminal potential than the average, such individuals may face stricter supervision and repressive measures. Such treatment of red-haired individuals is at least problematic if the prejudice is without any empirical foundation. But even if it could be statistically proven that red-haired individuals are on average prone to be more criminal than their black-haired counterparts, special treatment of all individuals with red hair would be problematic, because it is based on group characteristics and not on individual criminal potential. Third, the majority may impose excessive costs on a minority simply because it is not aware of these costs and, for these reasons, does not take the interests of the minority into account in the decision-making process.

Often it will be difficult to determine whether one of these specific dangers has been realised. Discriminatory intention or false stereotypes will often be difficult to prove.[45] However, that does not mean that our classification is without practical use. Even if we cannot observe discriminatory

[43] See Towfigh, *Parteien-Paradox*, pp. 116–17 (arguing that parties fail to represent the whole spectrum of opinions and interests prevalent in a democracy).

[44] Ely, *Democracy & Distrust*, p. 153.

[45] Ely, *Democracy & Distrust*, p. 138.

intent, we can resort to indirect proxies for intentional discrimination. The solution that most constitutional orders provide is the formalisation of individual-rights protection. Courts do not control whether minority interests have been violated. Rather, they review the violation of fundamental rights.

Some of these fundamental rights define circumstances in which the danger of minority discrimination is particularly prevalent. Most equal protection clauses enumerate causes of differentiation, such as race, gender, religion or ethnic origin, which are especially suspect.[46] In these cases, the danger of intentional discrimination is very likely.[47] Even if equal-protection clauses do not mention specifically susceptible causes for differentiation, courts often develop such classifications. The logic behind the tiered scrutiny test of the US Supreme Court in the context of the equal protection clause[48] is that the danger of intentional discrimination is much higher if the criterion for differentiation is race or sex instead of qualification or ability.[49]

Freedom of religion is another individual right that particularly aims at protecting minorities. The same can be said of the freedom of expression and related expressive liberties, such as artistic freedom or freedom of the press. These guarantees are primarily supposed to protect minority positions; the majority is rarely in need of institutional protection in order to be heard. Finally, procedural guarantees in the criminal procedure equally protect minorities. Criminal suspects often belong to a social group that is not particularly well represented in the political process.

Constitutional minority protection is thus an indirect protection. The constitution identifies typical situations in which minority discrimination is particularly prevalent. However, courts exercising judicial review do not determine whether minority interests have indeed been affected in each individual case. The protection of minorities is only the theoretical

46 See Article 9 (3) of the South African Constitution; Article 3 (3) of the German Constitution; Article15 (1) of the Canadian Charter of Rights and Freedoms.

47 Cass R. Sunstein, 'Public Values, Private Interests, and the Equal Protection Clause' (1982) *The Supreme Court Review* 127–66 at 140.

48 On the tiered scrutiny test, see Stephen A. Siegel, 'The Origin of the Compelling State Interest Test and Strict Scrutiny' (2006) 48 *American Journal of Legal History* 355–407; Adam Winkler, 'Fatal in Theory and Strict in Fact: An Empirical Analysis of Strict Scrutiny in the Federal Courts' (2006) 59 *Vanderbilt Law Review* 793–871; Richard H. Fallon, 'Strict Judicial Scrutiny' (2007) 54 *U.C.L.A. Law Review* 1267–337; E. Thomas Sullivan and Richard S. Frase, *Proportionality Principles in American Law. Controlling Excessive Government Actions* (New York: Oxford University Press, 2009), p. 53–66.

49 See John Hart Ely, 'The Centrality and Limits of Motivation Analysis' (1978) 15 *San Diego Law Review* 1155–61 at 1157; Sunstein, 'Public Values', 140.

justification for fundamental rights protection through judicial review. Fundamental rights thus do not exclusively protect minorities.[50] But if fundamental rights benefit members of the social majority, their protection is only a reflective one.

2.3 *Protection against Legislative Capture*

However, minorities may not only be the victims of unbounded majority decisions. Sometimes, the problem is precisely opposite if the political process is dominated by specific influential minorities.[51] The political process is not merely a free exchange of arguments in the political discourse, leading to a decision based on the rationality of the argument.[52] Instead, interest groups affect the political process and try to put specific topics on the political agenda and to influence the decision-making in their favour.[53] There are several empirical studies showing that politicians are susceptible to the pressure of strong lobby groups.[54]

This influence can take different forms.[55] First, interest groups can try to influence decision-making behaviour through party donations.[56] Second, they can be valuable sources of information if politicians lack the necessary expertise. However, the more politicians rely on information provided by interest groups, the more the latter have the opportunity to influence decisions through the presentation and selection of information that they pass on. Finally, lobby groups can put pressure on political actors through their influence on the electorate. Economic pressure groups can threaten to cut jobs or to shift the production abroad, whereas labour unions can influence elections through recommendations to their members.

[50] Christoph Möllers, 'Legalität, Legitimität und Legitimation des Bundesverfassungsgerichts', in Matthias Jestaedt *et al.* (eds.), *Das entgrenzte Gericht: Eine kritische Bilanz nach sechzig Jahren Bundesverfassungsgericht* (Berlin: Suhrkamp, 2011), pp. 281–422 at 342.

[51] Seminally, Mancur Olson, *The Logic of Collective Action: Public Goods and the Theory of Groups* (Cambridge: Harvard University Press, 1965).

[52] See Engel, 'Offene Gemeinwohldefinitionen', 26.

[53] See the instructive case study of Geoffrey P. Miller, 'Public Choice at the Dawn of the Special Interest State: The Story of Butter and Margarine' (1989) 77 *California Law Review* 83–131.

[54] See Thomas Stratman, 'What Do Campaign Contributions Buy? Deciphering Causal Effects of Money and Votes' (1991) 57 *Southern Economic Journal* 606–20; Laura I. Langbein, 'Lobbies and Political Conflict: The Case of Gun Control' (1993) 77 *Public Choice* 551–72; Robert E. Baldwin and Christopher S. Magee, 'Is Trade Policy for Sale? Congressional Voting on Recent Trade Bills' (2000) 105 *Public Choice* 79–101.

[55] See Hans Herbert von Arnim, *Gemeinwohl und Gruppeninteressen* (Frankfurt a.M.: Alfred Metzner Verlag, 1977), pp. 136–41.

[56] See Towfigh, *Parteien-Paradox*, pp. 107–9.

Lobbying is not problematic *per se*. Often, the political process is dependent on the information provided by economic actors in order to take an informed decision. The problem, however, is that incentives and resources are often not equally distributed among all stakeholders. The stronger the interest of a specific group in one area is, the more resources it will dedicate to lobbying. This, in turn, increases the probability of affecting the political decision-making process. If a specific decision entails large gains for a small group, but only small costs for each member of the large majority, the small group has significant incentives to promote its own cause.[57] By contrast, the majority faces a free-rider problem. As each individual only suffers a small loss, she has no incentives to finance any lobbying efforts.

For example, subsidies usually benefit small groups while they impose costs on every taxpayer. However, the share of each individual in financing any given subsidy is so small that it will usually neither encourage her to take action nor influence her voting behaviour.[58] By contrast, the group that is benefiting from the subsidy has strong incentives to invest money into lobbying and to tie the voting decision to the reception of the subsidy. For these reasons, politicians have incentives to meet the demands of well-organised interest groups in order to ensure their loyalty without having to fear significant sanctions of the disinterested majority.

Constitutions do not contain express prohibitions of excessive lobbying. However, certain fundamental rights may provide constitutional courts with instruments to counterbalance legislative capture.[59] As in the case of minority protection, direct control of legislative capture is difficult. On the one hand, lobbying efforts are often not transparent. Consequently,

[57] See Olson, *Collective Action*, p. 28.

[58] See Arthur T. Denzau and Michael C. Munger, 'Legislators and Interest Groups: How Unorganized Interests Get Represented' (1986) 80 *American Political Science Review* 89–106 at 103.

[59] Such doctrinal propositions can predominantly be found in the US constitutional law literature. See Jerry L. Mashaw, 'Constitutional Deregulation: Notes Toward a Public, Public Law' (1980) 54 *Tulane Law Review* 849–76 at 874–5; Sunstein, 'Public Values'; Richard A. Epstein, 'Toward a Revitalization of the Contract Clause' (1984) 51 *The University of Chicago Law Review* 703–51; Cass R. Sunstein, 'Naked Preferences and the Constitution' (1984) 84 *Columbia Law Review* 1689–732; Cass R. Sunstein, 'Interest Groups in American Public Law' (1985) 38 *Stanford Law Review* 29–87; Erwin Chemerinsky, 'The Vanishing Constitution' (1989) 103 *Harvard Law Review* 43–104 at 78–81. But see also the critique of this approach that is voiced by Einer R. Elhauge, 'Does Interest Group Theory Justify More Intensive Judicial Review?' (1991) 101 *Yale Law Journal* 31–110. For approaches to counter legislative capture in the German constitutional law literature, see v. Arnim, *Gemeinwohl*, pp. 285–303; Niels Petersen, 'The German Constitutional Court and Legislative Capture' (2014) 12 *International Journal of Constitutional Law* 650–69 at 654–46.

it is difficult to determine which legislative decisions are mainly due to interest-group pressure. On the other hand, lobbying is not problematic *per se*.[60] The problem occurs when the legislature enacts a certain measure *because of* interest group influence.[61] Certainly, we will rarely be able to observe the motivation of the legislature.[62] Furthermore, constitutional courts will often be reluctant to accuse the legislature of bad faith.[63]

The solution to this problem is again a formalisation of individual rights protection. The freedom of profession or the guarantee of property protection can be understood as rights that are supposed to protect individuals against capture.[64] There are two proxies for legislative capture.[65] An insufficient fit between measure and purpose indicates that the legislature intended to pursue other goals than the ones that are explicitly used to justify the measure.[66] A second proxy is legislative inconsistency. If the legislature is inconsistent or incoherent in pursuing certain goals, this can also be an indication that it also pursued secondary goals, such as particularistic interests.[67] The prevention of legislative capture is thus equally a guiding principle for the scope of judicial review. It gives us, at the same time, an external standard to evaluate whether courts were overly activist in exercising judicial review and an instrument to determine the proper standard of review when controlling the legislature.

2.4 *Guardians of the Political Process*

Judicial review also serves as an instrument to safeguard the integrity of the political process.[68] Courts act as competition agencies that try to prevent

60 Klaus Meßerschmidt, 'The Race to Rationality Review and the Score of the German Federal Constitutional Court' (2012) 6 *Legisprudence* 347–78 at 376.

61 Petersen, 'Capture', 658.

62 Ely, *Democracy & Distrust*, p. 138.

63 Petersen, 'Capture', 658.

64 See Epstein, 'Contract Clause' (who makes a similar case for guarantee of the protection of property).

65 Petersen, 'Capture', 659.

66 Frederick Schauer, 'Proportionality and the Question of Weight', in Grant Huscroft, Bradley W. Miller and Grégoire Webber (eds.), *Proportionality and the Rule of Law: Rights, Justification, Reasoning* (New York: Cambridge University Press, 2014), pp. 173–85 at 181–2.

67 Niels Petersen, 'Legislative Inconsistency and the "Smoking Out" of Illicit Motives' (2016) 64 *American Journal of Comparative Law* 501–25.

68 Seminally, Ely, *Democracy & Distrust*, pp. 105–34. See also Samuel Issacharoff and Richard H. Pildes, 'Politics as Markets: Partisan Lockups of the Democratic Process' (1998) 50 *Stanford Law Review* 643–717; Richard H. Pildes, 'The Theory of Political Competition'

collusion between political parties in cases in which the parties have parallel interests running counter to the interests of the citizenry.[69] Such a divergence between the interests of the political elites and the general public occurs principally in two areas. First, political parties have incentives to establish entry barriers for new entrants into political markets.[70] Such entry barriers can take various forms: They can lead from gerrymandering in majority election systems[71] to minimum quotas for representation in parliament in representative systems.[72] Furthermore, if parties are at least in part subsidised by the state, the established parties, which are represented in parliament, also have incentives to allocate a bigger share of the available resources to themselves.[73] Second, political actors have incentives to maximise the amount of privileges they receive from the state. Such privileges can be the remuneration or other benefits for members of parliament,[74] public subsidies for political parties or the allocation of public offices for party members.[75]

(1999) 85 *Virginia Law Review* 1605–26; Samuel Issacharoff, 'Gerrymendering and Political Cartels' (2002) 116 *Harvard Law Review* 593–648; Sujit Choudhry, "He Had a Mandate'; The South African Constitutional Court and the African National Congress in a Dominant Party Democracy' (2009) 2 *Constitutional Court Review* 1–86; Michael Pal, 'Breakdowns in the Democratic Process and the Law of Canadian Democracy' (2011) 57 *McGill Law Journal* 299–347; Niels Petersen, 'Verfassungsgerichte als Wettbewerbshüter des politischen Prozesses', in Dominik Elser *et al.* (eds.), *Das letzte Wort – Rechtsetzung und Rechtskontrolle in der Demokratie* (Baden-Baden: Nomos, 2014), pp. 59–78.

69 See Shapiro, *Democratic Theory*, pp. 60–1; Emanuel Towfigh, 'Demokratische Repräsentation im Parteienstaat', in Ulrich Jan Schröder and Antje von Ungern-Sternberg (eds.), *Aktualität der Weimarer Staatsrechtslehre* (Tübingen: Mohr Siebeck, 2011), pp. 211–34 at 222.

70 Michael Stolleis, 'Parteienstaatlichkeit – Krisensymptome des demokratischen Verfassungsstaats' (1986) 44 *Veröffentlichungen der Vereinigung der Deutschen Staatsrechtslehrer* 7–45 at 26–9; Issacharoff and Pildes, 'Politics as Markets'; Shapiro, *Democratic Theory*, p. 61.

71 On gerrymandering, see Issacharoff, 'Gerrymendering'.

72 On the latter, see Karl-Otto Zimmer, 'Nochmals: Zur verfassungsnäheren Gestaltung der 5-%-Klausel' (1985) 38 *Die Öffentliche Verwaltung* 101–2 at 102; Dieter Grimm, 'Politische Parteien', in Ernst Benda, Werner Maihofer and Hans-Jochen Vogel (eds.), *Handbuch des Verfassungsrechts der Bundesrepublik Deutschland* (Berlin: Walter de Gruyter, 2 edn. 1994), ch. 14 at para. 43; Martin Morlok, 'Parteienrecht als Wettbewerbsrecht', in Peter Häberle, Martin Morlok and Vassilios Skouris (eds.), *Festschrift für Dimitris Th. Tsatsos* (Baden-Baden: Nomos, 2003), pp. 408–47 at 435; Markus Krajewski, 'Kommunalwahlrechtliche Sperrklauseln im föderativen System' (2008) 61 *Die Öffentliche Verwaltung* 345–53 at 348.

73 Issacharoff and Pildes, 'Politics As Markets', 688–90.

74 Hans Herbert von Arnim, *Abgeordnetenentschädigung und Grundgesetz* (Landau: Pfälzische Verlagsanstalt, 1975), p. 72.

75 Stolleis, 'Parteienstaatlichkeit', 23–6.

Most of these practices are not negative per se. The question is rather one of the right degree.[76] Minimum quotas for parliamentary representation can have an important function in facilitating the formation of government in a representative system. State subsidies for political parties are supposed to weaken these parties' dependence on private donations and thus the influence of private donors. The remuneration and the benefit for parliamentarians should be attractive enough to convince talented young people of a career in politics. However, the danger is that these instruments are abused.

In this regard, elections are only an insufficient control mechanism.[77] On the one hand, there are information asymmetries between politicians and voters:[78] Voters rarely have the necessary information to evaluate what the right degree is. On the other hand, the voters lack alternatives if the established parties collude. Consequently, judicial review has the function to correct such instances of collusion. As in the case of minority protection and the prevention of legislative capture, courts will rarely pursue this goal openly. Instead, the functional understanding of judicial review has an implicit guiding function in the development of the constitutional doctrine.[79]

2.5 Correction of External Effects

Finally, political decision-making systematically disregards specific interests if decisions have positive or negative external effects. Decisions have external effects if they affect individuals who have not directly or indirectly participated in the decision-making process. Many political decisions have a redistributive effect – that is, their costs are not necessarily borne by the beneficiaries. Subsidies benefit the subsidised industries but are financed by the general taxpayers. Regulations establishing emission standards for factories impose costs on factory owners while they benefit the whole society because they contribute to cleaner air and water. Such redistributive measures are a common part of political decision-making. However, such decisions are problematic if the group that has to bear a significant part of the costs of a measure has not participated in the decision-making process.

[76] Pildes, 'Political Competition', 1614.

[77] Towfigh, *Parteien-Paradox*, pp. 128–9.

[78] Towfigh, 'Demokratische Repräsentation', 230.

[79] See Issacharoff and Pildes, 'Politics As Markets', 690–9; Petersen, 'Verfassungsgerichte als Wettbewerbshüter', pp. 66–73 (both for the German Constitutional Court).

Such external effects can be either of a territorial or of a temporal nature. Territorial external effects usually occur if the group that bears part of the costs is not part of the political community making the decision. Let us assume that a power plant is constructed close to the Eastern border of a state. If winds in the area blow primarily in Eastern direction, the Eastern neighbours are significantly affected by the pollution caused by the power plant. However, those neighbours neither benefit from the plant's electricity generation nor did they take part in the decision-making process about the plant's construction. For this reason, political actors have incentives to make decisions whose costs can be allocated to social groups that do not determine the composition of the political elites and thus do not have any sanctioning potential.[80]

However, it is doubtful whether constitutional courts are the appropriate actors to correct such external effects. Certainly, *Eyal Benvenisti* has recently made the case that courts sometimes implicitly cooperate in order to overcome transnational collective action problems.[81] However, such a cooperation of courts has its limits. Some global problems like climate change can probably not be addressed by a coordinated unilateral action of courts.[82] Instead, these issues rather have to be tackled through political cooperation. The role of courts in this respect is to take into account the potential of international cooperation to solve international collective-action problems when they control the delegation of sovereign power to international organisations. Conceptions of legitimacy that are rooted in the nation state are not appropriate standards of review in this respect.[83]

With regard to temporal external effects, judicial review might be able to play a more important role.[84] Temporal external effects usually occur if

[80] Emanuel Towfigh and Niels Petersen, 'Public and Social Choice Theory', in Emanuel Towfigh and Niels Petersen (eds.), *Economic Methods for Lawyers* (Cheltenham: Edward Elgar, 2015), pp. 121–45 at 132–3.

[81] Eyal Benvenisti, 'Reclaiming Democracy: The Strategic Uses of Foreign and International Law by National Courts' (2008) 102 *American Journal of International Law* 241–74.

[82] See Christoph Engel, 'Internationaler Umweltschutz: Systematik der Probleme und der Lösungen', in Jürgen Basedow, Klaus J. Hopt and Hein Kötz (eds.), *Festschrift für Ulrich Drobnig* (Tübingen: Mohr Siebeck, 1998), pp. 247–76 at 265.

[83] See Brun-Otto Bryde, 'Das Demokratieprinzip des Grundgesetzes als Optimierungsaufgabe', in Thomas Blanke (ed.), *Demokratie und Grundgesetz* (Baden-Baden: Nomos, 2000), pp. 59–70 at 65; Niels Petersen, 'The Democracy Concept of the European Union: Coherent Constitutional Principle or Prosaic Declaration of Intent?' (2005) 6 *German Law Journal* 1507–25.

[84] See Christoph Engel, 'The Constitutional Court – Applying the Proportionality Principle – as a Subsidiary Authority for the Assessment of Political Outcomes', in Christoph Engel and Adrienne Héritier (eds.), *Linking Politics and Law* (Baden-Baden: Nomos, 2003), pp. 285–314 at 305–6.

decisions have detrimental effects on future generations – that is, if they have immediate benefits, although the costs will be felt years or decades later. The most prominent examples stem from financial or environmental policy. A government can use debt to finance projects in order to gain additional votes. When the debts have to be paid back, the responsible politicians have often retired so that they are not accountable for the negative effects of their decisions.[85]

The situation is similar in the field of environmental policy. Emissions usually have long-term negative effects. The effects of measures aimed at the mitigation of climate change will only be felt in several decades, whereas the costs are already felt today. Many of the voters who today decide about the composition of the government may then not be alive anymore. At the same time, citizens who will feel the effect of environmental measures that are taken (or not taken) in 20 or 30 years often do not yet have a vote or might even not yet be born.

Consequently, judicial review can protect future generations if courts correct short-sighted political measures.[86] However, decisions in the field of public finance or the environment often require complex prognoses and specific expertise. Thus, courts might not be the appropriate actors to take an active role in this process.[87] The decisions of the German Constitutional Court on the European financial architecture show that the courts are increasingly confronted with such questions.[88] However, they also show that they may not yet be up to this challenge.

2.6 *Conclusion*

In this section, I have argued that judicial review has the function to correct political market failures. There are three types of situations in

[85] See Andreas Glaser, *Nachhaltige Entwicklung und Demokratie* (Tübingen: Mohr Siebeck, 2006), p. 331–2; Haltern, 'Demokratische Verantwortlichkeit', 566; Wolfgang Kahl and Andreas Glaser, 'Die Nachhaltigkeitsfähigkeit der parlamentarischen Demokratie', in Klaus Lange (ed.), *Nachhaltigkeit im Recht* (Baden-Baden: Nomos, 2003), pp. 9–38 at 10–3; Michael Kleiber, *Der grundrechtliche Schutz zukünftiger Generationen* (Tübingen: Mohr Siebeck, 2014), p. 5.

[86] Such propositions are, for example, developed by Glaser, *Nachhaltige Entwicklung*, pp. 362–4; Kleiber, *Schutz zukünftiger Generationen.*

[87] See Oliver Lepsius, 'Nachhaltigkeit und Parlament', in Wolfgang Kahl (ed.), *Nachhaltigkeit als Verbundbegriff* (Tübingen: Mohr Siebeck, 2008), pp. 326–50 at 335–8 (arguing that parliaments are the actors that are best suited to deal with such sustainability questions).

[88] See Entscheidungen des Bundesverfassungsgerichts [BVerfGE] vol. 129, p. 124; vol. 130, p. 318; vol. 132, p. 195; vol. 134, p. 366.

which courts play an important role. First, they act as arbiters in horizontal or vertical competency conflicts. Such conflicts between different institutions or different levels of a federal state cannot be resolved by the political process. Instead, they have to be referred to courts as external, neutral arbiters. Second, judicial review is supposed to protect minorities. The exercise of sovereign power has to be legitimised vis-à-vis the whole society, not only vis-à-vis the majority. This does not mean that the interests of all social groups always have to be realised to the largest extent. In a pluralistic society, such a requirement would not be realistic. However, the interests of all social actors have to be taken into account in the political process. To the extent that certain interests are underrepresented, courts have an important corrective function to ensure the accountability of the political actors with regard to underrepresented social groups.

Finally, judicial review can help to reduce the representation risks that are inherent in representative democracies. The political process sometimes creates incentive structures that lead to decisions that are contrary to the public interest. Political actors pursue special interests, look for their own material advantage or disregard long-term goals. Courts can try to correct these deficiencies of democratic decision-making at least partly through judicial review. We have seen that there are two types of representation risks: On the one hand, representatives may intentionally abuse their power; on the other hand, they can make bad decisions because they lack sufficient expertise.[89] The political market failures that were identified in this section are all rooted in the incentive structures of the political process. *Prima facie*, it thus seems plausible to restrict the corrective function of judicial review to the intentional abuse of power and to leave the correction of incompetence to the political process.[90]

However, such a differentiation would be unfeasible. If we wanted to restrict judicial review to the control of intentional abuses of power, we would have to analyse the actual motives of the legislature. As we have seen, however, these will often be difficult to determine. Consequently, we have to base the analysis on indirect proxies, such as the lack of fit between measure and purpose or legislative inconsistency.[91] However, these proxies

[89] See section 1 of this chapter.

[90] Such a demand is often made in German constitutional law scholarship. See Oliver Lepsius, 'Anmerkung' (2009) 64 *Juristenzeitung* 260–3 at 262; Philipp Dann, 'Verfassungsgerichtliche Kontrolle gesetzgeberischer Rationalität' (2010) 49 *Der Staat* 630–46 at 640–2; Möllers, 'Legalität', p. 399.

[91] See section 2.3 of this chapter.

can at the same time be signals of a lack of rationality.[92] The lack of fit between measure and purpose can be due either to implicit motives of the legislature or to a lack of diligence in the drafting process.

Furthermore, the lack of rationality in the legislative procedure can be the consequence of a specific incentive structure. Let us assume the legislature wants to introduce stricter supervision and control measures in order to combat organised crime more effectively. The effectiveness of these measures can be tested empirically. However, the legislature often does not have incentives to make such an empirical investigation. The political success of the measure depends on whether the general public *believes* that these measures are effective. However, the mere appeasement of the public is, in principle, no sufficient justification for the restriction of fundamental rights.

These considerations show that the lack of procedural or substantial "rationality" of the legislative measure is not necessarily due to the incompetence of the legislature. It may rather be the result of the prevailing incentive structure.[93] For this reason, it is impossible to distinguish between an admissible control of legislative motivation and an inadmissible review of legislative rationality. Rather, both are necessarily intertwined.

3. Vice and Virtue of Judicial Independence

The advantages of judicial review as a control mechanism for the political process have already been touched on. Judges enjoy a degree of independence that is unmatched by any other public institution. At first sight, this might call their democratic legitimacy into question. However, according to the conception that has been developed in this chapter, democratic legitimacy is not limited to the representation of the preferences of the societal majority. Instead, courts come into play where democratic accountability creates problematic incentives, such as in the cases of minority protection or external effects, or where accountability is no effective control mechanism. In such situations, the democratic weakness of courts, their lack of accountability, becomes their strength. It is precisely the independence of courts that enables them to exercise effective control of the legislature.[94]

92 Petersen, 'Legislative Inconsistency', 523.

93 Petersen, 'Common Wisdom Fallacy', 310.

94 Mauro Cappelletti, *The Judicial Process in Comparative Perspective* (Oxford: Clarendon Press, 1989), p. 176.

Critics of judicial review sometimes argue that courts are no less prone to mistakes than parliaments.[95] If it could not be established that courts are less likely to make mistakes than legislatures, they argue, the legislative decisions should be exclusively reserved to parliament with its more direct democratic legitimacy.[96] However, the advantage of judicial review is that courts have different incentives structures from legislatures.[97] The judicial independence counterbalances the partly problematic incentives in the political process. Furthermore, courts are further removed from interest group pressure than political actors.[98] This does not shield courts from making mistakes in individual cases. However, systematic mistakes are not to be expected to the same degree as in the political process.

A further argument that is often raised against judicial review is that courts are not in a better position to protect minorities than parliaments. If there were prejudices and reservations against certain minorities in the general population, then the judges would be prone to such reservations as well.[99] Certainly, judges may sometimes share the same prejudices as the general public. However, they usually have a higher level of education than the average citizen. Because education helps to reduce prejudices and to increase tolerance, we can usually assume that judges are more sensitive to the issue of minority protection than the general population. Moreover, it is not important that judicial review remains without mistakes in individual cases. Instead, judicial review is already a reasonable institution when courts correct more mistakes than they do themselves.[100]

4. Conclusion

In this chapter, I have argued that the principal function of judicial review is the correction of political market failures. However, this argument is

[95] Waldron, 'Case Against Judicial Review', 1399–401.

[96] See also Kramer, *The People Themselves*, p. 247, who calls the advocates of judicial review "modern aristocrats".

[97] Christoph Engel, 'Rechtswissenschaft als angewandte Sozialwissenschaft – Die Aufgabe der Rechtswissenschaft nach der Öffnung der Rechtsordnung für sozialwissenschaftliche Theorie', in Christoph Engel (ed.), *Methodische Zugänge zu einem Recht der Gemeinschaftsgüter* (Baden-Baden: Nomos, 1998), pp. 11–40 at 16.

[98] John Ferejohn, 'Judicializing Politics, Politicizing Law' (2002) 65 *Law and Contemporary Problems* 41–68 at 65; Engel, 'Constitutional Court', p. 300; Dimitris Kyritsis, 'Representation and Waldron's Objection to Judicial Review' (2006) 26 *Oxford Journal of Legal Studies* 733–51 at 747.

[99] Waldron, 'Case Against Judicial Review', 1404–5; Bellamy, *Political Constitutionalism*, p. 46.

[100] See v. Arnim, *Gemeinwohl*, p. 244.

not supposed to lead to the development of super-positive standards for judicial review. Apex courts do not control whether minority rights have been violated or whether the legislature has been captured in a particular situation. Instead, they use constitutional rights as normative standard of review. Such constitutional rights do not necessarily protect minorities.[101] Instead, the argument developed in this chapter is primarily a theoretical argument. It is supposed to provide an external justification for judicial review and thus a standard to determine whether courts engage in judicial activism.

However, this does not mean that the determination of the function of judicial review is without consequences for constitutional law doctrine. On the contrary, courts often have a large amount of discretion when interpreting the constitution. In such cases, the considerations on the legitimacy of judicial review can play an important role in determining the proper standard of review. They guide us in the design and development of constitutional law doctrine. One example is the central theme of this book – the proportionality test. In the next chapter, we will see that Bernhard Schlink, one of the most prominent critics of balancing in the context of the proportionality test, relies on an argument that is rooted in the division of powers: The balancing of competing values is the task of the legislature, not of courts.[102] However, this argument is not convincing if the legislature systematically fails to take into account certain relevant interests in its decision-making process, or if it attaches too much importance to specific special interests. We will come back to this point in the following chapter.[103]

The fact that the actual fundamental rights doctrine and the function of judicial review identified in this chapter are not identical does not impair the conception that was developed here. Instead, the formalisation of the fundamental rights doctrine renders important services. If courts were directly asked to protect minorities, we would run into difficult problems of determining which minorities are worthy of protection. Instead, fundamental rights identify certain situations in which discrimination of minorities is particularly prevalent. This does not mean that every violation of a fundamental right is indeed a case with minority concern. The same

[101] Möllers, 'Legalität', p. 342.

[102] Schlink, *Abwägung*, p. 190; Schlink, 'Verhältnismäßigkeit', p. 461. See also Webber, *Negotiable Constitution*, pp. 147–8.

[103] See ch. 2, section 1.4.

consideration applies with regard to legislative capture. Again, courts are not burdened with the task of identifying the motivation of the legislature and the factors that influenced the decision-making process. Instead, the formalisation of fundamental-rights doctrine allows us to identify cases in which the danger of capture is typically rather likely.

2

The Normative Debate on Balancing

The previous chapter discussed the legitimacy of judicial review in the abstract. This question will also play a central role in this chapter. However, we will turn to a concrete doctrinal argumentation structure – the proportionality test.[1] The proportionality test is a central doctrinal instrument in a two-step fundamental rights analysis. The second step, the justification analysis, involves a normative comparison between the infringed fundamental right and the pursued public aim or between two competing fundamental rights. However, constitutional texts usually do not determine how such conflicts are to be resolved.[2] Some limitations clauses enumerate certain aims that allow fundamental rights restrictions. Others are more general and only demand that the limitation be "reasonable and justifiable".[3]

In such a normative context, the proportionality test offers courts a doctrinal structure that allows them to resolve conflicts between competing values without having to establish abstract value hierarchies.[4] Instead, proportionality focuses on the circumstances of each individual case. The test consists of four steps: a measure restricting a fundamental right has to pursue a legitimate aim; it has to be rationally connected to this aim; there should not be a less restrictive alternative measure, which is equally effective; and, finally, the measure has to be proportionate – that is, it has to strike an appropriate balance between the fundamental right and the pursued public purpose.

The two pivotal steps of the test are the two latter ones. In economic terms, the less-restrictive-means test is a requirement of Pareto efficiency.[5]

[1] The argument developed in this chapter relies, in part, on Petersen, 'How to Compare'.

[2] Gabriele Britz, 'Prozedurale Lösung von Grundrechtskollisionen durch "grundrechtliches Vorverfahren"' (2003) 42 *Der Staat* 35–59 at 35–6.

[3] See, for example Article. 36 (1) of the South African Constitution.

[4] Stone Sweet and Mathews, 'Proportionality Balancing', 88; similarly Moshe Cohen-Eliya and Iddo Porat, 'American Balancing and German Proportionality: The Historical Origins' (2010) 8 *International Journal of Constitutional Law* 263–86 at 276.

[5] Jan-Reinard Sieckmann, *Regelmodelle und Prinzipienmodelle des Rechtssystems* (Baden-Baden: Nomos, 1990), pp. 224–5; David M. Beatty, 'Human Rights and the Rules of Law',

The core of this test is usually the question whether alternative measures would indeed be as effective as the chosen fundamental rights restriction. The most difficult step of the proportionality test is the last prong, the balancing test. Balancing principally requires a cost-benefit-analysis.[6] The balancing test does not compare the two competing values in the abstract. Instead, it takes the circumstances of each individual case into account. These are, in particular, the intensity of the fundamental rights restriction and the extent to which the legislative aim is promoted through the measure in question.[7]

Nevertheless, this last step of the proportionality test, the balancing stage, faces severe scholarly critique. It requires courts to attribute values to the competing rights. However, how are courts able to make such an evaluation if the constitution is moot with regard to the relative value of different constitutional rights? The following analysis will examine the two main strands of the critique that is voiced against the balancing test. Many authors argue that balancing requires the comparison of incommensurable values. As they do not see a rational standard for such a comparison, they claim that balancing leads to a subjective value decision of the deciding judges. The second strand of critique argues that the focus of proportionality on the circumstances of each individual case impairs legal certainty. For this reason, they advocate resorting to more categorical forms of argumentation.

We will see that both strands of critique are based on specific assumptions on the role of judicial review in a democratic system and on the value of legal certainty. The proposed remedies indeed mitigate some of the problems of proportionality. However, they come with their own drawbacks. I will argue that the discussion revolves in its core around a question of competency: Which institution should decide about certain fundamental value questions? Here, proportionality seems to be the best fit for the model of judicial review that was developed in the previous chapter.

in David M. Beatty (ed.), *Human Rights and Judicial Review: A Comparative Perspective* (Dordrecht: Martinus Nijhoff, 1994), pp. 1–56 at 47; Robert Alexy, 'Constitutional Rights, Balancing, and Rationality' (2003) 16 *Ratio Juris* 131–40 at 135; van Aaken, *Rational Choice*, p. 329; Rivers, 'Proportionality', 198; Cohen-Eliya and Porat, 'American balancing', 268; Giovanni Sartor, 'The Logic of Proportionality: Reasoning with Non-Numerical Magnitudes' (2013) 14 *German Law Journal* 1419–56 at 1448.

6 Van Aaken, *Rational Choice*, p. 330; Knill and Becker, 'Divergenz trotz Diffusion?', 458; Rivers, 'Proportionality', 180; Engel, 'Öffentliches Wirtschaftsrecht', para. 52; Portuese, 'Principle of Proportionality', 620.

7 Robert Alexy, *A Theory of Constitutional Rights* (Oxford: Oxford University Press, 2002), p. 51.

1. Balancing and the Comparison of Incommensurable Values

The critique of balancing first appeared in German constitutional law scholarship. The most prominent and also most elaborate critique was developed in Bernhard Schlink's dissertation on balancing in constitutional law.[8] Schlink argues that balancing is no rational tool of judicial argumentation because it requires a comparison of incommensurable values. Today, this critique is shared by various authors across different jurisdictions.[9] In the following, the main argument of the critics will be retraced. Then, I will analyse the response that was given by several advocates of the balancing test. The most prominent attempt to defend the rationality of balancing was *Robert Alexy*'s weight formula. However, I will argue that *Alexy* fails to rebut the arguments of the critics. Equally, attempts to use the Nash bargaining solution to rationalise balancing are not convincing. The final sub-section examines the alternative to balancing that Schlink proposes. He advocates a reduced form of the proportionality test without the balancing stage. However, his proposal makes certain presumptions about the role of judicial review, which are not compatible with the conception developed in the previous chapter.

1.1 The Incommensurability Critique

In order to understand the incommensurability critique, we have to take a closer look at different ways to establish relationships between two values. There are three different ways to establish such relationships. First, we can make relative assertions – that is, determine whether a specific good has a smaller, greater or equal value as the good of

[8] Schlink, *Abwägung*.

[9] See Aleinikoff, 'Age of Balancing', 972–6; Habermas, *Facts and Norms*, p. 259; Woolman, 'Out of Order?', 114–21; Leisner, *Abwägungsstaat*, p. 74; Blaauw-Wolf, 'Balancing of interests', 210; Schlink, 'Verhältnismäßigkeit', p. 460; Böckenförde, 'Schutzbereich', 190; Raue, 'Grundrechtsbeschränkungen', 85; Ralph Christensen and Andreas Fischer-Lescano, *Das Ganze des Rechts – Vom hierarchischen zum reflexiven Verständnis deutscher und europäischer Grundrechte* (Berlin: Duncker & Humblot, 2007), p. 357; Christensen and Lerch, 'Dass das Ganze das Wahre ist', 439–40; Tsakyrakis, 'Proportionality', 471; Webber, *Negotiable Constitution*, pp. 92–3; Webber, 'Proportionality', 194; Hillgruber, 'Ohne rechtes Maß?', 862; Isensee, 'Das Grundrecht als Abwehrrecht und als staatliche Schutzpflicht', ch. 191 at para. 136; Schlink, 'Proportionality in Constitutional Law', 291–302 at 299; Camilo de Oliveira, *Kritik der Abwägung*, pp. 205–10; Sales, 'Rationality', 236; Francisco J. Urbina, 'Incommensurability and Balancing' (2015) 35 *Oxford Journal of Legal Studies* 575–605.

comparison. Such a relation can be measured through ordinal scales.[10] An ordinal scale establishes a ranking of different values without determining the distance of these values to each other. This presupposes that the compared goods are comparable.[11] One example is the comparison of grades. We can say that an A is better than a B, and that a B is better than a C. However, we cannot say that a paper that was graded with an A is twice as good as a paper with a B, or that the difference in quality between a paper with an A and a paper with a B equals the qualitative difference between a B- and a C-graded paper.

Second, we can establish a relationship on a metric scale, which permits a statement about the ratio of two competing values. There are two types of metric scales. Interval scales allow us to make statements about the distance between two values. However, the scale lacks an absolute zero-point. The most prominent example is temperature scales, which have different zero-points depending on whether we measure the temperature in Celsius, Fahrenheit or Kelvin. However, we can say that the distance between 5 °C and 10 °C equals the distance between 20 °C and 25 °C, even if we transform the temperature into a different scale.[12] However, we cannot say that 20 °C is twice as hot as 10 °C, because here the different temperature scales would differ. On a Fahrenheit scale, the respective values would be 68° F and 50° F. Consequently, the multiplication of values is mathematically not defined if these values are measured on an interval scale.

Finally, we can also measure values on a ratio scale. Unlike interval scales, ratio scales possess an absolute zero-point so that we can make assessments of the relative importance of values. Examples for values that are measured on a ratio scale are weight, height or distance. A distance of 200 metres is twice as long as a distance of 100 metres. In order to come to this conclusion, it is not relevant whether the distance is measured in metres or yards, as both scales have the same zero-point. Consequently, we can divide and multiply values that are measured on a ratio scale. However, for the establishment of a ratio scale, it is not sufficient that the compared values are merely comparable. Instead, they have to be commensurable – that is, we have to be able to transpose them into a common normative scale or currency that allows us to determine the distance and the ratio of the individual values to each other.

[10] Schlink, *Abwägung*, p. 136.

[11] Ruth Chang, 'Introduction', in Ruth Chang (ed.), *Incommensurability, Incomparability, and Practical Reason* (Cambridge: Harvard University Press, 1997), pp. 1–34 at 6.

[12] On a Fahrenheit scale, the difference in both cases would be 9° F.

If the practice of judicial balancing only consisted of comparing the abstract values of competing interests to each other, it would be sufficient to measure these values on an ordinal scale. We would only need to determine which of the two values is more important. However, balancing does not merely consist of an abstract comparison of values.[13] Instead, courts have to take the circumstances of each individual case into account. This includes the intensity of the restriction of the fundamental right and the extent to which the public purpose is promoted by the measure in question.[14]

Consequently, we have to consider more than one factor on each side of the equation. If we wanted to translate the structure of the balancing test into a mathematical formula, we would have to relate the different factors through multiplication and division with each other.[15] However, the multiplication or division of different values is only mathematically defined if these values can be measured on a ratio scale.[16] For this reason, the values compared in the balancing test have to be commensurable – that is, we have to be able to translate them into a common normative currency.

In principle, there are two ways to compare the value of different constitutional rights with each other: On the one hand, we can look at the intrinsic value; on the other hand, we can determine the instrumental value of the right to achieve an external purpose.[17] With regard to the first possibility, it seems to be impossible to find a common normative currency to determine the intrinsic value of different constitutional rights on a ratio scale. At least, the constitutional text does not give any indications that would allow for the establishment of such a value scale.[18]

[13] Robert Uerpmann, *Das öffentliche Interesse: Seine Bedeutung als Tatbestandsmerkmal und als dogmatischer Begriff* (Tübingen: Mohr Siebeck, 1999), p. 282.

[14] Alexy, *Theory of Constitutional Rights*, p. 51.

[15] On this point, the most prominent critic and advocate of balancing agree. See Schlink, *Abwägung*, pp. 128–34 on the one hand and Robert Alexy, 'On Balancing and Subsumption: A Structural Comparison' (2003) 16 *Ratio Juris* 433–49 at 443–8 on the other.

[16] See generally Sebastian Goerg and Niels Petersen, 'Empirical Research and Statistics', in Emanuel Towfigh and Niels Petersen (eds.), *Economic Methods for Lawyers* (Cheltenham: Edward Elgar, 2015), pp. 146–76 at 157. With regard to balancing, see also Schlink, *Abwägung*, pp. 136–7.

[17] Cass R. Sunstein, 'Incommensurability and Kinds of Valuation: Some Applications in Law', in Ruth Chang (ed.), *Incommensurability, Incomparability, and Practical Reason* (Cambridge: Harvard University Press, 1997), pp. 234–54 at 235.

[18] Peter Lerche, *Übermaß und Verfassungsrecht* (Köln: Carl Heymann, 1961), p. 129; Schlink, *Abwägung*, pp. 134–5; Rainer Dechsling, *Das Verhältnismäßigkeitsgebot* (München: Franz Vahlen, 1989), pp. 18–21; Matthias Herdegen, 'Verfassungsinterpretation als methodische Disziplin' (2004) 59 *Juristenzeitung* 873–9 at 877; Herbert Bethge, 'Grundrechtskollisionen',

However, even if constitutional rights do not have an intrinsic value that can be measured on a ratio scale, they might have an instrumental value. Utilitarians would argue that every measure restricting fundamental rights has a specific positive or negative utility for the affected individuals.[19] We can draw an analogy to the world of economic exchanges. In principle, apples and pears are not comparable. Yet, we nevertheless compare them in daily life by translating their instrumental value into a common currency. Money is the measure for the value that individuals attribute to different, intrinsically not comparable goods.

Let us now conduct the following thought experiment: If we transfer this economic logic of the market for goods and services to the realm of constitutional rights, we could ask each concerned individual how much he or she would be willing to pay for a specific constitutional value. The willingness to pay would then be the common normative currency for the individual constitutional rights.[20] This willingness to pay would not have to be expressed in monetary terms. Instead, there are other possibilities to measure individual preferences. For example, we could ask individuals to what extent they would be willing to absorb pain in the form of electric shocks for pursuing a certain interest.[21] The more pain an individual would be willing to absorb, the more intense his or her preferences for a specific constitutional value would be.

Let us consider a concrete example: the conflict between the religious freedom of a female Muslim teacher who wants to wear a headscarf in school and the interest of the general society of a religiously neutral appearance of teachers.[22] On the one hand, we could ask the teacher how much she would be willing to pay for the right to carry the headscarf. On the other hand, we could ask Muslim and non-Muslim parents

in Detlef Merten and Hans-Jürgen Papier (eds.), *Handbuch der Grundrechte. Band III: Grundrechte in Deutschland: Allgemeine Lehren II* (Heidelberg: C. F. Müller, 2009), ch. 72 at para. 82; Matthias Cornils, 'Allgemeine Handlungsfreiheit', in Josef Isensee and Paul Kirchhof (eds.), *Handbuch des Staatsrechts der Bundesrepublik Deutschland. Band VII: Freiheitsrechte*, 3rd edn. (Heidelberg: C. F. Müller, 2009), ch. 168 at para. 102.

19 See James Griffin, 'Are There Incommensurable Values?' (1977) 7 *Philosophy and Public Affairs* 39–59; Donald H. Regan, 'Authority and Value: Reflection on Raz's Morality of Freedom' (1989) 62 *Southern Californian Law Review* 995–1095 at 1056–75.

20 Griffin, 'Are There Incommensurable Values?', 50–5. See also Ekkehard Hofmann, *Abwägung im Recht* (Tübingen: Mohr Siebeck, 2007), p. 298.

21 Jonathan Baron, *Thinking and Deciding* (Cambridge: Cambridge University Press, 3 edn. 2000), p. 390.

22 This example is modelled after a case before the German Federal Constitutional Court. See Entscheidungen des Bundesverfassungsgerichts [BVerfGE] vol. 108, p. 282.

how much they would be willing to pay to prohibit teachers from wearing headscarves in school. Depending on whether the Muslim teachers or the parents would be willing to pay more, the prohibition of headscarves for teachers in schools would either be justified or not.

However, such a practice would raise practical and normative difficulties. First, it would be difficult to determine the willingness to pay of the affected citizens. Courts cannot make an empirical inquiry about the affected groups' willingness to pay for each decision on fundamental rights. Even if they made such an inquiry, we would need instruments to make citizens credibly reveal their preferences.[23] As long as the payments or electric shocks are only imaginary, citizens would have incentives to overestimate their willingness to pay in order to strengthen their position. However, studies in which citizens are asked to make actual money transfers or receive electric shocks seem to be impractical.

Second, it is doubtful whether we could find an appropriate currency to compare the intensity of preferences between subjects.[24] At least if there are no transfer payments between the different affected groups, the monetary willingness to pay does not allow a comparison of different preferences because money has a decreasing marginal utility.[25] The higher the disposable income, the higher is the general willingness to pay.[26] An individual whose monthly income is €1,000 attributes a different value to €10 than an individual whose monthly income is €10,000. This problem is not resolved if we resort to non-monetary currencies. The willingness to absorb pain not only depends on the intensity of preferences but also on the general ability to absorb pain.

Third, the result of the comparison depends heavily on the number of people supporting the interests on each side of the equation. A minority might have strong preferences for a specific constitutional right. However, if it only forms a small part of the overall population, it might lose out even if the majority merely possesses very weak opposing preferences. However, if fundamental rights are precisely supposed to protect

[23] In economics, this problem is discussed under the concept of mechanism design. See Drew Fudenberg and Jean Tirole, *Game Theory* (Cambridge: MIT Press, 1991), pp. 243–318; Roger B. Myerson, in Steven M. Durlauf and Lawrence E. Blume (eds.), *The New Palgrave Dictionary of Economics: Vol. V*, 2 edn. (Basingstoke: Palgrave Macmillan, 2008), pp. 533–42 at 533.

[24] Schlink, *Abwägung*, pp. 166–7.

[25] Hans-Bernd Schäfer and Claus Ott, *Lehrbuch der ökonomischen Analyse des Zivilrechts* (Berlin: Springer Gabler, 5 edn. 2012), p. 26.

[26] Emanuel Towfigh, 'The Economic Paradigm', in Emanuel Towfigh and Niels Petersen (eds.), *Economic Methods for Lawyers* (Cheltenham: Edward Elgar, 2015), pp. 18–31 at 23.

minorities,[27] as we argued in the previous chapter, then the size of the groups supporting specific values cannot be a decisive factor in the balancing test.

None of these problems is necessarily unsolvable. Consequently, it is not logically impossible to translate individual preferences with regard to constitutional rights into a common currency that can be measured on a ratio scale. However, no convincing solutions have been offered yet. Consequently, the concept of determining the instrumental value of constitutional rights as a proxy for the balancing test in constitutional doctrine still faces too many challenges to be of any practical use.

1.2 *Alexy's Weight Formula and the Attempt to Rationalise Balancing*

The main advocate of balancing constitutional rights is the German legal philosopher, Robert Alexy. The balancing of competing constitutional principles forms the core of Alexy's book *A Theory of Constitutional Rights*.[28] Following Ronald Dworkin,[29] Alexy distinguished between two types of norms: rules and principles. Whereas rules have a binary structure, according to which they were either applicable or inapplicable, principles have optimisation requirements.[30] A conflict between two principles has to be resolved through the means of the proportionality test, the core of which is the balancing of the competing principles.[31] To the balancing critics, Alexy responded that rationality was not the same as complete determination.[32] He argued that judicial margins of discretion were a common feature of legal argumentation.[33] It was important that the result of the balancing test could be rationally justified. However, it was not necessary for there to be only one rationally justifiable result.[34]

In his later work, Alexy formally tried to justify the rationality of balancing.[35] For this purpose, he distinguished between the internal and the

[27] See ch. 1, section 2.2.
[28] Alexy, *Theory of Constitutional Rights*.
[29] Ronald Dworkin, *Taking Rights Seriously* (London: Duckworth, 1977), pp. 22–8.
[30] Alexy, *Theory of Constitutional Rights*, pp. 47–8.
[31] Id., pp. 66–7.
[32] Id., pp. 100–1.
[33] Alexy, 'On Balancing and Subsumption', 434–5.
[34] Alexy, *Theory of Constitutional Rights*, pp. 100–9.
[35] Alexy, 'Constitutional Rights'; Alexy, 'On Balancing and Subsumption'; Robert Alexy, 'Balancing, Constitutional Review, and Representation' (2005) 3 *International Journal of Constitutional Law* 572–81. However, he was not the first author to propose a mathematical justification of balancing. For an earlier formal attempt to justify balancing, see Heinrich Hubmann, 'Die Methode der Abwägung', in Heinrich Hubmann and Heinz Hübner (eds.), *Festschrift für Ludwig Schnorr von Carolsfeld* (Köln: Carl Heymanns Verlag, 1972), pp. 173–97.

external justification of balancing.[36] The internal justification possesses a formal structure, which can be expressed through the so-called weight formula.[37] This weight formula contains three factors: the abstract weights of the competing constitutional values (W), the intensity of interference (I) and the reliability of the empirical assumptions (R):[38]

$$W_{i,j} = \frac{I_i * W_i * R_i}{I_j * W_j * R_j}$$

If $W_{i,j}$ is larger than one, then principle *i* prevails. If the value of the formula is smaller than one, principle *j* prevails.[39] If $W_{i,j}$ equals one, there is a stalemate between the two principles.[40] In such a case, the restriction of the fundamental right would be justified because the legislature has a margin of appreciation. The external justification refers to the values that are attributed to the different factors of the formula. Alexy acknowledges that it is impossible to determine these values logically. Therefore, he only requires plausible reasons to be given for the assumption of specific values.[41]

Nevertheless, Alexy's weight formula faces two significant objections. To the extent that Alexy includes the abstract weight of the competing principles into his weight formula, he has to deal with the problem of incommensurability discussed in the previous sub-section. The attribution of abstract values to the competing principles is part of the external justification. The external justification does not need to meet the requirements of formal logical argumentation. Instead, plausible reasons are sufficient. However, it is not entirely clear what such reasons would look like. It rather seems, to cite a famous dictum by the late *Anthony Scalia*, that balancing is like the evaluation "whether a particular line is longer than a particular rock is heavy."[42]

[36] Alexy, 'On Balancing and Subsumption', 435.
[37] Id., 443–8; Alexy, 'Balancing', 575. For an attempt to modify the weight formula, see Carlos Bernal Pulido, 'The Rationality of Balancing' (2006) 92 *Archiv für Rechts- und Sozialphilosophie* 195–208.
[38] Alexy, 'On Balancing and Subsumption', 446.
[39] Id., 444.
[40] Id., 445.
[41] Alexy, 'Balancing', 576–7. On the external justification of balancing decisions, see also Jan-Reinard Sieckmann, 'Autonome Abwägung' (2004) 90 *Archiv für Rechts- und Sozialphilosophie* 66–85 at 79.
[42] *Bendix Autolite Corp. v. Midwesco Enterprises, Inc.* 486 U.S. 888 at 897 (1988).

However, even if we assume that it is possible to find arguments for the attribution of abstract values to the competing principles, Alexy cannot perform the mathematical operations that his weight formula requires. As we have seen, the multiplication or division of values requires these values to be measurable on a ratio scale.[43] But even Alexy himself acknowledges that it is impossible to determine the value of constitutional principles on a ratio scale.[44] If one performs the operations of Alexy's weight formula with ordinal values, though, the choice of the scale can already determine the result.[45]

1.3 Normalising the Weight of the Competing Values

Some authors try to mitigate the problem of incommensurability through normalisation. They do not include the abstract weight of the constitutional values into the equation, but only the degree of their realisation.[46] *Paul-Erik Veel* proposes an analogy to the Nash bargaining solution.[47] Nash has developed a solution for optimisation problems where the utility functions of different individuals are not comparable.[48] *Veel* applies Nash's solution to the problem of incomparable values. According to his

[43] See section 1.1 of this chapter. However, see also Matthias Klatt and Moritz Meister, 'Proportionality – a Benefit to Human Rights? Remarks on the I.CON Controversy' (2012) 10 *International Journal of Constitutional Law* 687–708 at 696; Matthias Klatt and Moritz Meister, *The Constitutional Structure of Proportionality* (Oxford: Oxford University Press, 2012), p. 63; Martin Borowski, 'On Apples and Oranges: Comment on Niels Petersen' (2013) 14 *German Law Journal* 1409–18 at 1413–5, who argue that it was sufficient to determine the competing values on an ordinal scale. Such an ordinal scale would indeed be sufficient if the formula only compared one factor on each side. However, as soon as the formula contains several values on each side that are related to each other through multiplication or division, the values have to be determined on a ratio scale.

[44] Alexy, *Theory of Constitutional Rights*, pp. 97–9.

[45] Schlink, *Abwägung*, pp. 136–7; Ekkehard Hofmann, 'Das Wohl der Allgemeinheit als Enteignungsvoraussetzung – Überlegungen zur Methodik der staatlichen Entscheidungsherstellung und ihrer gerichtlichen Kontrolle im Verwaltungs- und Verfassungsrecht', in Marc Bungenberg *et al.* (eds.), *Recht und Ökonomik* (München: C. H. Beck, 2004), pp. 161–88 at 173; Susnjar, *Proportionality*, pp. 206–11; Petersen, 'How to Compare', 1390.

[46] For formalised justification attempts, see Paul-Erik N. Veel, 'Incommensurability, Proportionality, and Rational Legal Decision-Making' (2010) 4 *Law & Ethics of Human Rights* 177–228; Engel, 'Öffentliches Wirtschaftsrecht', paras. 51–57. For a non-formalised approach that relies on the degree of realisation, see Virgílio Afonso da Silva, 'Comparing the Incommensurable: Constitutional Principles, Balancing and Rational Decision' (2011) 31 *Oxford Journal of Legal Studies* 273–301.

[47] Veel, 'Incommensurability'.

[48] John Forbes Nash, 'The Bargaining Problem' (1950) 18 *Econometrica* 155–62.

concept, every constitutional value has a cardinal value function v(x), which expresses the degree of realisation of the constitutional value.[49] *Veel*'s model is based on two assumptions: On the one hand, there are two possible measures, r1, s1 and r2, s2, which can have an effect on the competing constitutional values r and s (e.g., carrying out or abstaining from a restriction of a fundamental right); on the other hand, the two constitutional values enjoy a minimum standard of protection, which he calls ρ and ς, whereas $r_2 > r_1 > \rho$ and $s_1 > s_2 > \varsigma$. Under these circumstances, the first measure can be preferred to the second if[50]

$$\langle V(r_1) - v(\rho)\langle v(s_1) - v(\varsigma)\rangle > \langle v(r_2) - v(\rho)\rangle\langle v(s_2) - v(\varsigma)\rangle$$

Consequently, *Veel* does not compare the abstract values of the competing constitutional rights. He only compares their degree of realisation. If we refer again to *Scalia*'s image,[51] *Veel*'s approach does not compare the length of the line to the weight of the stone. Instead, it compares whether we add relatively more weight to the stone than we cut length from the line. A measure that would increase the weight of the stone by 20 percent while reducing the length of the line by 10 percent would be constitutional. By contrast, a measure that adds less on one side of the balance than it takes at the other would be disproportionate.

A similar line of argumentation can be found in a recent contribution by *Christoph Engel*.[52] *Engel* argues that the restriction of a fundamental right is justified if the utility u for the public interest is bigger than the costs c that are incurred by the restricted right – that is, u > c.[53] This equation can be transformed into u-c > 0 or into u-c > z, z being a predefined intervention threshold.[54] As u and c are incommensurable, both values cannot be subtracted from each other. However, it is possible to normalise the two values by dividing them through the maximally possible utility υ or the maximally possible costs γ:

$$\frac{u}{\upsilon} - \frac{c}{\gamma} > z$$

[49] Veel, 'Incommensurability', 199.
[50] Id., 200.
[51] See earlier note 42, and accompanying text.
[52] Engel, 'Öffentliches Wirtschaftsrecht', paras. 52–54.
[53] Id., para. 52.
[54] Id., para. 54.

As u and υ, as well as c and γ, each possess the same normative currency, both ratios can be subtracted from each other. Contrary to Veel, Engel's reference for the normalisation is not the constitutional right or the public purpose in the specific case but the maximally possible realisation of fundamental rights and the maximally possible realisation of public utility.

However, both approaches face objections. In particular, neither approach avoids attributing a specific weight to the competing values. Veel assumes that the competing values have exactly the same weight.[55] However, this assumption is problematic.[56] Even if we have two competing constitutional values, we have to justify why these values have the same importance.[57] Furthermore, restrictions of fundamental rights are not necessarily justified with the promotion of competing constitutional values. Many limitations clauses only require compelling reasons, or legitimate reasons, or reasonable and justifiable limitations. Therefore, any public purpose could, in principle, be an appropriate reason for the restriction of a fundamental right. However, if we assume under such circumstances that competing principles in the balancing test *always* have the same weight, we would deny that different rights and public purposes differ in social importance and that this difference in social importance should play a role in the balancing test.

By contrast, Engel's conception avoids a comparison between competing fundamental rights and public interests. However, he assumes that we can find a common normative currency for all fundamental rights and, at the same time, for all public interests. Therefore, the normalisation still requires us to relate all fundamental rights on a ratio scale to each other.[58] Furthermore, the same is necessary for all potential public interests. However, this task seems to be as difficult as the comparison between fundamental rights and public interests, particularly because both categories can overlap. The latter is the case if a fundamental right restriction is supposed to protect a competing fundamental right. However, to take a common conflict as an example, it seems impossible to translate freedom of the press and the celebrities' right to privacy into a common normative currency.

[55] Explicitly Veel, 'Incommensurability', 210–13.

[56] See also Rusteberg, *Gewährleistungsgehalt*, pp. 57–8.

[57] See Aharon Barak, 'Proportionality and Principled Balancing' (2010) 4 *Law & Ethics of Human Rights* 1–18 at 9 (arguing that rights which are formally on the same level in the normative hierarchy do not necessarily have the same social importance).

[58] See also Engel, 'Öffentliches Wirtschaftsrecht', para. 54 (acknowledging that his solution can only "partially" rationalise the balancing process).

1.4 The Critics' Alternative to Balancing

So far, we have collected evidence in this chapter that the critique of balancing has significant analytical force. However, what conclusions do we draw from this critique? We have to make comparisons of incommensurable choices every day in our daily life.[59] Even for legal decision-making, such comparisons are not unique.[60] Instead, they are an integral part of criminal or tort law.[61] Therefore, if balancing requires judges to compare incommensurable values, this only means that balancing decisions are not completely determined.[62] This does not immediately disqualify balancing as an instrument of judicial reasoning. Instead, we would have to find a more appropriate alternative in order to refute balancing as a doctrinal tool of judicial review.[63] The alternative proposed by *Schlink* is a reduced form of the proportionality test, which only consists of the first three steps and does not include a balancing stage.[64]

However, this proposal has significant normative problems. If courts cannot resort to balancing, the less-restrictive-means test gains importance. And that has a structural effect on the latter. This can be seen in the case law of the Canadian Supreme Court, which traditionally attributes a low significance to the balancing stage of the proportionality test.[65]

[59] Cass R. Sunstein, 'Incommensurability and Valuation in Law' (1994) 92 *Michigan Law Review* 779–861 at 793; Amartya Sen, *The Idea of Justice* (Cambridge: Harvard University Press, 2009), p. 241; Paul Craig, 'The Nature of Reasonableness Review' (2013) 66 *Current Legal Problems* 131–67 at 163.

[60] Julia Hänni, 'Rechtskonflikte, Wertefolgen und Inkommensurabilität', in Edward Schramm *et al.* (eds.), *Konflikte im Recht – Recht der Konflikte* (Stuttgart: Franz Steiner Verlag, 2010), pp. 173–85 at 180.

[61] Timothy Endicott, 'Proportionality and Incomennsurability', in Grant Huscroft, Bradley W. Miller and Grégoire Webber (eds.), *Proportionality and the Rule of Law: Rights, Justification, Reasoning* (New York: Cambridge University Press, 2014), pp. 311–42 at 323–6.

[62] Aleinikoff, 'Age of Balancing', 972; Schauer, 'Balancing', p. 310.

[63] See Aleinikoff, 'Age of Balancing', 1003; Stephen E. Gottlieb, 'The Paradox of Balancing Significant Interests' (1994) 45 *Hastings Law Journal* 825–66 at 827; Barak, 'Proportionality and Principled Balancing', 17; Craig, 'Nature of Reasonableness Review', 155; Petersen, 'How to Compare', 1388; Borowski, 'Apples and Oranges', 1409; Vicki C. Jackson, 'Constitutional Law in an Age of Proportionality' (2015) 124 *Yale Law Journal* 3094–196 at 3153. See also Dimitris Kyritsis, 'Whatever Works: Proportionality as a Constitutional Doctrine' (2014) 34 *Oxford Journal of Legal Studies* 395–415 at 415 (arguing that proportionality should be judged by whether it has a positive or negative effect on judicial decision-making).

[64] Schlink, *Abwägung*, pp. 192–219. See also Böckenförde, 'Schutzbereich', 190; von Bernstorff, 'Proportionality without balancing'.

[65] See Hogg, 'Section 1 Revisited', 23; Frank Iacobucci, 'Judicial Review by the Supreme Court of Canada under the Canadian Charter of Rights and Freedoms: The First Ten Years', in

However, without the balancing stage, courts have to cope with certain analytical weaknesses of the less-restrictive-means stage that are masked if courts can rely on balancing to deal with these issues.

The core of the less-restrictive-means test is the question whether a potentially less-restrictive alternative measure is as effective in achieving the public purpose as the reviewed measure. This estimation requires an empirical prognosis. In many cases, there will be uncertainty regarding the two measures that are compared.[66] How should courts deal with such uncertainty? Some authors demand that measures only be accepted as potentially less restrictive if they are bound to be as effective as the reviewed measure.[67] However, such a strict interpretation of the less-restrictive-means test would make proportionality an extremely blunt sword.

By contrast, a less-strict interpretation would require judges to make complex normative and empirical evaluations in the context of the less-restrictive-means test.[68] Let us consider an example: In *RJR-MacDonald v. Canada*, the Canadian Supreme Court had to decide about the constitutionality of a ban on tobacco advertising and an obligation of the tobacco industry to print unattributed warnings on the cigarette packages.[69] The crucial question of the case was whether an alternative to the total ban on tobacco advertising was available that was less restrictive to the freedom of expression. The court discussed a partial ban that excluded purely informational advertising, reminders of package appearance, and information about the relative tar content or about new brands as a potentially less restrictive alternative. However, the judges disagreed about whether this partial ban was as effective as the total ban enacted by the Canadian legislature. The majority concluded that the

David M. Beatty (ed.), *Human Rights and Judicial Review: A Comparative Perspective* (Dordrecht: Martinus Nijhoff Publishers, 1994), pp. 93–133 at 121; Leon E. Trakman, William Cole-Hamilton and Sean Gatien, 'R. v. Oakes 1986–1997: Back to the Drawing Board' (1998) 36 *Osgoode Hall Law Journal* 83–149 at 103; Peter W. Hogg, *Constitutional Law of Canada, Vol. 2* (Ontario: Thomson Carswell, 5 edn. 2007), p. 153.

66 See David Bilchitz, 'Does balancing adequately capture the nature of rights?' (2011) 25 *SA Public Law* 423–44 at 423.

67 This is, for example, demanded by Jörg Pöße, 'Der Einschätzungsspielraum des Gesetzgebers als Gegenstand verfassungsgerichtlicher Kontrollbeschränkung', in Martin Nolte (ed.), *Kontrolle im verfassten Rechtsstaat* (Kiel: Lorenz-von-Stein-Institut, 2002), pp. 33–46 at 44.

68 See Lothar Hirschberg, *Der Grundsatz der Verhältnismäßigkeit* (Göttingen: Verlag Otto Schwartz & Co., 1981), p. 172–5; Andreas von Arnauld, *Die Freiheitsrechte und ihre Schranken* (Baden-Baden: Nomos, 1999), p. 263.

69 *RJR-MacDonald v. Canada (Attorney General)* [1995] 3 S.C.R. 199.

legislator had the burden of proof to show that the partial ban was less effective and thus concluded that the total ban failed the less restrictive means test.[70] The judges' margin of discretion is thus shifted from the evaluation of competing normative values to the evaluation of conflicting social science evidence.

Furthermore, there is uncertainty in the scholarly debate about how to deal with external effects in the context of the less-restrictive-means test.[71] How should we consider a less-restrictive means that pursues the public interest with equal effectiveness but imposes burdens on third persons? What about an alternative means that is more costly for public finances? Does a more costly measure generally disqualify as a less restrictive means? Or are even significantly higher costs irrelevant in the evaluation of the alternative measure? Some authors propose compromises: Whether higher costs should be taken into account is supposed to depend on the extent to which the restriction of the fundamental right is reduced.[72] However, such a proposal introduces balancing considerations into the less-restrictive-means test.

Finally, there are certain situations where most people would agree that a measure is evidently disproportionate. However, it is difficult to capture them with the reduced form of the proportionality test. For example, a pneumoencephalography is an extremely painful medical procedure that allows doctors to see the brain structure more clearly. If such a procedure is used for the prosecution of a minor criminal offence, this clearly seems to be out of proportion.[73] Schlink acknowledges this result, but proposes to resolve the case on the level of the legitimate aim.[74] However, this solution seems to introduce balancing into the determination of the legitimate aim and thus only shifts the problem from the balancing stage to one of the other prongs of the proportionality test.

[70] Id. at 344.

[71] See Christoph Engel, 'Das legitime Ziel als Element des Übermaßverbots', in Winfried Brugger, Stephan Kirste and Michael Anderheiden (eds.), *Gemeinwohl in Deutschland, Europa und der Welt* (Baden-Baden: Nomos, 2002), pp. 103–72 at 113–32; Wojciech Sadurski, *Rights before Courts: A Study of Constitutional Courts in Postcommunist States of Central and Eastern Europe* (Dordrecht: Springer, 2005), p. 269–70; Kai Möller, 'Proportionality: Challenging the critics' (2012) 10 *International Journal of Constitutional Law* 709–31 at 714.

[72] See Mark Elliott, 'Proportionality and Deference: The Importance of a Structured Approach', in Christopher Forsyth et al. (eds.), *Effective Judicial Review: A Cornerstone of Good Governance* (Oxford: Oxford University Press, 2010), pp. 264–86 at 280

[73] BVerfGE 17, 108.

[74] Schlink, *Abwägung*, p. 206.

These questions are less urgent if courts can resort to the traditional form of the proportionality test, as they are much easier to integrate into the structure of the balancing test. However, in the reduced form of the proportionality test, they pose a dilemma: Either we accept that the judicial discretion that was identified as the main problem of the balancing stage shifts to one of the other three stages of the proportionality test.[75] Then, however, we would have gained very little from introducing the reduced form of proportionality. Or else we stick to a strict interpretation of the first three elements of the proportionality test. In that case, however, proportionality would become extremely ineffective.[76] Almost every fundamental-rights restriction would pass the test without problems.

Schlink seems to prefer the latter option.[77] However, such strict application of the reduced form of the proportionality test implicitly presupposes a specific conception of the function and the legitimacy of judicial review that is rather sceptical of the institution.[78] As we have seen, Schlink rejects balancing because it confers too much discretion to judges. He argues that the value decisions that are necessarily part of every balancing test should be attributed to the legislature, not to constitutional courts.[79] The rationality argument thus turns into a competency argument.[80] The critics fear that balancing does not impose sufficient methodological limits on

[75] See Saurer, 'Globalisierung des Verhältnismäßigkeitsgrundsatzes', 31.

[76] David Bilchitz, 'Necessity and Proportionality: Towards a Balanced Approach?', in Liora Lazarus, Christopher McCrudden and Nigel Bowles (eds.), *Reasoning Rights: Comparative Judicial Engagement* (Oxford: Hart, 2014), pp. 41–62 at 50.

[77] Schlink, 'Verhältnismäßigkeit', p. 457.

[78] See von Arnauld, *Freiheitsrechte*, p. 264; Frederick Schauer, 'Freedom of Expression Adjudication in Europe and the United States: A Case Study in Comparative Constitutional Architecture', in Georg Nolte (ed.), *European and US Constitutionalism* (Cambridge: Cambridge University Press, 2005), pp. 49–69 at 64; Petersen, 'How to Compare', 1407. See also Alison L. Young, 'Proportionality Is Dead: Long Live Proportionality!', in Grant Huscroft, Bradley W. Miller and Grégoire Webber (eds.), *Proportionality and the Rule of Law: Rights, Justification, Reasoning* (New York: Cambridge University Press, 2014), pp. 43–66 at 65, according to whom the structure of fundamental rights review and the question of the legitimacy of judicial review are necessarily intertwined.

[79] Schlink, *Abwägung*, p. 190; Schlink, 'Verhältnismäßigkeit', pp. 461–2. See also Ernst-Wolfgang Böckenförde, 'Grundrechte als Grundsatznormen' (1990) 29 *Der Staat* 1–31 at 20–1; Webber, *Negotiable Constitution*, pp. 147–8; Tsakyrakis, 'Proportionality', 472; Hillgruber, 'Ohne rechtes Maß?', 862.

[80] Julian Rivers, 'Constitutional Rights and Statutory Limitations', in Matthias Klatt (ed.), *Institutionalized Reason: The Jurisprudence of Robert Alexy* (Oxford: Oxford University Press, 2012), pp. 248–71 at 253.

courts.[81] Therefore, they consider it to be an instrument that grants too much power to courts.[82]

However, this argument can only convince *prima facie*. Adrian Vermeule recently pointed out that constitutions always try to strike a balance between different representation risks.[83] It is a common mistake in constitutional law doctrine to try to minimise one representation risk while disregarding a connected one.[84] When critics of balancing try to avoid balancing because of its analytical difficulties, they run into exactly this problem. They focus exclusively on one specific risk, judicial self-empowerment. At the same time, they neglect the risks that go with the political process.

The previous chapter has shown that the political process is subject to significant representation risks.[85] These dangers cannot be captured through the reduced form of proportionality if interpreted strictly.[86] In the end, we therefore have to strike a balance between the representation risks caused by the political process and the risk of judicial self-empowerment of apex courts exercising judicial review. To get this balance right is partly an empirical question. We have to estimate the actual extent of these dangers that we have only described analytically. In the course of this book, it will not be possible to examine all factors of the equation. However, we will analyse one side by analysing the proportionality case law of three influential courts. This will allow us to get a better picture about whether balancing indeed increases the danger of judicial self-empowerment.

2. Ad-hoc Balancing and the Impairment of Legal Certainty

A second strand of critique primarily targets the ad-hoc character of balancing. As balancing does not merely compare abstract values, but takes into account the circumstances of each individual case, some authors fear

81 Schauer, 'Balancing', p. 310.

82 See Haltern, 'Integration als Mythos', 69; Leisner, *Abwägungsstaat*, pp. 170–3; Benvindo, *Limits of Constitutional Adjudication*, pp. 31–81; Classen, 'Verhältnismäßigkeit', p. 653; Huscroft, 'Proportionality and Pretense', 255.

83 Adrian Vermeule, *The Constitution of Risk* (New York: Cambridge University Press, 2014), p. 2.

84 Id., pp. 27–87.

85 See ch. 1, section 2.

86 Andreas von Arnauld, *Die Freiheitsrechte und ihre Schranken*, (Baden-Baden: Nomos, 1999), p. 264; Wolfram Cremer, *Freiheitsgrundrechte: Funktionen und Strukturen* (Tübingen: J. C. B. Mohr, 2003), p. 222; Aharon Barak, 'Proportional Effect: The Israeli Experience' (2007) 57 *University of Toronto Law Journal* 369–82 at 382.

that balancing diminishes legal certainty.[87] For this reason, several authors have recently proposed alternative models of fundamental-rights review in order to strengthen rule-based forms of argumentation. They primarily rely on categorical forms of argumentation and the establishment of bright-line rules.[88] Some combine categorical reasoning with principled balancing and a reduced form of the proportionality test.[89]

However, legal certainty is no ontological value that has to be pursued at any cost.[90] Instead, we have to strike a balance between legal certainty and perfect fit – that is, adapting to the circumstances of each individual case.[91] Legal certainty increases with more detailed and less flexible rules. However, strict rules have the tendency to be over- and under-inclusive.[92] They often include cases that they are not supposed to include. At the same time, they do not capture situations that they should capture. Furthermore, they are often developed for a specific context. If they are applied outside of this context, the original justification may not be applicable anymore.[93]

Consequently, strict rules are not per se preferable to flexible principles. Instead, both have advantages and disadvantages. Rules lead to less than optimal decisions, whereas principles provide less legal certainty. Whether to prefer rules or principles thus depends on the context.[94] In some areas

[87] Forsthoff, *Staat in der Industriegesellschaft*, p. 140; Fritz Ossenbühl, 'Maßhalten mit dem Übermaßverbot', in Peter Badura and Rupert Scholz (eds.), *Wege und Verfahren des Verfassungslebens: Festschrift für Peter Lerche* (München: C. H. Beck, 1993), pp. 151–64 at 157; Thomas Vesting, 'Gegenstandsadäquate Rechtsgewinnungstheorie – eine Alternative zum Abwägungspragmatismus des bundesdeutschen Verfassungsrechts?' (2002) 41 *Der Staat* 73–90 at 75; Raue, 'Grundrechtsbeschränkungen', 86; Jestaedt, 'Abwägungslehre', pp. 267–8; Webber, *Negotiable Constitution*, pp. 110–11; Rusteberg, *Gewährleistungsgehalt*, pp. 69–70; von Bernstorff, 'Kerngehaltsschutz', 183; Hillgruber, 'Ohne rechtes Maß?', 863; José Juan Moreso, 'Ways of Solving Conflicts of Constitutional Rights: Proportionalism and Specificationism' (2012) 25 *Ratio Juris* 31–46, p. 38; Sales, 'Rationality', 236; von Bernstorff, 'Proportionality without balancing', p. 67. See also Francisco J. Urbina, 'Is It Really That Easy? A Critique of Proportionality and 'Balancing as Reasoning'' (2014) 27 *Canadian Journal of Law and Jurisprudence* 167–92 at 184–92 (arguing that "balancing as moral reasoning" impairs legal certainty).

[88] See Webber, *Negotiable Constitution*, pp. 110–14; Tsakyrakis, 'Proportionality'; von Bernstorff, 'Proportionality without balancing', pp. 75–82.

[89] Von Bernstorff, 'Proportionality without balancing', pp. 71–5.

[90] Frederick Schauer, *Playing by the Rules: A Philosophical Examination of Rule-Based Decision-Making in Law and Life* (Oxford: Clarendon Press, 1993), p. 140; Engel, 'Freiheit und Autonomie', para. 70.

[91] Aleinikoff, 'Age of Balancing', 979–80; von Arnauld, *Freiheitsrechte*, p. 260.

[92] See Schauer, *Rules*, pp. 31–4.

[93] Oliver Lepsius, 'Kritik der Dogmatik', in Gregor Kirchhof, Stefan Magen and Karsten Schneider (eds.), *Was weiß Dogmatik?* (Tübingen: Mohr Siebeck, 2012), pp. 39–62 at 56–7.

[94] Schauer, *Rules*, pp. 141–5.

of law, legal certainty plays a crucial role. The most prominent example is criminal law. Here, we take sub-optimal decisions into account to guarantee a high degree of legal certainty. The prohibition of *nulla poena sine lege* takes into account that certain behaviour is not punished, even if it appears to be morally reprehensible if we do not dispose of a clear normative basis for the punishment.

In other situations, the costs of wrong decisions are negligible while the decision-making costs for each individual case would be prohibitive so that we equally resort to rules.[95] Most democratic systems have introduced a minimum age for voting because they want to ensure that voters are sufficiently mature. However, instead of testing in each individual case whether voters possess sufficient maturity, there is usually a rule according to which citizens are allowed to vote if they reach a certain age, for example, eighteen years. This rule is over- and under-inclusive because it excludes a mature sixteen-year-old girl, whereas it includes an immature twenty-year-old woman. However, testing the maturity of each individual citizen would be very costly, and it would involve difficult normative issues. At the same time, the social costs of over- and under-inclusion do not seem to be very significant.

But there are also legal principles that have the function of allowing for greater flexibility in the treatment of individual cases while reducing legal certainty.[96] One example from contract law would be the principle of *good faith*. If critics now argue that legal certainty has to be the predominant guiding principle for designing fundamental rights review, they would have to argue that constitutional law is an area of law in which legal certainty is more important than fit. Intuitively, such a proposition is not immediately plausible because constitutions contain many open-textured norms. Therefore, constitutional law arguably rather focuses on flexibility than on legal certainty.

If we turn our focus from theory to practice, the dichotomy between legal certainty and fit becomes less important than it seems at first sight.[97] On the one hand, balancing does not exclude the formation of rules. Similar cases are usually decided in the same way.[98] To illustrate this assumption,

[95] See Martti Koskenniemi, '"The Lady Doth Protest Too Much": Kosovo, and the Turn to Ethics in International Law' (2002) 65 *Modern Law Review* 159–75 at 169.

[96] Klaus Stern, 'Zur Entstehung und Ableitung des Übermaßverbots', in Peter Badura and Rupert Scholz (eds.), *Wege und Verfahren des Verfassungslebens* (München: C. H. Beck, 1993), pp. 165–75 at 175.

[97] See also Gottlieb, 'Paradox', 860; Ossenbühl, 'Abwägung im Verfassungsrecht', 909.

[98] See Carlos Bernal Pulido, 'The Migration of Proportionality across Europe' (2013) 11 *NZJPIL* 483–515 at 514.

let us consider the jurisprudence of the South African Constitutional Court. In several decisions, the South African Court had to decide on the constitutionality of reverse onus clauses. In the first case, in *S. v. Mbatha*, the Court relied on the proportionality test to strike down a reverse onus clause.[99] However, in subsequent cases, it simply relied on the precedent established in *S. v. Mbatha* without engaging in a detailed balancing test.[100]

On the other hand, rules do not completely determine legal decisions either. Most cases that come to an apex court will not be completely predetermined by a clear rule – otherwise, they would not have made it that far.[101] However, if a rule is not directly applicable to a specific case, judges have the discretion to distinguish, to modify the existing rule or to create a new sub-rule.[102] Judges try to correct for the over- or under-inclusiveness of a rule through an analogy or restrictive interpretation.[103] Therefore, the dichotomy of rules and principles is less sharp than it seemed to be prima facie. Instead, judges have the flexibility to decide cases on their individual merits in a rule-dominated system also. At the same time, this reduces the legal certainty that the rules were supposed to ensure.

If we accept this line of reasoning, then balancing has one significant advantage: It is more transparent than categorical argumentation.[104] Balancing forces the judges to mention the factors that determine their decision explicitly. By contrast, categorical reasoning often entails implicit balancing.[105] Therefore, it often conceals the reasons that guided the

[99] *S v. Mbatha* 1996 (2) SA 464 (CC).

[100] *S v. Ntsele* 1997 (11) BCLR 1543; *S v. Mello* 1998 (3) SA 712 (CC).

[101] George L. Priest and Benjamin Klein, 'The Selection of Disputes for Litigation' (1984) 13 *Journal of Legal Studies* 1–55; Frederick Schauer, 'A Comment on the Structure of Rights' (1993) 27 *Georgia Law Review* 415–34 at 433; Tonya L. Putnam, 'Courts without Borders: Domestic Sources of U.S. Extraterritoriality in the Regulatory Sphere' (2009) 63 *International Organization* 459–90 at 472–3.

[102] See Wolfgang Hoffmann-Riem, 'Grundrechtsanwendung unter Rationalitätsanspruch' (2004) 43 *Der Staat* 203–33 at 211–2.

[103] See Engel, 'Rechtswissenschaft als angewandte Sozialwissenschaft', p. 14; Martti Koskenniemi, *From Apology to Utopia: The Structure of the International Legal Argument* (Cambridge: Cambridge University Press, 2005), pp. 592–3.

[104] Wolfgang Kahl, 'Vom weiten Schutzbereich zum engen Gewährleistungsgehalt' (2004) 43 *Der Staat* 167–202 at 189–93.

[105] Kathleen M. Sullivan, 'Post-Liberal Judging: The Roles of Categorization and Balancing' (1992) 63 *University of Colorado Law Review* 293–317 at 311; Moritz Meister, *Das System des Freiheitsschutzes im Grundgesetz* (Berlin: Duncker & Humblot, 2011), pp. 113–14; Ilmer Dammann, *Der Kernbereich der privaten Lebensgestaltung. Zum Menschenwürde- und Wesensgehaltsschutz im Bereich der Freiheitsgrundrechte* (Berlin: Duncker & Humblot, 2011), pp. 185–97; Klatt and Meister, 'Proportionality – a benefit to human rights?', 701; Klatt and Meister, *Proportionality*, p. 49. But see also T. M. Scanlon, 'Adjusting Rights and

decision.[106] Considered from this perspective, it is not balancing, but categorical reasoning that facilitates judicial self-empowerment.[107] However, we will come back to this question on later occasions in this book.[108]

3. Proportionality and the Role of Judicial Review

At its core, the discussion on the appropriateness of balancing as a doctrinal instrument of judicial review is not primarily a discussion on methodological rationality.[109] If we require the balancing test to determine judicial decisions completely, we impose standards of rationality to it that we do not apply in other areas of legal reasoning.[110] The judge as a mere *bouche de la loi* is an illusion that does not pass the test of reality. The critics of balancing rather criticise the margin of discretion that balancing confers to judges.

However, the persuasiveness of the critique rests on an empirical premise and two normative axioms. Empirically, the critics assume that the judicial margin of discretion is wider in the context of balancing than in the context of rule-based legal reasoning.[111] The normative axioms concern the function of law and the role of courts in the political process. Whether balancing is normatively desirable depends on the resolution of two fundamental tensions: the tension between legal certainty and fit, on the one hand, and the tension between an effective control of the legislature and the preservation of legislative autonomy, on the other.

We have seen that categorical forms of argumentation either neglect the demands of fit or are less transparent than arguments based on balancing. I will, therefore, focus on the second tension that deals with the role of judicial review in a democratic society. Critics of balancing are usually also

Balancing Values' (2004) 72 *Fordham Law Review* 1477–86; Juan Antonio García Amado, 'Abwägung versus normative Auslegung' (2009) 40 *Rechtstheorie* 1–42 (arguing that all balancing decisions can be reconstructed as cases of normative interpretation).

106 Kahl, 'Vom weiten Schutzbereich', 190–2.

107 Stephen Gardbaum, 'A Democratic Defense of Constitutional Balancing' (2010) 4 *Law & Ethics of Human Rights* 77–106 at 90–2; Lepsius, 'Kritik der Dogmatik', pp. 43–5; Stephen Gardbaum, 'Proportionality and Democratic Constitutionalism', in Grant Huscroft, Bradley W. Miller and Grégoire Webber (eds.), *Proportionality and the Rule of Law: Rights, Justification, Reasoning* (New York: Cambridge University Press, 2014), pp. 259–83 at 273.

108 See, in particular, ch. 5, section 7.

109 Schauer, 'Balancing', p. 310.

110 Uerpmann, *Öffentliches Interesse*, pp. 278–83; Alexy, 'On Balancing and Subsumption', 448; Barak, 'Proportional Effect', 382.

111 See Schauer, 'Balancing', pp. 311–5.

sceptical about the virtue of strong judicial review.[112] From their perspective, balancing fails to respect the boundaries between judicial and political decision-making.[113]

There are two possible ways to react to this critique. On the one hand, we can accept that political discretion is an inherent part of judicial decision-making.[114] In the previous chapter, we have seen that we cannot simply leave the delimitation of competing spheres of freedom to the political process, as the latter can be biased.[115] Therefore, judicial discretion may be the price that we have to pay for an effective control of political decision-making. On the other hand, methodological constraints are not necessarily the only constraints that judges face. Judicial decisions are influenced by several factors. Doctrine is just one of them. But courts also have institutional constraints. For this reason, the actual discretion that judges have might be far more restricted than the methodological discussion makes it appear. The question to what extent institutional constraints are able to restrict the use of balancing will be at the centre of the empirical analysis in the following chapters.

112 Mathews and Stone Sweet, 'All Things in Proportion?', 122.

113 See Schlink, *Abwägung*, p. 190; Böckenförde, *Lage der Grundrechtsdogmatik*, p. 54; Schlink, 'Verhältnismäßigkeit', pp. 461–2; Webber, *Negotiable Constitution*, pp. 147–8; Hillgruber, 'Ohne rechtes Maß?', 862; Sales, 'Rationality', 225; Camilo de Oliveira, *Kritik der Abwägung*, pp. 223–31; von Bernstorff, 'Proportionality without balancing', p. 66.

114 Martin Borowski, *Grundrechte als Prinzipien* (Baden-Baden: Nomos, 2 edn. 2007), p. 123; David Robertson, *The Judge as Political Theorist: Contemporary Constitutional Review* (Princeton: Princeton University Press, 2010), pp. 16–17.

115 See ch. 1, section 2.

3

Balancing and Judicial Legitimacy

Whereas the first two chapters laid out the normative foundations of this book, we will now change the perspective. The normative discussion on balancing has not given us a satisfactory answer about whether it is an appropriate instrument of constitutional review. On the one hand, balancing gives judges a significant amount of discretion. On the other hand, it is necessary for an effective control of the legislature. For this reason, the remaining chapters of this book will analyse whether Constitutional or Supreme Court judges do indeed use the discretion that balancing provides for judicial activism. This chapter has a dual purpose. The first part looks at the institutional constraints faced by courts that exercise judicial review. It analyses whether we can expect judges to use balancing as an instrument of judicial self-empowerment. Theory predicts that judges will be rather reluctant to use balancing as an instrument for judicial activism, as this could undermine the judges' legitimacy. The second part will outline the research design and the case selection for the empirical analysis that is supposed to test this theoretical hypothesis in the three subsequent chapters.

1. A Theory of Balancing

The proportionality test is the core of the fundamental-rights doctrine of many constitutional courts. The popularity of the proportionality test is not difficult to understand. Proportionality offers courts a formal argumentation structure to resolve conflicts between individual rights and competing rights or public interests. The courts can avoid expressing abstract preferences for one value over another and thus refrain from establishing hierarchies of competing values.[1] This non-hierarchical approach has two advantages: On the one hand, it gives courts room for manœuvre.[2]

[1] Stone Sweet and Mathews, 'Proportionality Balancing', 88.

[2] See Theunis Roux, 'Principle and Pragmatism on the Constitutional Court of South Africa' (2009) 7 *International Journal of Constitutional Law* 106–38 at 133–4.

They can confine themselves to resolving the case at hand without setting precedents for future situations that are difficult to predict.[3] On the other hand, this approach expresses respect for the position of each of the parties.[4] It does not fundamentally discredit the abstract legitimacy of one of the positions. Instead, the ruling is based on the circumstances of the individual case.[5]

However, the critique of balancing suggests that balancing has a fundamental methodological deficit. A doctrinal instrument that grants judges flexibility may also open the door for judicial activism. That is why many scholars argue that balancing is an instrument of judicial self-empowerment.[6] But this critique is usually not based on a systematic analysis of judicial practice. At best, it refers to individual cases as anecdotal evidence. Furthermore, it assumes that the open analytical structure of balancing automatically leads to judicial activism. However, this argument overlooks the fact that courts face not only methodological but also institutional constraints.[7]

1.1 Judicial Power and Judicial Legitimacy

In the 1930s, the US Supreme Court repeatedly struck down statutes that were enacted as part of Franklin D. Roosevelt's "New Deal" legislation.[8] Roosevelt reacted by proposing a reform of the election system for the judges to the Supreme Court. Under this so-called court-packing plan, the president had the right to appoint up to six new members to the Supreme Court, one for each Justice over the age of 70. This reform would have tilted the majority in the Supreme Court in Roosevelt's favour. The initiative ultimately failed because of public resistance. However, it was not

[3] Alec Stone Sweet, *Governing with Judges: Constitutional Politics in Europe* (Oxford: Oxford University Press, 2000), p. 142; Kranenpohl, 'Die Bedeutung von Interpretationsmethoden und Dogmatik', 401. On the importance of judicial flexibility, see also Robertson, *Judge as Political Theorist*, p. 282.

[4] Stone Sweet and Mathews, 'Proportionality Balancing', 90; Wojciech Sadurski, 'Reasonableness and Value Pluralism in Law and Politics', in Giorgio Bongiovanni, Giovanni Sartor and Chiara Valentini (eds.), *Reasonableness and Law* (Dordrecht: Springer, 2009), pp. 129–46 at 140; Hailbronner, *Traditions and Transformations*, p. 120.

[5] See David M. Beatty, *The Ultimate Rule of Law* (Oxford: Oxford University Press, 2004), pp. 169–71.

[6] See ch. 2, section 1.1.

[7] On the role of institutional constraints, see Friedman, 'Politics of Judicial Review', 316–20.

[8] On the extent of this judicial resistance, see Richard H. Pildes, 'Is the Supreme Court a "Majoritarian" Institution?' (2010) *The Supreme Court Review* 103–58 at 129–30.

without consequences. After the reform proposal, the Supreme Court gave up its resistance against "New Deal" legislation and stopped invalidating laws as unconstitutional.

The "court-packing plan" may be the most famous example of a severe political conflict between judiciary and executive. But it is by far not the only one. Today, the German Constitutional Court may be considered one of the strongest courts in Europe. But this has not always been the case. After the establishment of the court in the 1950s, there was initially strong political resistance against the court. Chancellor Konrad Adenauer and his Minister of Justice, Thomas Dehler, feared that the Court might be an obstacle to their plan of establishing a European Defense Community. On several occasions, Dehler tried to damage the authority of the court and to deny the competency of the court to rule on the matter because he deemed it to be a purely political issue.[9] The government equally planned to reform the composition of the court. Judges of the German Constitutional Court needed a two-thirds majority to be elected. This mechanism was supposed to avoid extreme partisanship by requiring the support of at least parts of the opposition. The reform plan intended to reduce the necessary quorum to a simple majority, which would have strengthened the power of the government to select judges according to their political preferences. Furthermore, the two senates of the court should have been merged and the number of judges significantly reduced.[10] However, the plan ultimately failed because the opposition refused to support them.

Even though both reform plans of courts exercising constitutional review failed in the end, they illustrate the arsenal of sanctions against the judiciary of which politicians dispose.[11] Depending on the institutional framework, the legislature can also narrow the court's competencies, cut the budget or redesign the election rules for judges in order to guarantee

[9] Manfred Baldus, 'Frühe Machtkämpfe – Ein Versuch über die historischen Gründe der Autorität des Bundesverfassungsgerichts', in Thomas Henne and Arne Riedlinger (eds.), *Das Lüth-Urteil aus (rechts-)historischer Sicht* (Berlin: Berliner Wissenschafts-Verlag, 2005), pp. 237–48 at 241–2; Oliver W. Lembcke, 'Das Bundesverfassungsgericht und die Regierung Adenauer – vom Streit um den Status zur Anerkennung der Autorität', in Robert Christian van Ooyen and Martin H. W. Möllers (eds.), *Das Bundesverfassungsgericht im politischen System* (Wiesbaden: VS Verlag für Sozialwissenschaften, 2006), pp. 151–61 at 156–7.

[10] See Heinz Laufer, *Verfassungsgerichtsbarkeit und politischer Prozeß* (Tübingen: J. C. B. Mohr, 1968), pp. 169–206; Richard Häußler, *Der Konflikt zwischen Bundesverfassungsgericht und politischer Führung* (Berlin: Duncker & Humblot, 1994), pp. 40–7 (giving a detailed account of the reform plans).

[11] See Friedman, 'Politics of Judicial Review', 314 (who argues that the potential to sanction the judiciary already disciplines the latter).

that a majority of judges are favourable to the government's policies.[12] Furthermore, courts exercising judicial review are dependent on the political branches to implement their judgments.[13] They have no sword that could force politics to comply with their rulings. It is told that the former US president Andrew Jackson once said, after the US Supreme Court had handed down a decision of which he disapproved: "John Marshall has made his decision, now let him enforce it."[14] When the German Constitutional Court issued its decision on religious symbols in classrooms,[15] the ruling was insufficiently implemented.[16] In December 1995, the *Neue Zürcher Zeitung*, the most important Swiss daily newspaper, remarked that the decision had not changed anything in the daily life of Bavarian schools.[17]

These considerations show that courts are, to a certain extent, dependent on the cooperation of the political branches when they exercise constitutional review.[18] They can secure the cooperation of politics in two ways. On the one hand, they can exploit institutional conflicts within the political branches.[19] Such institutional conflicts occur primarily in federal systems. Here, the state governments and legislatures may see the court as a guarantor against a disproportional concentration of power

[12] See Laufer, *Verfassungsgerichtsbarkeit*, pp. 167–9.

[13] See Heinz Klug, 'Introducing the Devil: An Institutional Analysis of the Power of Constitutional Review' (1997) 13 *South African Journal on Human Rights* 185–208 at 189; Schulze-Fielitz, 'Das Bundesverfassungsgericht in der Krise des Zeitgeists', 27; Roland Lhotta, 'Das Bundesverfassungsgericht als politischer Akteur: Plädoyer für eine neo-institutionalistische Ergänzung der Forschung' (2003) 9 *Swiss Political Science Review* 142–53 at 143; Andrej Lang, 'Wider die Metapher vom letzten Wort: Verfassungsgerichte als Wegweiser', in Dominik Elser *et al.* (eds.), *Das letzte Wort – Rechtsetzung & Rechtskontrolle in der Demokratie* (Baden-Baden: Nomos, 2014), pp. 15–37.

[14] Cited in Jean Edward Smith, *John Marshall: Definer of a Nation* (New York: Henry Holt, 1996), p. 518.

[15] See earlier, Introduction.

[16] Steffen Detterbeck, 'Gelten die Entscheidungen des Bundesverfassungsgerichts auch in Bayern? – Zur prozessualen Bedeutung der Kruzifix-Entscheidung vom 16.5.1996 und zur Deutung von § 31 I BVerfGG' (1996) 49 *Neue Juristische Wochenschrift* 426–32 at 426–7; Michael Stolleis, 'Überkreuz – Anmerkungen zum Kruzifix-Beschluß (BVerfGE 93, 1–37) und seiner Rezeption' (2000) 83 *Kritische Vierteljahresschrift für Gesetzgebung und Rechtswissenschaft* 376–87 at 383.

[17] Neue Zürcher Zeitung, 16 December 1995, cited in Vanberg, *Politics of Constitutional Review*, p. 4.

[18] Vanberg, *Politics of Constitutional Review*, p. 6.

[19] JoAnne Sweeney, 'Creating a More Dangerous Branch: How the United Kingdom's Human Rights Act has Empowered the Judiciary and Changed the Way the British Government Creates Law' (2013) 21 *Michigan State International Law Review* 301–35 at 318; Erin F. Delaney, 'Judiciary Rising: Constitutional Change in the United Kingdom' (2014) 108 *Northwestern University Law Review* 543–605 at 577.

on the federal level.[20] At the same time, the court may also help the federal institutions to implement their policy goals within the individual states.[21]

On the other hand, courts can also confront the political branches directly. In such a case, their judicial power depends on the legitimacy they enjoy.[22] The stronger the public acceptance of a court is, the more politicians have to fear losing electoral support if they openly refuse to implement judicial decisions.[23] If a court enjoys a high degree of legitimacy, noncompliance is usually perceived as a violation of the fundamental rules of democracy.[24] In contrast, if a court lacks acceptance, politicians who oppose the implementation of judgments do not jeopardise electoral approval. Legitimacy is thus a central source of judicial power.[25]

[20] See Dietrich Herrmann, 'Akte der Selbstautorisierung als Grundstock institutioneller Macht von Verfassungsgerichten', in Hans Vorländer (ed.), *Die Deutungsmacht der Verfassungsgerichtsbarkeit* (Wiesbaden: VS Verlag für Sozialwissenschaften, 2006), pp. 141–73 at 166.

[21] See Barry Evan Friedman and Erin F. Delaney, 'Becoming Supreme: The Federal Foundation of Judicial Supremacy' (2011) 111 *Columbia Law Review* 1137–93 at 1152–9.

[22] Vanberg, *Politics of Constitutional Review*, pp. 49–53; Walter F. Murphy and Joseph Tanenhaus, 'Publicity, Public Opinion, and the Court' (1990) 84 *Northwestern University Law Review* 985–1023; Lee Epstein, Jack Knight and Olga Shvetsova, 'The Role of Constitutional Courts in the Establishment and Maintenance of Democratic Systems of Government' (2001) 35 *Law & Society Review* 117–63 at 125; Christoph Engel, 'Delineating the Proper Scope of Government: A Proper Task for a Constitutional Court?' (2001) 157 *Journal of Institutional and Theoretical Economics* 187–219 at 213; Clifford James Carrubba, 'A Model of the Endogenous Development of Judicial Institutions in Federal and International Systems' (2009) 71 *Journal of Politics* 55–69 at 65; Sascha Kneip, *Verfassungsgerichte als politische Akteure* (Baden-Baden: Nomos, 2009), p. 199; Silvia von Steinsdorff, 'Verfassungsgerichte als Demokratie-Versicherung? Ursachen und Grenzen der wachsenden Bedeutung juristischer Politikkontrolle', in Klemens H. Schrenk and Markus Soldner (eds.), *Analyse demokratischer Regierungssysteme: Festschrift für Wolfgang Ismayr* (Wiesbaden: VS Verlag für Sozialwissenschaften, 2010), pp. 479–98 at 492; Lang, 'Wider die Metapher vom letzten Wort', p. 27.

[23] Georg Vanberg, 'Verfassungsgerichtsbarkeit und Gesetzgebung: Zum politischen Spielraum des Bundesverfassungsgerichts', in Steffen Ganghof and Philip Manow (eds.), *Mechanismen der Politik – Strategische Interaktion im deutschen Regierungssystem* (Frankfurt a.M.: Campus Verlag, 2005), pp. 183–213 at 188; André Brodocz, *Die Macht der Judikative* (Wiesbaden: VS Verlag für Sozialwissenschaften, 2009), p. 99.

[24] Vanberg, *Politics of Constitutional Review*, p. 74.

[25] Hans Vorländer, 'Deutungsmacht – Die Macht der Verfassungsgerichtsbarkeit', in Hans Vorländer (ed.), *Die Deutungsmacht der Verfassungsgerichtsbarkeit* (Wiesbaden: VS Verlag für Sozialwissenschaften, 2006), pp. 9–33 at 24; Barry Evan Friedman, *The Will of the People: How Public Opinion Has Influenced the Supreme Court and Shaped the Meaning of the Constitution* (New York: Farrar, Straus and Giroux, 2009), p. 375.

If we consider the concept of legitimacy more closely, we can distinguish two types of legitimacy – specific and diffuse legitimacy.[26] Specific legitimacy refers to the concrete case. It measures the acceptance of specific judgments. By contrast, diffuse legitimacy focuses on the institution of a Constitutional or Supreme Court. Even if people disagree with a specific judgment, they may nevertheless support its implementation because they respect the institution as such.[27] There is certainly a connection between both forms of legitimacy.[28] Diffuse legitimacy depends on specific legitimacy. If a court renders decisions that meet strong public resistance, it will also lose some general acceptance as an institution.[29] However, this is a long process: One unpopular decision will not damage the institutions as such so that specific and diffuse legitimacy may well diverge in concrete cases.

The stronger the diffuse legitimacy of a court is, the more politicians have to expect to lose votes if they openly resist a decision of a constitutional court.[30] This may even be the case if the decision itself was unpopular.[31] If the court itself is widely accepted, the non-implementation of its decisions or the sanctioning of the institution is usually perceived as a violation of the rules of the democratic game.[32] By contrast, if a court does not enjoy public support, political sanctions will barely have consequences for the political elites. Electors will not punish them if they damage an unpopular institution. Legitimacy is thus a crucial power resource of a court exercising constitutional review.[33] Only widespread

[26] Seminally David Easton, *A Systems Analysis of Political Life* (New York: John Wiley, 1965), pp. 267–77; David Easton, 'A Re-Assessment of the Concept of Political Support' (1975) 5 *British Journal of Political Science* 435–57.

[27] James L. Gibson, 'Institutional Legitimacy, Procedural Justice, and Compliance with Supreme Court Decisions: A Question of Causality' (1991) 25 *Law & Society Review* 631–6 at 635.

[28] Gregory A. Caldeira and James L. Gibson, 'The Etiology of Public Support for the Supreme Court' (1992) 36 *American Journal of Political Science* 635–64.

[29] Anke Grosskopf and Jeffery J. Mondak, 'Do Attitudes Toward Specific Supreme Court Decisions Matter? The Impact of Webster and Texas v. Johnson on Public Confidence in the Supreme Court' (1998) 51 *Political Research Quarterly* 633–54.

[30] Vanberg, 'Verfassungsgerichtsbarkeit und Gesetzgebung', p. 188; Brodocz, *Macht der Judikative*, p. 99.

[31] See Pildes, 'Is the Supreme Court a "Majoritarian" Institution?', 130–1 (showing that the resistance against Roosevelt's court-packing plan was based on a respect for the institution, while Roosevelt and his policies enjoyed widespread support).

[32] Vanberg, *Politics of Constitutional Review*, p. 74.

[33] Friedman, *Will of the People*, p. 375.

public support allows courts to take decisions involving significant costs for the political majority.

The legitimacy of courts relies on the perception that courts are neutral arbiters basing their decisions on legal considerations.[34] One of the principal lines of defending the legitimacy of constitutional review in continental Europe is to stress the different rationality of legal decisions of constitutional courts when compared to political decisions of the legislature.[35] If a court were perceived as a political actor with its own political agenda, this would undermine its legitimacy and thus weaken its institutional position.[36]

One certainly cannot expect the general public to follow the methodological intricacies of the constitutional jurisprudence closely. The daily business of courts usually flies under the radar of public attention. In high-profile cases, public opinion focuses more on the result than on the reasoning. Over time, a dubious methodological approach may nevertheless affect the public reputation and thus the general acceptance of a court. The link between the court's legitimacy and its style of argumentation is provided by the legal academy and the media.[37] If the vast majority of legal academics disapproved the methodological approach of the court and accused the latter of judicial activism, the image of the court as a neutral arbiter would be severely damaged. For this reason, the effectiveness of a specific doctrine presupposes that it is accepted as a legal argument within constitutional law scholarship.

[34] Stone Sweet, *Governing with Judges*, pp. 199–200; Martin Shapiro, 'The Success of Judicial Review and Democracy', in Martin Shapiro and Alec Stone Sweet (eds.), *On Law, Politics, and Judicialization* (Oxford: Oxford University Press, 2002), pp. 149–83 at 165; Uwe Kranenpohl, *Hinter dem Schleier des Beratungsgeheimnisses – Der Willensbildungs- und Entscheidungsprozess des Bundesverfassungsgerichts* (Wiesbaden: VS Verlag für Sozialwissenschaften, 2010), p. 409; Georg Vanberg, 'Constitutional Courts in Comparative Perspective: A Theoretical Assessment' (2015) 2015.18 *Annual Review of Law and Social Science* 167–85 at 179; see also Or Bassok, 'The Two Countermajoritarian Difficulties' (2012) 31 *Saint Louis University Public Law Review* 333–82 at 370; Ulrich Sieberer, 'Strategische Zurückhaltung von Verfassungsgerichten – Gewaltenteilungsvorstellungen und die Grenzen der Justizialisierung' (2006) 16 *Zeitschrift für Politikwissenschaft* 1299–323 at 1308.

[35] See Ferejohn, 'Judicializing Politics, Politicizing Law', 45; Robertson, *Judge as Political Theorist*, p. 383; Möllers, 'Legalität', p. 328.

[36] Gregory A. Caldeira, 'Neither the Purse nor the Sword: Dynamics of Public Confidence in the Supreme Court' (1986) 80 *American Political Science Review* 1209–26.

[37] See Friedman, *Will of the People*, p. 378; Bassok, 'The Two Countermajoritarian Difficulties', 367 (on the role of the media in shaping the public image of courts).

1.2 *Balancing and Judicial Legitimacy*

In order to ensure their own legitimacy, courts will frame even highly political decisions in doctrinal terms.[38] However, the simple framing in doctrinal terms may not be enough to secure legitimacy. Critics of a constitutional court, who want to weaken the court's institutional position, will often point to the political nature of a particular decision.[39] For this reason, the court's argumentation frameworks have to be accepted by the legal discourse as doctrinal arguments.[40] Consequently, if a significant part of the legal academy came to the conclusion that balancing is nothing more than a disguising of political considerations, the legitimacy of the court would be severely damaged.[41] For this reason, constitutional courts will be sensitive to the methodological problems of balancing.[42] They have to develop strategies to dissipate the suspicion that they are taking political decisions when they are applying the proportionality test.

When analysing the potential harm that balancing may cause to judicial legitimacy, we have to distinguish three situations. If a court wants to confirm a piece of legislation, balancing does not pose any legitimacy issues. The court confirms a legislative decision and thus does not interfere with the political branches. It cannot be accused of being activist or having a political agenda. If the court reverses decisions of lower courts without implicitly reviewing the statutory basis of these decisions, there is a conflict between courts. This may also involve a conflict about the scope of the competencies of the competing courts, and there are often political considerations at stake. From an institutional perspective, however, the constitutional court does not transgress the border to the political branches.[43]

38 Stone Sweet, *Governing with Judges*, p. 200.

39 See Friedman, *Will of the People*, pp. 114–15 and 202.

40 See Engel, 'Delineating the Proper Scope of Government', 212.

41 Id., 212.

42 Cf. Adam Shinar, 'Method and Culture in American Constitutional Law: A Critique of *Proportionality and Constitutional Culture*' (2014) 10 *Israel Review of Legal Studies* 137–58 at 157–8 (arguing that the US Supreme Court will be reluctant to adopt the proportionality test because it has come under such heavy fire in the legal literature).

43 See Fritz Ossenbühl, 'Verfassungsgerichtsbarkeit und Fachgerichtsbarkeit – Gedanken zur Wahrung der Verfahrensgrundrechte', in Rolf Stödter and Werner Thieme (eds.), *Hamburg – Deutschland – Europa: Festschrift für Hans Peter Ipsen* (Tübingen: J.C.B. Mohr, 1977), pp. 129–41 at 129; Schlink, 'Verhältnismäßigkeit', p. 461; Christoph Möllers, *Gewaltengliederung: Legitimation und Dogmatik im nationalen und internationalen Rechtsvergleich* (Tübingen: Mohr Siebeck, 2005), p. 144; Oliver Lepsius, 'Die Chancen und Grenzen des Grundsatzes der Verhältnismäßigkeit', in Matthias Jestaedt and Oliver Lepsius (eds.), *Verhältnismäßigkeit: Zur Tragfähigkeit eines verfassungsrechtlichen Schlüsselkonzepts*

If a court wants to strike down legislation as unconstitutional, it comes into conflict with the legislature. If it bases such a decision on the balancing stage of the proportionality test, it has to justify why its valuation of the competing interests at stake is superior to the valuation of the legislature. For this reason, we should expect courts to be particularly guarded about using balancing in such a situation. They will try to base their decisions on alternative arguments or to rationalise the balancing exercise in order to signal that they refrain from making a political judgment.

This does not mean that courts totally refrain from balancing. However, the likelihood of courts resorting to balancing when reviewing legislation depends on two factors. First, a court will balance more often the stronger its institutional position is. If a court enjoys widespread public support, it has less political and methodological constraints. A weak court, in contrast, will try to avoid an argumentation framework that appears to be "political" and that could undermine its legitimacy. Second, the use of balancing considerations depends on the level of acceptance of balancing as a "legal" argument in the legal discourse. The more balancing is accepted as a doctrinal instrument, the more the constitutional court will rely on balancing when reviewing legislative decisions.

Finally, even if courts use balancing as a doctrinal instrument, they do not necessarily hide judicial activism behind balancing considerations. Institutional strength is not constant. Instead, public acceptance can decrease if the image of an activist court persists. The open analytical structure of balancing may *prima facie* facilitate infusing of the balancing test with political considerations. However, because of this activist potential, there is also higher scrutiny of balancing decisions. Furthermore, the openness of the analytical structure increases the transparency of the test and may thus rather have a disciplining effect. For this reason, we should expect balancing courts to exercise self-restraint when they are balancing. If they use balancing to overturn a piece of legislation, they will try to rationalise balancing through auxiliary arguments or to signal self-restraint through other means.

2. The Research Design

The hypotheses developed in the previous section stand in contrast to the argument that constitutional courts use balancing as an instrument for

(Tübingen: Mohr Siebeck, 2015), pp. 1–41 at 10; similarly also Brun-Otto Bryde, *Verfassungsentwicklung: Stabilität und Dynamik im Verfassungsrecht der Bundesrepublik Deutschland* (Baden-Baden: Nomos, 1982), p. 325.

judicial activism. For this reason, these hypotheses will be tested empirically in the following chapters. The primary focus will be on the assumption that courts are reluctant to use balancing extensively when they invalidate a piece of legislation. To test the hypotheses, I will classify arguments used in the case law of three constitutional or supreme courts. Such a classification gives us a sense of the extent to which courts base their decisions on balancing and whether they rely on auxiliary arguments in the process. In the following, I will first explain the selection of the courts and the cases that are included in the analysis. I will then describe the classification of the different arguments that is the basis of the analysis.

2.1 Case Selection

The study analyses the case law of three different constitutional courts: The German Federal Constitutional Court, the Canadian Supreme Court and the South African Constitutional Court. These three courts have been selected for two reasons. First, they are among the domestic courts that exercise constitutional review and have, at the same time, the longest history of applying the proportionality test. The German Constitutional Court was the first court to apply proportionality as an instrument of constitutional review.[44] Its use of the proportionality test dates back to the late 1950s.[45] The Canadian Supreme Court developed the proportionality test as an instrument of individual rights review in 1986.[46] Finally, the South African Constitutional Court has relied on proportionality since 1995, shortly after its establishment.[47] Because of the long history of applying proportionality, a greater number of cases are available for our analysis. This allows a more reliable classification of the case law and the identification of potential historical trends.[48]

Secondly, the three selected courts stem from different legal traditions. One approach in comparative qualitative studies is the "most different cases" approach.[49] According to this approach, the non-essential variables should

[44] Stone Sweet and Mathews, 'Proportionality Balancing', 74.

[45] See Entscheidungen des Bundesverfassungsgerichts [BVerfGE] vol. 7, p. 377.

[46] *R v. Oakes* [1986] 1 S.C.R. 103.

[47] *S v. Makwanyane* 1995 (3) SA 391 (CC).

[48] See Gary King, Robert O. Keohane and Sidney Verba, *Designing Social Inquiry: Scientific Inference in Qualitative Research* (Princeton: Princeton University Press, 1994), pp. 29–31 (on the importance of increasing the quantity of observations).

[49] See Ran Hirschl, *Comparative Matters: The Renaissance of Comparative Constitutional Law* (Oxford: Oxford University Press, 2014), pp. 253–6.

differ significantly in the observed systems, but be similar for the main variables of the analysis.[50] If we can observe the same phenomenon in very different contexts, it is likely that the observation is not dependent on the specificity of the selected cases, but that it can also be observed in systems not included in the study. For this reason, I chose three courts that stem from different legal families. The German Federal Constitutional Court is a Civil Law court, whereas the Canadian legal system is part of the Common Law tradition. The South African law, finally, is rooted both in Roman law and British common law.[51] This selection is supposed to control for the influence of the legal tradition. The theoretical hypothesis suggested that the use of balancing is influenced by constitutional constraints. By selecting courts from different legal cultures, I would like to show that this hypothesis is valid across different legal cultures.

The analysis concentrates on decisions overturning or invalidating a piece of legislation. We have seen that, in these cases, the institutional conflict between judiciary and legislature is particularly pronounced.[52] Concerning the German Constitutional Court, the analysis concentrates on all cases in which the Court held that a law violated a fundamental right of the German Constitution. However, there is one important exception: The German fundamental rights doctrine distinguishes between "liberty" and "equality" rights. The study only focused on the former category of rights. Judgments not related to liberty rights were not examined because the Constitutional Court does not regularly resort to proportionality in these cases and the status of the proportionality test in the context of equal protection is unclear.[53] The period of observation starts with the very first decision of the German Federal Constitutional Court in 1951 and ends in December 2015.

With regard to the Canadian Supreme Court, the analysis comprises all cases in which the Court held that a statute was inconsistent with the Canadian Charter of Rights and Freedoms.[54] The period of observation starts in 1985 with *Big M Drug Mart*, the first significant decision on the interpretation of the Charter,[55] and ends in December 2015. In the South African jurisprudence, all cases in which a statute was invalidated and

[50] Id.

[51] Konrad Zweigert and Hein Kötz, *An Introduction to Comparative Law* (Tony Weir trl., Oxford: Oxford University Press, 3rd edn, 1998), pp. 231–5.

[52] See ch. 3, section 1.2.

[53] See Lübbe-Wolff, 'Principle of Proportionality', 13.

[54] Canadian Charter of Rights and Freedoms, Part I of the Constitution Act, 1982, being schedule B to the Canada Act 1982, ch. 11.

[55] *R. v. Big M Drug Mart* [1985] 1 S.C.R. 295.

which refer to Article 36 of the South African Constitution were analysed. Article 36 of the South African Constitution establishes a general exceptions clause, which applies to all fundamental rights. Excluded from the analysis are thus, among others, all cases dealing with socioeconomic rights because the Court usually does not resort the general limitations clause in Article 36 of the Constitution. Instead, it relies on a reasonableness test in these cases.[56] The period of observation starts with the establishment of the South African Constitutional Court in 1995 and ends in December 2015. In all three jurisdictions, I also analysed individual cases confirming a piece of legislation or reviewing decisions of lower courts. However, these cases were not selected in a systematic manner. Such a systematic selection was not necessary because these cases are only used for exemplification.

2.2 *Classification of Judicial Arguments*

An analysis of judicial arguments requires rules, according to which these arguments are classified. I will first start with some general observations before describing the individual arguments in detail. Constitutional courts have several alternatives to balancing. First, they can use a different prong of the proportionality test. If a law does not pursue a legitimate aim, if there is no rational connection between measure and purpose, or if there is a less restrictive means, the court does not need to resort to balancing. Other alternatives to balancing are less obvious. Nevertheless, all three analysed courts also based the constitutional incompatibility of statutes on arguments outside the proportionality test. Substantially, they can rely on consistency considerations or legitimate expectations. Procedurally, they can impose burdens of justification on the legislature or require additional procedural guarantees to decrease the likelihood of fundamental rights violations by the administration.

In the context of proportionality, I relied primarily on how the courts classified the arguments themselves. If a court labelled the test it used as

[56] See *Government of the Republic of South Africa v. Grootboom* 2001 (1) SA 46 (CC). For a reconstruction of the Constitutional Court's jurisprudence on socioeconomic rights, see James Fowkes, *Building the Constitution: The Practice of Constitutional Interpretation in post-apartheid South Africa* (Cambridge: Cambridge University Press, 2016), ch. 8. Cf. also Stephen Gardbaum, 'Positive and Horizontal Rights: Proportionality's Next Frontier or a Bridge Too Far?', in Vicki Jackson and Mark Tushnet (eds.), *Proportionality: New Frontiers, New Challenges* (New York: Cambridge University Press, forthcoming) (explaining why the proportionality test is not a suitable test for positive rights).

a less-restrictive-means test, I did not second-guess this classification. I referred to the auto-classification for two reasons. On the one hand, it is easier to measure. Whether an argument is indeed a less-restrictive-means argument or implicit balancing can often be subject to debate. On the other hand, the auto-classification gives us some interesting information. If a court frequently hides balancing behind the less-restrictive-means test, it is an indication that it considers balancing to be problematic. Implicit balancing would thus be an instrument to strengthen the court's own legitimacy by hiding normative valuations behind apparently neutral empirical considerations.

However, the evaluation of the arguments did not exclusively rely on the self-classification of the analysed courts. Instead, I classified the arguments myself in certain cases for two reasons. On the one hand, courts often do not label what they are doing. For example, the category of procedural arguments is one that is not based on judicial self-classification, but one that was constructed for the purposes of this study. Another example is consistency or coherency considerations. Even though the German Constitutional Court has developed an explicit consistency test (*Folgerichtigkeit*), the Court often uses consistency considerations in decisions without labelling them as such. The South African Constitutional Court and the Canadian Supreme Court also rely on consistency arguments without explicitly saying so.

Using these different classifications allows us to see a different argumentation structure in the judicial decisions. One of the hypotheses developed earlier was that courts do not only refrain from balancing, but that they also try to rationalise balancing by using auxiliary arguments. Simply classifying an argument as balancing argument would thus not do justice to a decision where the justices use auxiliary considerations in one of the steps in the proportionality test. For this reason, we have to designate these auxiliary arguments as such. If the courts combined several arguments, this was indicated accordingly in the codification of the judgments. For example, if a court used an additional consistency argument to justify why a decision was disproportionate, the decision was designated as a consistency and a balancing decision. An exception was only made when one argument was totally consumed by the other – that is, if the statute was considered disproportionate solely because it was inconsistent.

This account already reveals that a classification of judicial arguments is not free of subjective evaluations of the researcher. However, a subjective element is unavoidable in social science research. I can only create transparency. For this reason, I have relegated the classification of all judgments to the Appendix. This allows every reader to get his or her own idea of the concrete classifications. In the following, I will describe the individual arguments that construct the classification scheme according to which all judgments were evaluated.

2.2a. Balancing

The starting point for the qualification of an argument as a balancing argument is the self-classification of the court. This is relatively easy in the case law of the Canadian Supreme Court. The Canadian Court always labels the different steps of the proportionality test explicitly. By contrast, it is more difficult to rely on the self-classification in the judgments of the German and the South African Constitutional Court. In cases without a specific labelling, I used two identification heuristics – one positive and one negative. On the one hand, I classified those arguments as balancing in which the courts compared the importance of competing aims – that is, the restricted individual right and the public aim pursued by the restriction when dealing with the facts of the case.[57] This analysis is not limited to a comparison of the abstract values of the competing aims. Rather, courts often perform a cost-benefit analysis, in which they compare the positive effect of a measure with the extent of the fundamental rights restriction.[58] Statements about the importance of a purpose in the concrete case or the severity of a concrete fundamental rights restriction were thus seen as indications that a court was indeed balancing. On the other hand, balancing is a residual category in the proportionality test.[59] Consequently, if a court applied the proportionality test without specifying the specific step, an argument was qualified as a balancing argument if it could not be attributed to any other category.

2.2b. Proportionality Arguments other than Balancing

Other than balancing, the proportionality test consists of three steps: the legitimate aim, the rational connection between measure and purpose, and the less-restrictive-means test. Reviewing the legitimate aim of a

[57] See Mattias Kumm and Alec D. Walen, 'Human Dignity and Proportionality: Deontic Pluralism in Balancing', in Grant Huscroft, Bradley W. Miller and Grégoire Webber (eds.), *Proportionality and the Rule of Law: Rights, Justification, Reasoning* (New York: Cambridge University Press, 2014), pp. 67–89 at 69. See also Möller, *Constitutional Rights*, pp. 137–40 (offering a broader definition of balancing) and Gottlieb, 'Paradox', 839 (arguing that balancing is an undefinable category).

[58] On the formal structure of balancing, see Alexy, 'On Balancing and Subsumption'.

[59] Kumm and Walen, 'Human Dignity', p. 69.

measure only involves normative considerations, whereas the other two steps revolve around empirical questions. Sometimes they are not easy to separate. Whether an argument is classified as a rational-connection argument or a less-restrictive-means argument often depends on the point of reference.[60] If we assume that the deterring effect of the death penalty is not stronger than the deterring effect of a long prison sentence, it may be disproportionate for two reasons. If the aim of introducing capital punishment were to create *additional* deterrence, the death penalty would lack a rational connection to this purpose under our assumption. If the aim were deterrence in general, there would be a rational connection, but a long prison sentence would be a less-restrictive means. As courts often do not specify whether they are relying on a rational-connection or a less-restrictive-means argument, both arguments will be placed in the same category.

Legitimate aim: The legitimate aim refers to the normative value of the purpose that the legislature tries to achieve with its fundamental rights restriction. If a legislative measure pursues an illegitimate purpose, it violates the constitution automatically. There is no need to consider the abstract value of the restricted fundamental right or the severity of the restriction. However, determining standards for evaluating the legitimacy of the purpose of a measure is a complex task. Therefore, the criterion could pose classification problems: Some decisions in which a legitimate aim was denied could, in fact, be based on an implicit balancing. For this reason, only those judgments were classified as being based on the legitimate-aim test if the discussion focused exclusively on the restrictive measure without considering the importance of the restricted right or the extent of the restriction.

Rational connection and less restrictive means: Concerning the rational-connection and the less-restrictive-means test, the starting point of the analysis was the self-classification of the respective court. If the court indicated that a measure lacked rational connection to the purpose or that it was not necessary to achieve the latter, the argument was qualified accordingly. In cases where the court did not expressly indicate which test it was using, the argument was qualified as rational-connection or less-restrictive-means argument if the court inquired into the empirical assumptions of the legislature without making a normative comparison between competing legal values. The core of the rational-connection test

[60] Similarly, Reimer, 'Verhältnismäßigkeit im Verfassungsrecht', p. 66.

is an empirical analysis regarding the causal connection between measure and purpose. In the less-restrictive-means test, courts have to look at both competing values separately. They do not have to evaluate the importance of the purpose, but only to analyse potential alternative means to achieve the same purpose. The most important step in this analysis is the comparison of the effectiveness of the actual measure and the potential alternatives, which again requires an empirical analysis.

Overbreadth: Finally, the South African Constitutional Court and the Canadian Supreme Court sometimes resort to the argument that a particular measure is overbroad. The structure of the overbreadth argument is very similar to the less-restrictive-means test.[61] Legislatures often rely on typifications. The typifying legislatures make the assumption that the observation of a certain set of facts typically implies specific consequences even if there is no complete correlation between the observed facts and the assumed consequences. Such a typification is the more problematic the weaker the correlation between these two factors is. A measure is usually qualified as overbroad if the legislature could have differentiated with regard to the facts – that is, if it could have created an exception for a specific group that did not need to be covered by the measure for the latter to achieve its aim. Overbreadth is usually qualified as such by the courts. For this reason, the classification was usually based on the labelling by the specific court.

2.2c. Substantive Arguments Outside of Proportionality

Consistency and coherency arguments: The three analysed courts often base decisions on consistency or coherency arguments. However, these arguments are not always labelled as such. The German Constitutional Court imposes a requirement of congruity (*Folgerichtigkeit*) on the German legislature.[62] The two other courts do not have an explicit test. However,

[61] See Iain Currie and Johan de Waal, *The Bill of Rights Handbook*, 6th edn. (Lansdowne: Juta, 2013), p. 184.

[62] See, e.g., BVerfGE 19, 101 at 116; BVerfGE 21, 160 at 172; BVerfGE 105, 73 at 125; BVerfGE 107, 27 at 46–47; BVerfGE 116, 164 at 180; BVerfGE 117, 1 at 30; BVerfGE 121, 317 at 360; BVerfGE 122, 210 at 231; BVerfGE 125, 175 at 225. For an evaluation of this development, see Simon Bulla, 'Das Verfassungsprinzip der Folgerichtigkeit und seine Auswirkungen auf die Grundrechtsdogmatik' (2008) 1 *Zeitschrift für das Juristische Studium* 585–96; Lothar Michael, 'Folgerichtigkeit als Wettbewerbsgleichheit – Zur Verwerfung von Rauchverboten in Gaststätten durch das BVerfG' (2008) 63 *Juristenzeitung* 875–82; Gerd Morgenthaler, 'Gleichheit und Rechtssystem – Widerspruchsfreiheit, Folgerichtigkeit', in Rudolf Mellinghoff and Ulrich Palm (eds.), *Gleichheit im Verfassungsstaat. Symposium aus Anlass des 65. Geburtstages von Paul Kirchhof* (Heidelberg: C. F. Müller, 2008), pp. 51–66; Lepsius,

they also overturn legislation on the basis of inconsistency. Furthermore, the German Constitutional Court implicitly often uses consistency considerations outside the formalised congruity test. Consistency or coherency arguments can come in three forms. First, courts review the internal consistency of a measure. If the legislature claims to pursue a certain aim, but if parts of the specific measure contradict this purpose, the measure is qualified as (internally) inconsistent. Second, courts sometimes refer to the external coherence of a measure. The external coherence is lacking if the legislature has made different evaluations of the addressed problem or danger in comparable situations. Finally, consistency arguments may appear in the form of historical consistency requirements. Historical consistency comes into play when the legislature changes a law in a way that leads to a more severe restriction of individual rights even though there was no obvious deficiency under the previous regime. Consistency or coherency arguments may appear as independent arguments justifying the invalidity of a piece of legislation. However, they are predominantly used as auxiliary arguments in order to strengthen the plausibility of considerations within different prongs of the proportionality test. Historical inconsistency may be an indication that a specific law was not "necessary" because less burdensome measures in the past did not pose any efficiency issues. Furthermore, if the legislature does not pursue the same aim with the same intensity in different contexts, this may be an indication that it does attribute particular importance to the issue, which may in turn be a factor in the balancing test.

'Anmerkung'; Christian Bumke, 'Die Pflicht zur konsistenten Gesetzgebung' (2010) 49 *Der Staat* 77–105; Joachim Englisch, 'Folgerichtiges Steuerrecht als Verfassungsgebot', in Klaus Tipke *et al.* (eds.), *Gestaltung der Steuerrechtsordnung: Festschrift für Joachim Lang* (Köln: Verlag Dr. Otto Schmidt, 2010), pp. 167–220; Dann, 'Verfassungsgerichtliche Kontrolle gesetzgeberischer Rationalität'; Mehrdad Payandeh, 'Das Gebot der Folgerichtigkeit: Rationalitätsgewinn oder Irrweg der Grundrechtsdogmatik?' (2011) 136 *Archiv des öffentlichen Rechts* 578–615; Matthias Cornils, 'Rationalitätsanforderungen an die parlamentarische Gesetzgebung im demokratischen Rechtsstaat' (2011) 126 *Deutsches Verwaltungsblatt* 1053–61 at 1054; Lerke Osterloh, 'Folgerichtigkeit: Verfassungsgerichtliche Rationalitätsanforderungen in der Demokratie', in Michael Bäuerle, Philipp Dann and Astrid Wallrabenstein (eds.), *Demokratie-Perspektiven: Festschrift für Brun-Otto Bryde* (Tübingen: Mohr Siebeck, 2013), pp. 429–42; Anna Leisner-Egensperger, 'Die Folgerichtigkeit – Systemsuche als Problem für Verfassungsbegriff und Demokratiegebot' (2013) 66 *Die Öffentliche Verwaltung* 533–9; Niels Petersen, 'Gesetzgeberische Inkonsistenz als Beweiszeichen: Eine rechtsvergleichende Analyse der Funktion von Konsistenzargumenten in der Rechtsprechung' (2013) 138 *Archiv des öffentlichen Rechts* 108–34.

Legitimate expectations: In some cases, courts invalidate laws because they violate legitimate expectations. For the coding exercise, we can rely on the self-classification of the courts. They usually state explicitly when legitimate expectations are violated. The German Constitutional Court sometimes balances in the context of the legitimate expectations test.[63] It compares the normative value of protecting legitimate expectations with the legislative interest to implement a change of the law as quickly as possible. Nevertheless, it appears justified to treat the balancing in the context of the legitimate-expectations test differently than proportionality balancing. When a court finds that a law violates legitimate expectations, it does not second-guess the fundamental policy decision of the legislature. The judges only require the legislature to put in place an adequate transitional arrangement. Consequently, a decision based on the violation of legitimate expectations invalidates a piece of legislation only for a limited period and/or a limited circle of addressees.

Categorical arguments: Categorical arguments are the diametrical opposite of balancing.[64] A categorical understanding of fundamental rights does not include a balancing between the importance of the fundamental right and the public purpose. Rather, it merely determines the scope of the fundamental right. If a state measure touches this scope, it automatically violates the fundamental right. Thus, there is no balancing of competing interests. Instead, the core of the argument revolves around the abstract definition of the fundamental right.

Deductive reasoning: In particular, the German Constitutional Court often deploys a deductive style of argumentation. If the court relies on deductive reasoning, it deduces an abstract normative standard from a fundamental right. In a second step, it applies this standard to the norm under review. Deductive reasoning is often combined with additional arguments. In many cases, the deducted standards are operationalised through equality or consistency considerations. Such combinations were indicated accordingly in the coding of the judgments.

Equality considerations: All three of the analysed constitutions contain equal protection guarantees. However, the German Constitutional Court sometimes also uses equality considerations in the context of other fundamental rights. These equality considerations may be used as part of the proportionality test. A measure may then be considered disproportionate because it discriminates without justification. In other cases,

[63] BVerfGE 31, 94 at 99; 51, 356 at 363–68; 68, 272 at 285–86.

[64] On the concept, see von Bernstorff, 'Proportionality without balancing'.

equality considerations are used to operationalise standards identified through deductive reasoning.

2.2d. Procedural Arguments

There are two types of procedural arguments. One category of procedural arguments refers to the (administrative) procedure that is established by the norm under review. By contrast, a second category refers to the (legislative) procedure that established the norm.

Procedural considerations: Courts often use procedural considerations in the context of the proportionality test. The court does not take issue with the substantive aim that is pursued by the legislature. However, it requires additional procedural safeguards to protect the fundamental rights of the concerned individuals. For example, it might require participatory rights or means of judicial or administrative review. The procedural requirements are thus meant to raise the quality of administrative decisions infringing upon individual rights and to minimise unnecessary violations of fundamental rights.

Such procedural arguments also contain an element of implicit balancing. Additional procedural safeguards usually decrease the efficiency of the administrative procedure.[65] They impose additional costs or extend the time of the procedure. Courts thus have to compare the diminished efficiency of the administrative procedure with the heightened protection of the individual right in question. However, the scope of procedural balancing is usually limited. The legislative purpose of the individual rights limitation is not second-guessed in principle. It only concerns the price the legislature has to pay in the form of additional procedural guarantees in order to achieve its aim.

Some arguments are hybrids between substantive and procedural arguments. One example for such hybrids is determinacy considerations. Sometimes determinacy is considered to be a substantive requirement that is supposed to increase legal certainty.[66] However, determinacy also has a procedural aspect, which concerns the distribution of powers

[65] On the costs and benefits of additional procedural safeguards, see Vermeule, *Constitution of Risk*, pp. 141–62.

[66] See Hans-Jürgen Papier and Johannes Möller, 'Das Bestimmtheitsgebot und seine Durchsetzung' (1997) 122 *Archiv des öffentlichen Rechts* 177–211 at 179; Katharina Sobota, *Das Prinzip Rechtsstaat* (Tübingen: Mohr Siebeck, 1997), pp. 497–8; Eberhard Schmidt-Aßmann, 'Der Rechtsstaat', in Josef Isensee and Paul Kirchhof (eds.), *Handbuch des Staatsrechts der Bundesrepublik Deutschland. Band II: Verfassungsstaat* (Heidelberg: C. F. Müller, 3rd edn, 2004), ch. 26 at para. 85.

between legislature and executive.[67] If courts qualify a norm as indeterminate, they argue that it defers more power to the executive than would be appropriate.

Review of the legislative procedure: A second type of procedural argument does not concern the administrative procedure that is established by a statute. Instead, it focuses on the legislative procedure establishing the statute. This predominantly concerns the question of whether the legislature has taken its decision on a sound empirical basis and whether it has taken the interests of all relevant actors into account. One instrument for reviewing the legislative procedure is the construction of a margin of appreciation or a burden of justification. If the legislature enjoys a margin of appreciation, it has discretion about how to act in situations of uncertainty. By contrast, if courts impose a burden of proof on the legislature, the legislature can only act if there is sufficient certainty about the nature of the problem and the effect of the proposed legislation. Arguments concerning the legislative procedure are rarely a sufficient condition for invalidating a piece of legislation. Predominantly, they are auxiliary arguments supporting substantive claims of the judgment. In the coding process, such an auxiliary nature was indicated accordingly.

[67] See Konrad Hesse, 'Bestand und Bedeutung der Grundrechte in der Bundesrepublik Deutschland' (1978) 5 *Europäische Grundrechte Zeitschrift* 427–38 at 435; Papier and Möller, 'Das Bestimmtheitsgebot', 179–80; Armin von Bogdandy, *Gubernative Rechtsetzung* (Tübingen: Mohr Siebeck, 2000), p. 191; Emanuel Towfigh, 'Komplexität und Normenklarheit' (2009) 48 *Der Staat* 29–73 at 63–5.

4

Proportionality as a Doctrinal Construction

Doctrinal instruments are not discovered but constructed. There is neither a natural structure of the proportionality test, nor is proportionality necessitated by the nature of certain constitutional provisions.[1] Instead, proportionality is a consequence of the way in which individual rights are conceptualised. If rights are not seen as trumps, but as *prima facie* prohibitions whose infringements can be justified, courts need tools to resolve conflicts between competing interests. Therefore, courts rely on proportionality because they perceive it to be the most useful argumentation framework for this task. This also means that proportionality can be applied in very different ways by the various courts, even though its formal structure is always the same.

If we look at the case law of the three analysed courts, there are, at first glance, significant differences in the use of the proportionality test. The Canadian Supreme Court and the German Constitutional Court both use the traditional four-step structure of the proportionality test, consisting of the legitimate aim, the rational-connection test, the less-restrictive-means test, and the balancing of the public purpose and the individual right. However, the emphasis is different. For the German Constitutional Court, the most important stage is the last one, the balancing of the competing aims.[2] By contrast, the Canadian Supreme

[1] But see Alexy, *Theory of Constitutional Rights*, p. 66; Nils Jansen, 'Die normativen Grundlagen rationalen Abwägens im Recht', in Jan-Reinard Sieckmann (ed.), *Die Prinzipientheorie der Grundrechte* (Baden-Baden: Nomos, 2007), pp. 39–57 at 55; Martin Borowski, 'Abwehrrechte als grundrechtliche Prinzipien', in Jan-Reinard Sieckmann (ed.), *Die Prinzipientheorie der Grundrechte* (Baden-Baden: Nomos, 2007), pp. 81–104 at 92 (arguing that proportionality was necessitated by the structure of individual rights).

[2] See Ossenbühl, 'Abwägung im Verfassungsrecht', 906; Isensee, 'Bundesverfassungsgericht', 1090; Schiedermair, 'Bundesverfassungsgericht', p. 483; Lindner, *Grundrechtsdogmatik*, p. 217; Kommers, 'Germany: Balancing Rights and Duties', p. 202; Grimm, 'Proportionality', 393; Cohen-Eliya and Porat, 'The hidden foreign law debate', 399; Jestaedt, 'Phänomen Bundesverfassungsgericht', p. 146; Lepsius, 'Die maßstabsetzende Gewalt', pp. 206–7; Classen,

Court resolves most cases in the third step, the less-restrictive-means test.[3]

The structure of the proportionality test employed by the South African Constitutional Court seems to differ markedly from the case law of its German or Canadian counterparts. The South African Court has explicitly rejected the structured approach consisting of four different steps. In its *Manamela* judgment, it held:

> It should be noted that the five factors expressly itemised in section 36 are not presented as an exhaustive list. They are included in the section as key factors that have to be considered in an overall assessment as to whether or not the limitation is reasonable and justifiable in an open and democratic society. In essence, the Court must engage in a balancing exercise and arrive at a global judgment on proportionality and not adhere mechanically to a sequential check-list.[4]

The South African Constitutional Court thus considers the same factors as its Canadian and German counterparts. However, these factors are not sequential steps, but rather part of the overall balancing exercise.[5]

This *prima facie* description of the different uses of proportionality could evoke the impression that the Canadian Supreme Court exercises more deference with respect to the legislature than the German Constitutional Court and the South African Constitutional Court, which rely to a much larger extent on balancing.[6] However, in this and the following chapters,

'Verhältnismäßigkeit', p. 652; Lübbe-Wolff, 'Principle of Proportionality', 15; Hailbronner, *Traditions and Transformations*, p. 118. But see also Heinrich Scholler, 'Der Grundsatz der Verhältnismäßigkeit im deutschen Verfassungs- und Verwaltungsrecht', in Nikolaos Alivizatos *et al.* (eds.), *Essays in Honour of Georgios I. Kassimatis* (Athens: Ant. N. Sakkoulas Publishers, 2004), pp. 307–21 at 315 (asserting that balancing has "no particular importance" in the case law of the German Constitutional Court).

3 See David M. Beatty, 'The Canadian Charter of Rights: Lessons and Laments' (1997) 60 *Modern Law Review* 481–98 at 484; Trakman, Cole-Hamilton and Gatien, 'Oakes', 103; Hogg, *Constitutional Law*, p. 128.

4 *S v. Manamela* 2000 (3) SA 1 (CC) at para. 32.

5 Ziyad Motala and Cyril Ramaphosa, *Constitutional Law* (Oxford: Oxford University Press, 2002), p. 417; Gerhard van der Schyff, *Limitation of Rights: A Study of the European Convention and the South African Bill of Rights* (Nijmegen: Wolf Legal Publishers, 2005), p. 278; Stuart Woolman and Henk Botha, 'Limitations', in Stuart Woolman, Michael Bishop and Jason Brickhill (eds.), *Constitutional Law of South Africa* (Cape Town: Juta, 2nd edn, 2006), ch. 34 at para. 34.93; Heinz Klug, *The Constitution of South Africa: A Contextual Analysis* (Oxford: Hart, 2010), p. 117; Koutnatzis, 'Verfassungsvergleichende Überlegungen', 51; Currie and Waal, *Bill of Rights*, p. 164; Pierre de Vos and Warren Freedman, *South African Constitutional Law in Context* (Cape Town: Oxford University Press, 2014), p. 350.

6 See Stephen Gardbaum, 'Limiting Constitutional Rights' (2007) 54 *UCLA Law Review* 789–854 at 843; Koutnatzis, 'Verfassungsvergleichende Überlegungen', 57–8.

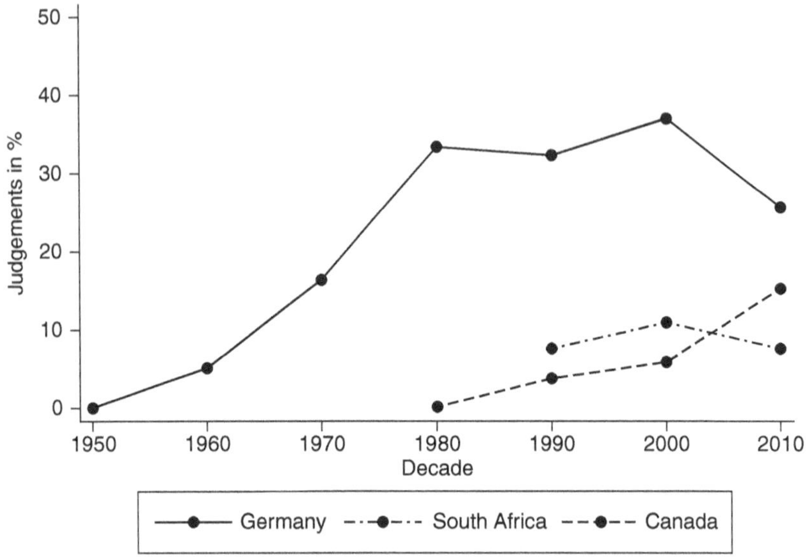

Graph 4.1 The Evolution of Balancing

I would like to draw a more nuanced picture. In this chapter, we will have a look at the results of the empirical analysis. This analysis seems to confirm our first impressions on the German Constitutional Court and the Canadian Supreme Court. In Germany, balancing is the predominant argumentation framework in the German fundamental rights jurisprudence, whereas the Canadian Supreme Court relies to a large extent on the less-restrictive-means test. However, we will see historical trends that show a shift towards balancing in both courts, even though this shift is more pronounced in the German case (Graph 4.1).

The biggest surprise, however, comes from the analysis of the South African case law. Although the structure of the test employed in South Africa suggests an extensive use of balancing, the court refrains from balancing in almost all cases. Technically, of course, the court resorts to balancing in all cases because of the mentioned one-step structure of its proportionality test. If we look more closely at the arguments that the court uses to tip the scale in cases in which it overturns a piece of legislation, it turns out that the court, in fact, rather relies on less-restrictive-means or rational-connection arguments. In the following, I will first present the results of the empirical analysis (section 1). In a second step, I will then look for explanations for the historical trend in Germany (section 2) and

Canada (section 3), as well as for the absence of balancing in South Africa (section 4).

1. The Results of the Empirical Analysis

The analysis of the German Constitutional Court confirms our first impression that balancing is the predominant argumentation framework (Table 4.1). However, what is more striking is the historical trend (Graph 4.1). In almost three decades after the foundation of the court, balancing only played a marginal role when the court justified the constitutional incompatibility of a statute. From 1951 to 1977, the court struck down a statute only four times because it deemed the law to be disproportionate. If the court resorted to proportionality arguments, it usually based its decision on the lack of a rational connection between means and end or the existence of a less-restrictive means. This picture changed towards the end of the 1970s. In the thirty-seven years from 1978 to 2014, the court based about one-third of its decisions, in which it overturned a piece of legislation, on balancing considerations. In relative terms, balancing became the most important argumentation framework from the 1980s onwards.

As expected, the picture is different if we look at the case law of the Canadian Supreme Court (Table 4.2). Overall, the less-restrictive-means test is the predominant argumentation framework. It accounts for almost two thirds of all decisions in which a piece of legislation was overturned. However, there are also some surprises in this respect. Some authors have claimed that balancing does not play any role in the jurisprudence of the Canadian Supreme Court.[7] Our empirical analysis suggests otherwise.[8] Whereas balancing is not as prevalent as in the German constitutional jurisprudence, it accounts for more than 5 percent of all decisions. Furthermore, we also observe a trend (Graph 4.1). However, the latter finding comes with a caveat. For the current decade, the total number of observed cases in which the Canadian Supreme Court invalidated a piece of legislation and relied on the limitation clause of section 1 of the Canadian Charter is rather small. Therefore, we have to observe the future development and see whether this tendency is confirmed or whether what seemed to be a trend was simply an artefact of the small number of cases.

[7] See Trakman, Cole-Hamilton and Gatien, 'Oakes', 103; Hogg, *Constitutional Law*, p. 153.

[8] See also Gardbaum, 'Limiting Constitutional Rights', 833 (challenging the assumption that the Canadian Supreme Court totally refrains from balancing).

Table 4.1 *Classification of Arguments in Decisions of the German Constitutional Court*

Years	Qty	LEG(%)	LRM(%)	BAL(%)	EQU(%)	CON(%)	EXP(%)	PRC(%)	DET(%)	DED(%)	CAT(%)
1950s	12	0	25	0	8.3	16.7	8.3	33.3	16.7	0	0
1960s	39	10.3	20.5	5.1	18	2.6	12.8	20.5	5.1	5.1	2.6
1970s	37	5.4	21.6	16.2	16.2	5.4	21.6	8.1%	10.8	5.4	0
1980s	48	4.2	20.8	33.3	14.6	8.3	10.4	12.5	8.3	4.2	0
1990s	37	5.4	27	32.4	8.1	13.5	10.8	13.5	2.7	18.9	0
2000s	46	0	15.2	37	4.4	26.1	4.4	30.4	17.4	13	4.4
2010s	31	0	6.5	25.8	6.5	22.6	22.6	29	29	9.7	3.2
Total	250	4	19.4	24.4	11.2	13.4	12.8	19.6	12	8.8	1.6

Some decisions can be based on more than one type of argument, so that the lines will usually add up to more than 100%. The classification contains the following types of arguments: LEG – legitimate purpose; LRM – rational connection or less-restrictive means; BAL – balancing; EQU – equal protection; CON – consistency or coherency arguments; EXP – protection of legitimate expectations; PRC – procedural arguments; DET – lack of determinacy; DED – deductive reasoning; CAT – categorical arguments.

Table 4.2 *Classification of Arguments in Decisions of the Canadian Supreme Court*

Years	Qty	LEG(%)	LRM(%)	OVB(%)	BAL(%)	PRC(%)	DET(%)	CON(%)	BUJ(%)
1980s	10	10	70	20	0	10	0	20	20
1990s	27	3.7	55.6	22.2	3.7	14.8	11.1	3.7	25.9
2000s	17	11.8	64.7	5.9	5.9	17.6	0	17.6	23.5
2010s	13	0	69.2	7.7	15.4	23.1	0	7.7	15.4
Total	67	6	62.7	14.9	6	16.4	4.4	10.4	22.4

Some decisions can be based on more than one type of argument, so that the lines will usually add up to more than 100%. The classification contains the following types of arguments: LEG – legitimate purpose; LRM – rational connection or less restrictive means; OVB – overbreadth; BAL – balancing; CON – consistency or coherency arguments; PRC – procedural arguments; DET – lack of determinacy; BUJ – burden of justification.

Table 4.3 *Classification of Arguments in Decisions of the South African Constitutional Court*

Years	Qty	LEG(%)	LRM(%)	OVB(%)	BAL(%)	CON(%)	PRC(%)	BUJ(%)
1990s	13	7.7	61.5	53.8	7.7	7.7	7.7	23.1
2000s	18	33.3	27.8	33.3	11.1	16.7	16.7	16.7
2010s	13	0	84.6	15.4	7.7	15.4	15.4	7.7
Total	44	15.9	54.5	31.8	9.1	13.6	13.6	15.9

Some decisions can be based on more than one type of argument, so that the lines will usually add up to more than 100%. The classification contains the following types of arguments: LEG – legitimate purpose; LRM – rational connection or less restrictive means; OVB – overbreadth; BAL – balancing; CON – consistency or coherency arguments; PRC – procedural arguments; BUJ – burden of justification.

If we look at the data from the analysis of the South African Constitutional Court, we observe a significant discrepancy between our expectations and the actual findings (Table 4.3). The structure of the proportionality test in South Africa made us assume that balancing is the predominant argumentation framework in the South African jurisprudence. However, the empirical analysis suggests differently. Balancing only plays a marginal role. Instead, the South African Court mainly relies on rational-connection, less-restrictive-means and overbreadth arguments.

In the following sections, we will analyse the reasons for these empirical patterns. In Germany and Canada, the focus will be on the (potentially) historical trends. Regarding South Africa, the reasons why the Constitutional Court abstains from balancing will be examined more closely.

2. The Rise of Balancing in the German Fundamental Rights Adjudication

Although balancing was formally part of the proportionality test in Germany from the beginning, the court did not rely on it very much in the early years when striking down statutes of the legislature.[9] The starting point of using proportionality as an instrument of fundamental rights

[9] The argument in this section was previously developed in Petersen, 'Balancing and Judicial Self-Empowerment'.

review was the pharmacy judgment,[10] which the court handed down in 1958.[11] This judgment principally relied on less-restrictive-means and consistency considerations and is thus typical for the early case law of the court. This changed at the end of the 1970s when the court increasingly relied on balancing when overturning legislative decisions. However, in its early jurisprudence, the Court did not totally refrain from balancing. Instead, it used balancing in cases in which it either confirmed a piece of legislation or in which it corrected decisions of lower courts. This observation corresponds to the hypotheses developed in the previous chapter: the use of balancing while turning against the legislature increases once the Constitutional Court has solidified its own institutional position.

2.1 *The Pharmacy Judgment as a Starting Point*

In the pharmacy judgment, the German Constitutional Court held that a licensing scheme for pharmacies in the state of Bavaria was incompatible with the freedom of profession enshrined in Article 12 of the constitution. The applicant – ironically a refugee from the communist Eastern part of Germany – had intended to open a pharmacy in the Bavarian village of Traunreut. The administrative authority had denied the request because the establishment of a new pharmacy was not in the public interest. The already existing pharmacy was supposed to be sufficient to serve the inhabitants of Traunreut with the necessary medicinal products.

There are two interesting points to note about this case. First, the Constitutional Court had cautiously raised the suspicion that the scheme was actually set up to protect the existing pharmacies against competition.

[10] Entscheidungen des Bundesverfassungsgerichts [BVerfGE] vol. 7, p. 377.

[11] See Eberhard Grabitz, 'Der Grundsatz der Verhältnismäßigkeit in der Rechtsprechung des Bundesverfassungsgerichts' (1973) 98 *Archiv des öffentlichen Rechts* 568–616 at 569–70; Stern, 'Zur Entstehung und Ableitung des Übermaßverbots', p. 172; Stephanie Heinsohn, 'Der öffentlichrechtliche Grundsatz der Verhältnismäßigkeit', PhD thesis, University of Münster (1997), p. 69; Helmuth Schulze-Fielitz, 'Wirkung und Befolgung verfassungsgerichtlicher Entscheidungen', in Peter Badura and Horst Dreier (eds.), *Festschrift 50 Jahre Bundesverfassungsgericht. Erster Band: Verfassungsgerichtsbarkeit, Verfassungsprozeß* (Tübingen: Mohr Siebeck, 2001), pp. 385–420 at 396; Grimm, 'Proportionality', 385; Stone Sweet and Mathews, 'Proportionality Balancing', 108; Jestaedt, 'Phänomen Bundesverfassungsgericht', p. 122; Christian Hillgruber, 'Grundrechtsschranken', in Josef Isensee and Paul Kirchhof (eds.), *Handbuch des Staatsrechts der Bundesrepublik Deutschland. Band IX: Allgemeine Grundrechtslehren* (Heidelberg: C. F. Müller, 3rd edn, 2011), ch. 201 at para. 52. Elements of proportionality can be found in decisions before the *pharmacy* judgment. See, for example, BVerfGE 7, 198 at 215–19; 7, 320 at 326.

It qualified the licensing scheme as a quantitative access restriction and argued that in such circumstances

> [t]here is a significant danger of [the legislative decision] being influenced by *illicit motives*; in particular, it seems likely that the access restriction is supposed to protect those who are already part of the profession against competition – a motive that, according to common opinion, cannot ever justify an infringement of the freedom of profession.[12]

The court did not draw the consequence to examine the motivation of the legislature. Instead, it used its observation as a reason to justify a particularly strict standard of scrutiny for the legislative decision.[13]

Second, while framing the standard of review in the abstract, the court used a balancing rhetoric. It argued that the freedom of profession was supposed to protect individual liberty, while the limitations clause contained in the provision aimed to protect the public interest.[14] It continued:

> If one tries to accommodate both objectives, which are equally legitimate in a social constitutional democracy, as effectively as possible, the resolution can only be found *through a thorough balancing* of the importance of the opposite and possibly competing interests."[15]

However, in the further course of the judgment, the court avoided basing its reasoning on a balancing of the competing interests. Instead, it used a combination of less-restrictive-means and coherency arguments.[16] The Bavarian government had argued that an unrestrained freedom to establish new pharmacies would lead to a fierce competition between

[12] BVerfGE 7, 377 at 408 (emphasis added) (translation by the author. The German original reads as follows: "Die Gefahr des Eindringens sachfremder Motive ist daher besonders groß; vor allem liegt die Vermutung nahe, die Beschränkung des Zugangs zum Beruf solle dem Konkurrenzschutz der bereits im Beruf Tätigen dienen – ein Motiv, das nach allgemeiner Meinung niemals einen Eingriff in das Recht der freien Berufswahl rechtfertigen könnte.").

[13] Anna-Bettina Kaiser, 'Das Apothekenurteil des BVerfG nach 50 Jahren – Anfang oder Anfang vom Ende der Berufsfreiheit?' (2008) *30 Juristische Ausbildung* 844–50 at 850; Petersen, 'Capture', 665.

[14] BVerfGE 7, 377 at 404.

[15] Id. at 405 (emphasis added) (translation by the author. The German original reads as follows: "Sucht man beiden – im sozialen Rechtsstaat gleichermaßen legitimen – Forderungen in möglichst wirksamer Weise gerecht zu werden, so kann die Lösung nur jeweils in sorgfältiger Abwägung der Bedeutung der einander gegenüberstehenden und möglicherweise einander geradezu widerstreitenden Interessen gefunden werden.").

[16] Schlink, *Abwägung*, pp. 53–4; Schulze-Fielitz, 'Wirkung und Befolgung verfassungsgerichtlicher Entscheidungen', p. 396; Becker, 'Verhältnismäßigkeit', para. 5.

the pharmacies and compromise their economic soundness.[17] In such an environment, the pharmacies might be inclined to violate obligations concerning prescriptions, quality control of the medical drugs and education of the personnel in order to increase their revenue. Furthermore, an excessive supply of pharmaceutical drugs may increase the consumption of these drugs and enhance addiction.

The constitutional court rejected these arguments. It found that the access restriction was not necessary to secure the economic soundness of the pharmacies.[18] To justify this less-restrictive-means argument, the court raised a simple economic consideration: The establishment of a pharmacy required a significant initial investment. For this reason, a pharmacist usually made an economic assessment whether the investment would pay off before he established a new pharmacy.[19] Therefore, an abundant increase of pharmacies was unlikely. Instead, the market already took care of the problem that the licensing scheme was supposed to address. The court supported these theoretical considerations with reference to the situation in Switzerland: the Swiss had not restricted the establishment of new pharmacies, and the system was working just fine.[20]

In the pharmacy judgment, the German Constitutional Court started to develop a formal argumentation framework to resolve conflicts between individual rights and competing public purposes. The judgment is characteristic of many early decisions of the court. The court used balancing rhetoric, but refrained from a comparison of the abstract value of the competing interests. Instead, it framed its decision as a review of legislative rationality by putting an emphasis on the empirical assumptions underlying the economic regulation. In the end, it overturned the legislation because it had serious doubts about the effectiveness of the chosen regulatory scheme.

2.2 *The Pre-balancing Period*

In the early case law, the argumentation patterns follow the general lines that we have observed in our analysis of the pharmacy judgment.[21] When the court applied the principle of proportionality, it used predominantly

[17] See BVerfGE 7, 377 at 413–14.
[18] Id. at 415–21.
[19] Id. at 420.
[20] Id. at 415–16.
[21] See section 2.1 of this chapter.

rational-connection and less-restrictive-means arguments.[22] Moreover, it often resorted to consistency and coherency arguments[23] or challenged the lacking protection of legitimate expectations.[24] Another illustrative example of the early approach is the cash-on-delivery (COD) ruling, in which the constitutional court overturned a law prohibiting the COD shipment of live animals.[25] The challenged statute aimed to protect animal health. It was supposed to avoid long transport times that could occur if the purchaser refused to accept the delivered animal.

Substantially, the court based its verdict on two principal arguments. On the one hand, it found that the legislation was overbroad because it targeted even those shipments that did not involve a considerable danger of harm for the animals.[26] Furthermore, an empirical assessment of the situation had shown that only a tiny fraction of all shipments had been returned to the sender.[27] Not all of the shipments had been returned because the purchaser had rejected the animals. Some were due to other reasons, for example, false mailing addresses or the absence of the addressee.[28] For these reasons, the Court found that there was no sufficient rational connection between measure and purpose.[29] On the other hand, the court made a coherency argument. The legislature had extended the prohibition of COD even to express shipments. At the same time, it had not demanded that all deliveries be expedited. The court noted that the transport time for non-express shipments often exceeded the total time of returned express deliveries. Therefore, it found the legislation to be inconsistent.[30]

Finally, the court supported its substantial arguments by an inquiry into the legislative process. It noted that the prohibition of COD shipments had been introduced in the legislation without giving the concerned professions

[22] Equally, Lepsius, 'Chancen und Grenzen', p. 16. See, for example, BVerfGE 7, 320 at 325–6; 7, 377 at 419–23 and 439–41; 9, 39 at 52–5 and 58–62; 11, 30 at 46–7; 11, 168 at 188; 12, 144 at 148–50; 13, 290 at 315–17; 17, 269 at 277–80; 17, 306 at 315–16; 19, 330 at 338–40; 21, 261 at 268–70; 21, 271 at 283; 30, 1 at 31–2; 30, 227 at 245–6; 30, 336 at 354–5; 34, 71 at 79; 34, 165 at 198; 36, 47 at 60 and 63; 36, 146 at 166; 40, 371 at 383; 41, 378 at 396–7.

[23] See, for example, BVerfGE 7, 377 at 429–30, 435–7, 439; 8, 1 at 26–7; 25, 236 at 251–2.

[24] See, for example, BVerfGE 2, 380 at 403; 13, 206 at 213; 13, 261 at 270–1; 15, 167 at 209; 18, 429 at 439; 24, 75 at 97–103; 30, 367 at 385–91; 31, 94 at 99; 31, 275 at 293; 32, 1 at 28; 43, 242 at 288; 43, 291 at 393–4.

[25] BVerfGE 36, 47.

[26] Id. at 60.

[27] Id. at 61–2.

[28] Id. at 63.

[29] Id.

[30] Id.

an opportunity to state their views.[31] Furthermore, it highlighted that some of the reasons that were mentioned in the legislative procedure to justify the prohibition had subsequently proven to be wrong.[32] For this reason, the legislature could not have considered all relevant factors in the balancing process and had thus been guided by incomplete and inaccurate considerations.[33] Through this reasoning, the court highlighted the lack of rationality in the legislative process. On the one hand, it pointed out failures of the legislative procedure. The legislature had neither made a sufficient factual inquiry nor considered all relevant factors. On the other hand, it showed how these deficiencies of the legislative process affected the substance of the legislation by highlighting that it was overbroad and inconsistent.

Balancing decisions were very rare in the first twenty-five years of the court's jurisprudence. The first decision came in 1962, when the court overturned a law that extended the limit on shopping hours to vending machines.[34] These vending machines were only profitable when they operated for 24 hours. At the same time a 24-hour operation did not compromise the existence of competing shops. For this reason, the court held that the law imposed a disproportionate burden on the operators of vending machines.[35] Before 1978, there were only three more rulings in which the constitutional court overturned a law based on balancing considerations.[36] As in the vending machine case, the stakes for the legislature in these decisions were fairly low. The change of direction came in 1978 and 1979, when the court used balancing in four judgments[37] – that is, in exactly as many as in the twenty-seven years before.

2.3 *The Second Period: Balancing as the Predominant Argumentation Framework*

From 1978 onwards, balancing has become the predominant argumentation framework. Relatively speaking, the court has used balancing to overturn a law more often than any other argument. Still, even in the last three decades, it has not based the constitutional incompatibility of a law on balancing in more than roughly one-third of its decisions. The confidence

31 Id. at 60.
32 Id. at 61.
33 Id. at 64.
34 BVerfGE 14, 19.
35 Id. at 23–4.
36 See BVerfGE 21, 173 at 182–3; 31, 229 at 243–4; 34, 165 at 198.
37 See BVerfGE 47, 285 at 322–35; 49, 382 at 400–2; 52, 1 at 36; 52, 257 at 366.

of the constitutional court in utilising balancing considerations is particularly visible in a decision on the status of transsexuals from May 2008.[38] In this decision, the court relied on balancing even though the case seemed to be a textbook example for the less-restrictive-means test. The applicant, who was born in 1929, had been married since 1952. For a long time, he had felt that he belonged to the female gender. Therefore, he underwent gender reassignment surgery in 2002. However, he was denied a respective change of his civil status because the civil status could, according to the then-applicable law, only be changed if he got divorced first.

With this provision, the legislature had intended to prevent matrimonies of same-sex couples. In 2001, however, the legislature had passed a new law that allowed civil unions of same-sex couples. Since then, the legislative purpose could have been attained through a less-restrictive means: the transformation of the matrimony into a civil union upon request of the couple. Nevertheless, the court resorted to balancing in its reasoning. It argued that the divorce requirement imposed a disproportionate burden on the applicant and thus violated his right to privacy.[39] When the court discussed the possible consequences, however, it explicitly advised the legislature of the possibility to transform the matrimony into a civil union as one possible option.[40]

2.4 *Balancing and the Review of Decisions of Civil and Criminal Courts*

In the previous sections, we saw that the constitutional court was reluctant to use balancing considerations in the first almost three decades of its existence when it overturned a law. However, that does not mean that the court did not balance at all in its judgments. On the contrary: Even in the time from the 1950s to the late 1970s, there are many decisions in which the court resorted to balancing. First, the court balanced when it confirmed the constitutionality of a law.[41] For two reasons, this is not surprising. On the one hand, balancing is a necessary step in the doctrine of the proportionality test when the law has passed the first three steps of the test. On the other

[38] BVerfGE 121, 175.

[39] Id. at 194–202.

[40] Id. at 203.

[41] See, for example, BVerfGE 9, 338 at 346; 10, 89 at 103–7; 13, 97 at 113–22; 13, 181 at 187–90; 14, 263 at 282–4; 15, 235 at 243–4; 16, 147 at 174–83; 21, 245 at 259–60; 23, 50 at 59–60; 25, 1 at 22–3; 27, 1 at 8; 28, 191 at 200; 30, 1 at 32–3; 32, 54 at 75–6; 33, 367 at 378–82; 37, 1 at 22–3; 38, 61 at 92 and 94–5; 39, 210 at 234; 50, 290 at 350–1 and 365.

hand, balancing does not raise the suspicion of the court interfering with the political sphere because the court confirms the legislative decision.

Second, the constitutional court balanced when it reviewed decisions of lower courts.[42] The seminal case is the *Lüth* judgment, which was handed down in January 1958 – five months before the pharmacy judgment.[43] The case concerned a statement of Erich Lüth, who was the director of the press office in Hamburg at the time. Lüth had called for a boycott of the latest film of the director Veit Harlan, who had directed several anti-Semitic films in Nazi Germany. After the producer and the distributor of Harlan's film had obtained an injunction against Lüth, which asked him to refrain from calling for a boycott against the film, Lüth turned to the constitutional court. He argued that the injunction violated his freedom of expression.

The decision is of seminal importance for two reasons. On the one hand, the court extended its own jurisdiction to the review of decisions of civil courts even if these decisions were not based on an unconstitutional law.[44] It argued that fundamental rights not only contained obligations for the legislature but also bound private law courts when they decided on conflicts between individuals.[45] On the other hand, the court introduced the balancing test for the first time.[46] It resorted to a "balancing of the

[42] See, for example, BVerfGE 7, 198 at 215–29; 12, 113 at 124–7; 16, 194 at 203; 17, 108 at 118–20; 22, 114 at 123–4; 24, 278 at 282–8; 34, 238 at 248–51; 35, 202 at 221–38. The Constitutional Court does not always engage in balancing itself. In many decisions, it frames its argument as a mere review of whether the lower court has considered all relevant factors in the balancing test. However, the level of scrutiny varies. In some decisions, the Constitutional Court simply states that the civil or criminal court has failed to assess the scope of a fundamental right properly, but leaves the final balancing decision to the court of first instance; *see*, for example, BVerfGE 27, 72 at 82–8; 27, 344 at 352–3. But in the vast majority of cases, the constitutional court predetermines the result of the balancing test in its decision. This applies, in particular, to the initially cited cases.

[43] BVerfGE 7, 198 at 215–19.

[44] Rainer Wahl, 'Lüth und die Folgen – Ein Urteil als Weichenstellung für die Rechtsentwicklung', in Thomas Henne and Arne Riedlinger (eds.), *Das Lüth-Urteil aus (rechts-)historischer Sicht* (Berlin: Berliner Wissenschafts-Verlag, 2005), pp. 371–97 at 375; Hans Vorländer, 'Die Deutungsmacht des Bundesverfassungsgerichts', in Robert Christian van Ooyen and Martin H.W. Möllers (eds.), *Das Bundesverfassungsgericht im politischen System* (Wiesbaden: VS Verlag für Sozialwissenschaften, 2006), pp. 189–99 at 190; Robertson, *Judge as Political Theorist*, p. 50; Jestaedt, 'Phänomen Bundesverfassungsgericht', p. 93; Bomhoff, *Balancing*, p. 77; Dominik Rennert, 'Die verdrängte Werttheorie und ihre Historisierung' (2014) 53 *Der Staat* 31–59 at 32.

[45] BVerfGE 7, 198 at 203–12.

[46] Jacco Bomhoff, 'Lüth's 50th Anniversary: Some Comparative Observations on the German Foundations of Judicial Balancing' (2008) 9 *German Law Journal* 121–4 at 122; Michaela Hailbronner, 'Rethinking the Rise of the German Constitutional Court: From Anti-Nazism to Value Formalism' (2014) *International Journal of Constitutional Law* 626–49 at 647.

fundamental right contained in Art. 5 para. 1 sent. 1 of the Constitution [i.e., the freedom of expression] and the rights and values that restrict its exercise" for the resolution of the conflict between the applicant's freedom of expression and Harlan's professional reputation.[47] On both sides of the equation, it considered the extent to which the competing interests were affected. On the one hand, it analysed the motives of Lüth's statement, and on the other, it examined the intensity of the restriction of Harlan's rights.

The court found that Lüth had intended to protect the reputation of the German film industry abroad and to fend off any Nazi influences.[48] It qualified the applicant's concern for the German reputation as "significant".[49] Furthermore, it acknowledged that it was necessary to interfere with Harlan's interests in order to pursue this purpose.[50] On the other side, the court argued that the statement did not infringe the core of Harlan's identity as an artist.[51] Lüth had exercised neither physical nor legal force, and Harlan was not denied permission to continue working in the film business.[52] For this reason, the court held that the injunction violated the applicant's freedom of expression.

In the *Lüth* judgment, the court thus displayed a typical balancing of competing interests. It evaluated and compared the importance of the competing interests and the intensity, with which they were affected. The *Lüth* judgment was no exception in the early years.[53] Moreover, the court did not apply balancing considerations only while reviewing the decisions of civil courts. Instead, it also overturned several decisions of criminal courts in which it found measures of criminal procedure to be disproportionate.[54] In one decision, the constitutional court reversed a decision to investigate an accused by means of a pneumoencephalography, an extremely painful procedure that facilitated reproduction of the brain structure as an X-ray image.[55] As the applicant was accused of a misdemeanour, the court held that the severity of the bodily harm caused by the measure was disproportionate with respect to the severity of the crime.

[47] BVerfGE 7, 198 at 215.
[48] Id. at 216–18.
[49] Id. at 216 (In the original, it says: "eine für das deutsche Volk sehr wesentliche Frage").
[50] Id. at 217.
[51] Id. at 220–1.
[52] Id. at 221.
[53] See *supra* note 42.
[54] See, for example, BVerfGE 16, 194 at 203; 17, 108 at 118–20; 22, 114 at 123–4; 34, 238 at 248–51; 35, 35 at 39–40.
[55] BVerfGE 17, 108 at 118–20.

In a different decision, the constitutional court overturned a judgment in which the High Court had based a conviction on audiotape recordings as evidence.[56] The constitutional court argued that the High Court had not sufficiently justified why it believed that the criminal offence had been so severe that it outweighed the right to privacy of the accused.[57] These examples show that the constitutional court widely used balancing as a doctrinal instrument in some of its early landmark decisions when reviewing lower-court decisions, even though it was rather reluctant to use balancing when declaring a law unconstitutional.

2.5 *Balancing and the Institutional Strength of the Constitutional Court*

How do we explain these observations? In the previous chapter, we saw that the probability of a court balancing depends on two factors. On the one hand, a court is more likely to use balancing considerations the stronger its institutional position is. On the other hand, it will lean on balancing more strongly the more balancing is accepted as a doctrinal argumentation framework in the legal community.

The institutional strength of a court is not constant. We can rather assume that it develops over time.[58] Constitutional courts need to gain the trust of the citizenry in order to increase their public support.[59] Some studies in political science show that the legitimacy of constitutional courts generally increases over time, as courts had more opportunities to attract public support.[60] Initially, however, the constitutional courts are mostly concerned with establishing their institutional position and securing their independence. Tom Ginsburg even calls it a paradox: In order to gain power, constitutional courts often have to exercise self-restraint and to choose carefully the cases in which they want to confront legislature and executive.[61] This was not any different for the German Constitutional Court.[62] In the previous chapter, we saw that the German Constitutional

[56] BVerfGE 34, 238.
[57] Id. at 251.
[58] Herrmann, 'Akte der Selbstautorisierung', p. 142.
[59] Georg Vanberg, 'The Will of the People: A Comparative Perspective on Friedman' (2010) *Michigan State Law Review* 717–28 at 720–1.
[60] James L. Gibson, Gregory A. Caldeira and Vanessa A. Baird, 'On the Legitimacy of National High Courts' (1998) 92 *American Political Science Review* 343–58 at 355.
[61] Tom Ginsburg, *Judicial Review in New Democracies: Constitutional Courts in Asian Cases* (Cambridge: Cambridge University Press, 2003), p. 95.
[62] Brodocz, *Macht der Judikative*, p. 171.

Court faced strong political resistance from the Adenauer government in the 1950s.[63] Consequently, when the court developed the proportionality test in the late 1950s, it did not yet have the same institutional strength that it enjoys today.[64]

We can, therefore, assume that the institutional position of the German Constitutional Court was much stronger at the end the 1970s than in the 1950s when the court developed the proportionality test. When the court started to use balancing as an argumentation framework to overturn legislation more consistently at the end of the 1970s, it had gained sufficient institutional strength and self-confidence for such a doctrinal move.

Furthermore, it is no new phenomenon that courts develop doctrinal frameworks for situations in which they target less powerful actors, and then turn them against more powerful ones once the doctrine has been accepted in the legal discourse. Barry Friedman and Erin Delaney have shown in a study that the US Supreme Court developed certain doctrines initially when reviewing state measures.[65] In these cases, the court backed the federal government against the states. However, once the doctrine was established, the court also turned it against the federal government.[66]

Similarly, the German Constitutional Court could develop the balancing doctrine when reviewing the decisions made by lower courts or when confirming a piece of legislation. When it confirmed legislation, it confirmed the decision of the political branches. When it reviewed decisions of civil or criminal courts, the review of these decisions was arguably in the interest of politics.[67] There had been a deep-rooted suspicion against the general judiciary among the delegates of the Parliamentary Council who drafted the German constitution.[68] The judiciary had played a crucial role in the Third Reich, stabilising and supporting the regime by interpreting

[63] See ch. 3, section 1.1.

[64] See Brun-Otto Bryde, 'Der Beitrag des Bundesverfassungsgerichts zur Demokratisierung der Bundesrepublik', in Robert Christian van Ooyen and Martin H. W. Möllers (eds.), *Das Bundesverfassungsgericht im politischen System* (Wiesbaden: VS Verlag für Sozialwissenschaften, 2006), pp. 321–31 at 323; Hailbronner, *Traditions and Transformations*, p. 3.

[65] Friedman and Delaney, 'Becoming Supreme'.

[66] Id. 1188–92.

[67] See Hailbronner, 'Rethinking the rise of the German Constitutional Court', 638 (arguing that the *Lüth* decision was very much in the interest of the political elites across all major parties).

[68] Donald P. Kommers, *Judicial Politics in West Germany: A Study of the Federal Constitutional Court* (Beverly Hills: Sage, 1976), p. 75.

the existing laws through the lens of Nazi ideology.[69] However, it was practically impossible to replace the whole judiciary because there would not have been enough competent judges to do the job.[70] This was one of the reasons why a constitutional court that was not part of the traditional judicial hierarchy was created and awarded the exclusive competency to overturn laws that it found to be unconstitutional.[71] Furthermore, among the first judges who were elected to the constitutional court, a considerable number had openly resisted the Nazi regime.[72]

When the constitutional court ceased the authority to review decisions of the civil courts by also extending the scope of fundamental rights to private relations in *Lüth*, it dealt with a case that catered to the suspicion against the general judiciary. *Lüth* was thus ideal for claiming the review authority.[73] The applicant was a prominent state official who had spoken up against a film director with a significant Nazi past. When the civil courts issued an injunction against *Lüth*, they trivalised Harlan's role in the Third Reich. The constitutional court could thus emphasise its role as the guardian of the fundamental values of post-war Germany.[74] It could also introduce the balancing framework and develop it without undermining its own legitimacy.

At the same time, the perception of proportionality and balancing in German constitutional law scholarship changed quite fundamentally. In the late 1950s and early 1960s, there was a controversial debate about whether the proportionality test was only an instrument of reviewing

69 Seminally, Bernd Rüthers, *Die unbegrenzte Auslegung: Zum Wandel der Privatrechtsordnung im Nationalsozialismus* (Tübingen: Mohr Siebeck, 1968).

70 Issacharoff, *Fragile Democracies*, p. 142.

71 Kommers, *Judicial Politics*, p. 75; Issacharoff, *Fragile Democracies*, p. 144–5.

72 Richard Ley, 'Die Erstbesetzung des Bundesverfassungsgerichtes' (1982) 13 *Zeitschrift für Parlamentsfragen* 521–41 at 532; Brun-Otto Bryde, 'Die Rolle der Verfassungsgerichtsbarkeit in Umbruchsituationen', in Joachim Jens Hesse, Gunnar Folke Schuppert and Katharina Harms (eds.), *Verfassungsrecht und Verfassungspolitik in Umbruchsituationen* (Baden-Baden: Nomos, 1999), pp. 197–210 at 201; Christoph Schönberger, 'Anmerkungen zu Karlsruhe', in Matthias Jestaedt *et al.* (eds.), *Das entgrenzte Gericht: Eine kritische Bilanz nach sechzig Jahren Bundesverfassungsgericht* (Berlin: Suhrkamp, 2011), pp. 9–76 at 30; Michael Stolleis, *Geschichte des öffentlichen Rechts in Deutschland. Vierter Band: Staats- und Verwaltungsrechtswissenschaft in West und Ost 1945–1990* (München: C. H. Beck, 2012), pp. 147–54; Issacharoff, *Fragile Democracies*, p. 143–4; Collings, *Democracy's Guardians*, p. 6.

73 See also Thomas Henne, '"Von 0 auf Lüth in 6 1/2 Jahren" – Zu den prägenden Faktoren der Grundsatzentscheidung', in Thomas Henne and Arne Riedlinger (eds.), *Das Lüth-Urteil aus (rechts-)historischer Sicht* (Berlin: Berliner Wissenschafts-Verlag, 2005), pp. 197–222 at 217–8; Lepsius, 'Die maßstabsetzende Gewalt', p. 192 on the significance of the Nazi background of the case.

74 Bryde, 'Beitrag', p. 324; Stolleis, *Geschichte des öffentlichen Rechts IV*, p. 165.

courts and the executive, or whether it could also be applied to review legislation.[75] In an influential book, Peter Lerche argued that courts should rather be reluctant to apply the balancing test when reviewing legislation.[76] In the late 1970s, scholarly resistance against balancing had not totally disappeared.[77] However, balancing was predominantly accepted as a doctrinal instrument of fundamental rights review.[78] The German Constitutional Court could thus apply the balancing test to the review of legislation without having to fear a significant critical scrutiny of this move in the legal academy.

3. Balancing in the Jurisprudence of the Canadian Supreme Court

The Canadian Supreme Court introduced the proportionality test quite early as a doctrinal instrument of its individual rights jurisprudence. In *Oakes*, the court used proportionality in order to operationalise the general limitation clause in section 1 of the previously adopted Canadian Charter on Fundamental Rights. Until very recently, the less-restrictive-means prong had the centre stage in the court's proportionality test. However, there are some voices in the Canadian constitutional law literature observing a recent turn towards balancing, even though it is still too

[75] On this debate, see Rupprecht von Krauss, *Der Grundsatz der Verhältnismäßigkeit* (Hamburg: Kommissionsverlag Ludwig Appel, 1955), pp. 42–7. See also Ottmar Pohl, 'Ist der Gesetzgeber bei Eingriffen in die Grundrechte an den Grundsatz der Verhältnismäßigkeit gebunden?', PhD thesis, University of Köln (1959) (arguing that proportionality could not be applied when reviewing the legislature).

[76] Lerche, *Übermaß*, p. 224.

[77] See Forsthoff, *Staat in der Industriegesellschaft*, pp. 137–42; Schlink, *Abwägung*.

[78] See Peter Häberle, *Die Wesensgehaltsgarantie des Art. 19 Abs. 2 Grundgesetz* (Karlsruhe: Verlag C. F. Müller, 1962), pp. 31–9; Manfred Gentz, 'Zur Verhältnismäßigkeit von Grundrechtseingriffen' (1968) 21 *Neue Juristische Wochenschrift* 1600–7 at 1604–5; Peter Wittig, 'Zum Standort des Verhältnismäßigkeitsgrundsatzes im System des Grundgesetzes' (1968) 21 *Die Öffentliche Verwaltung* 817–25; Grabitz, 'Grundsatz der Verhältnismäßigkeit', 575–81; Christian Starck, 'Staatliche Organisation und staatliche Finanzierung als Hilfen zu Grundrechtsverwirklichungen?', in Christian Starck (ed.), *Bundesverfassungsgericht und Grundgesetz. Festgabe aus Anlaß des 25jährigen Bestehens des Bundesverfassungsgerichts. Zweiter Band: Verfassungsauslegung* (Tübingen: J. C. B. Mohr, 1976), pp. 480–526 at 482; Jürgen Schwabe, *Probleme der Grundrechtsdogmatik* (Darmstadt 1977), pp. 319–23; Peter Badura, Fritz Rittner and Bernd Rüthers, *Mitbestimmungsgesetz 1976 und Grundgesetz* (München: C. H. Beck, 1977), p. 196; Rudolf Wendt, 'Der Garantiegehalt der Grundrechte und das Übermaßverbot' (1979) 104 *Archiv des öffentlichen Rechts* 414–74 at 455–6; Robert Alexy, 'Zum Begriff des Rechtspinzips', in Werner Krawietz *et al.* (eds.), *Argumentation und Hermeneutik in der Jurisprudenz* (Berlin: Duncker & Humblot, 1979), pp. 59–87.

early to tell whether this trend is just an outlier or expression of a fundamental change in the Canadian jurisprudence. The final subsection tries to speculate whether the Canadian case law will mirror the German one or whether it will return to its previous equilibrium.

3.1 *The Establishment of Proportionality in Oakes*

Prima facie, the constellation in the Canadian Supreme Court's *Oakes* decision looked rather unremarkable. The court had to deal with a reverse onus clause that established the rebuttable assumption that a person found to be in the possession of drugs was, in fact, trafficking these drugs. The court seized the opportunity to clarify the interpretation of the limitation clause in section 1 of the Canadian Charter of Rights and Freedoms that had been enacted only a few years earlier. The Chief Justice stated for a unanimous court that section 1 "involves 'a form of proportionality test' ".[79] He specified the proportionality test as follows:

> First, the measures adopted [. . .] must be rationally connected to the objective. Second, the means, even if rationally connected to the objective in this first sense, should impair 'as little as possible' the right or freedom in question [. . .]. Third, there must be a proportionality between the effects of the measures which are responsible for limiting the Charter right or freedom, and the objective which has been identified as of "sufficient importance".[80]

It is notable that the court introduced the test with relatively little fanfare.[81] A few months earlier, the court had already hinted in an obiter dictum in *Big M Drug Mart* that it could use the proportionality test in order to specify section 1 of the Canadian Charter.[82] When introducing proportionality in Oakes, the court referred to this obiter dictum. There is, however, one significant difference. Whereas *Big M Drug Mart* limited the proportionality test to the less-restrictive-means stage,[83] the court included the balancing stage when defining the proportionality test in *Oakes*.[84]

When applying the developed standard to the concrete case, however, the court did not need to make use of the last step. Instead, it decided that

[79] *R. v. Oakes* [1986] 1 S.C.R. 103 at 139.
[80] Id.
[81] Stone Sweet and Mathews, 'Proportionality Balancing', 117.
[82] *R. v. Big M Drug Mart Ltd.* [1985] 1 S.C.R. 295 at 352.
[83] Id.
[84] Stone Sweet and Mathews, 'Proportionality Balancing', 117–18.

the reverse onus clause already lacked a rational connection to its purpose: The possession of a small amount of narcotics did not allow the inference that the person was actually trafficking the drug; for this reason, the norm could lead to results "which would defy both rationality and fairness".[85] The use of the rational-connection stage of the *Oakes* test was characteristic for the subsequent jurisprudence of the Canadian Supreme Court. When the court invalidated a piece of legislation, it relied either on rational-connection or – to an even larger degree – on less-restrictive-means considerations.[86]

3.2 *The Emphasis on the Less-restrictive-means Test*

Almost two-thirds of all decisions in our dataset are based on the rational-connection or the less-restrictive-means test.[87] One example for this reliance on less-restrictive means is the court's decision in *Andrews*.[88] The judgment dealt with a provision that required Canadian citizenship to be admitted to the bar in British Columbia. The court held that this citizenship requirement violated the prohibition of discrimination in section 15 (1) of the Canadian Charter.

The government of British Columbia had advanced two arguments in order to justify the citizenship requirement. On the one hand, citizenship ensured that the lawyers admitted to the bar were familiar with the local affairs; on the other hand, citizenship was an expression of the commitment to the Canadian society. However, the court found that the measure was not even rationally connected to these aims.[89] There would have been more efficient and less-restrictive means to achieve the same purposes. Concerning the familiarity with local affairs, a test would have been the more effective requirement than citizenship.[90] Canadian citizenship did not necessarily imply that individuals have indeed spent enough time in Canada to be familiar with the local affairs. At the same time, foreign residents could be as familiar with the local affairs as Canadian residents. For this reason, requiring a test could have been a less-restrictive means.[91]

85 *R. v. Oakes* [1986] 1 S.C.R. 103 at 142.
86 Beatty, 'Canadian Charter', 484; Trakman, Cole-Hamilton and Gatien, 'Oakes', 103; Hogg, *Constitutional Law*, p. 128.
87 See earlier Table 4.2.
88 *Andrews v. Law Society of British Columbia* [1989] 1 S.C.R. 143 at 155–57.
89 Id. at 155–57.
90 Id. at 156.
91 Id.

Furthermore, the court argued that citizenship was not rationally connected to being loyal to the Canadian society.[92] On the one hand, citizenship does not ensure that individuals are loyal to the Canadian society. On the other hand, there are many foreign residents who are deeply committed to the Canadian society without being citizens. Swearing an oath of allegiance may thus be a less-restrictive means to ensure the attachment of lawyers to the values of the Canadian society.[93] This reasoning certainly implies specific normative valuations.[94] Nevertheless, the judgments show the commitment of the court to rely on rational-connection and less-restrictive-means arguments instead of balancing.

However, the Canadian Supreme Court did not totally refrain from balancing when invalidating laws.[95] Instead, there are individual cases in which it relied on balancing.[96] In *Logan*, the court invalidated a criminal law provision that attributed criminal liability to a person for the actions of his partner even if the latter exceeded the criminal actions that were agreed upon.[97] The respondents in *Logan* had been convicted of attempted murder because one of their partners had shot a victim in the neck and severely injured her while robbing a convenience store even though the robbers had previously agreed not to use their guns. The court held that the provision of the criminal code, which allowed convicting a person of an act that this person had neither committed nor intended, was disproportionate because it allowed for the conviction of an intentional act, even though the accused was only guilty of negligence.[98]

A second decision of the court in *Sharpe* concerned a provision of the criminal code punishing the possession of child pornography.[99] The court acknowledged that the criminalisation of the possession of child pornography was, in principle, a legitimate aim.[100] However, the provision went too far. The justices argued that the inclusion of drawings that were produced by the accused himself and that were only dedicated to his personal use and of "privately created visual recordings of lawful sexual activity made by or depicting the person in possession and intended only for private use" added "little to

[92] Id.
[93] Id. at 200 (per LaForest J.).
[94] See, for example, id. at 190–92 (per McIntyre and Lamer JJ. dissenting).
[95] Gardbaum, 'Limiting Constitutional Rights', 833.
[96] *R. v. Logan* [1990] 2 S.C.R. 731; *R. v. Sharpe* [2001] 1 S.C.R. 45 at 98.
[97] *R. v. Logan* [1990] 2 S.C.R. 731.
[98] Id. at 747.
[99] *R. v. Sharpe* [2001] 1 S.C.R. 45 at 106–09.
[100] Id. at para. 82.

the protection the law provides children".[101] For this reason, the inclusion of these materials was deemed to be disproportionate.[102]

However, these two decisions are exceptions.[103] They amount to less than 5 percent of all cases in which a legislative act was invalidated before 2009.[104] Contrary to the German Federal Constitutional Court, the Canadian Supreme Court was not only reluctant to use balancing in cases in which it overturned legislation, but even in cases in which it confirmed legislation. The court usually put the main emphasis of its justification analysis on the rational-connection or the less-restrictive-means test.[105] Notwithstanding certain exceptions,[106] the Court utilised the balancing stage only for checking the plausibility of the result attained in the previous stages of the proportionality test.[107]

3.3 *A Recent Turn to Balancing?*

In recent years, Canadian constitutional law scholarship has observed a turn to balancing in the jurisprudence of the Canadian Supreme Court.[108] The turning point that is identified in the literature is the judgment in *Hutterian Brethren* from 2009.[109] In *Hutterian Brethren*, members of an aboriginal community challenged a photo requirement for driver's licences because it violated their freedom of religion. They claimed that

[101] Id. at para. 110.

[102] Id.

[103] See Errol P. Mendes, 'The Crucible of the Charter: Judicial Principles v. Judicial Deference in the Context of Section 1' (2005) 27 *Supreme Court Law Review* 47–104 at 96–100.

[104] See earlier Table 4.2.

[105] See, for example, *R. v. Edwards Books and Art Ltd.* [1986] 2 S.C.R. 713; *Canadian Newspapers Co. v. Canada (Attorney General)* [1988] 2 S.C.R. 122; *Irwin Toy Ltd v. Quebec (Attorney General)* [1989] 1 S.C.R. 927; *R. v. Chaulk* [1990] 3 S.C.R. 1303; *R. v. Keegstra* [1990] 3 S.C.R. 697; *Rodrigeuz v. British Columbia (Attorney General)* [1993] 3 S.C.R. 519; *Little Sisters Book and Art Emporium v. Canada (Minister of Justice)* [2000] 2 S.C.R. 1120; *Harper v. Canada* [2004] S.C.R. 827; *Newfoundland (Treasury Board) v. Newfoundland and Labrador Assn. of Public and Private Employees (N.A.P.E.)* 2004 S.C.C. 66.

[106] See, for example, *RWDSU v. Saskatchewan* [1987] 1 S.C.R. 460; *B.C.G.E.U. v. British Columbia (Attorney General)* [1988] 2 S.C.R. 214; *Canada (Attorney General) v. JTI-Macdonald Corp.* [2007] 2 S.C.R. 610.

[107] See Iacobucci, 'Judicial Review', p. 121 (arguing that the balancing stage usually only contains a "resume" of the previous stages).

[108] Sara Weinrib, 'The Emergence of the Third Step of the Oakes Test in Alberta v. Hutterian Brethren of Wilson Colony' (2010) 68 *University of Toronto Faculty of Law Review* 77–97 at 77; Patrick Monahan and Chanakya Sethi, 'Constitutional Cases 2010: An Overview' (2011) 54 *Supreme Court Law Review* 3–53 at 14.

[109] *Alberta v. Hutterian Brethren of Wilson Colony* [2009] 2 S.C.R. 567.

their religious laws prohibited them from making photos of themselves. The court held that the provision restricted the freedom of religion, but that this restriction was justified. In the justification analysis, the court put the main emphasis on the balancing stage.[110] The court argued that the photo requirement was supposed to prevent the occurrence of identity theft because, without a picture, the driver's licence could be used by any third person.[111] The court deemed that the achievement of this purpose was more important than the limitation of the freedom of religion was severe. Driving was no indispensable activity because the community could employ professional drivers.[112] For this reason, the picture requirement did not touch the core of the freedom of religion.[113]

The simple fact that the court relied on balancing does not make the decision a turning point in the Canadian jurisprudence yet. *Hutterian Brethren* is not the first decision confirming a piece of legislation that is primarily based on the balancing stage.[114] However, two things are noteworthy about *Hutterian Brethren*. First, the court intensively discussed the value of the last stage of the proportionality test.[115] In its reasoning, the majority of the court referred to a lecture, which the former president of the Israeli Supreme Court, Aharon Barak, had given at a conference in Toronto in 2006.[116] Second, the Supreme Court placed the balancing stage at the centre of the proportionality test in some subsequent decisions.[117] In these decisions, the court expressly referred to its judgment in *Hutterian Brethren*.[118]

This development was at first limited to decisions in which the Canadian Supreme Court confirmed legislative decisions: In *Toronto Star* and *CBC*, the court confirmed that certain restrictions for the media to report from judicial proceedings were justified limitations of the freedom of the press.[119] By contrast, the Supreme Court still followed the traditional approach in decisions challenging a piece of legislation. In 2012,

[110] Id. at 604–15.
[111] Id. at 592.
[112] Id. at 613–4.
[113] Id. at 615.
[114] See, for example, the cases cited in note 106.
[115] *Hutterian Brethren* [2009] 2 S.C.R. 567 at 604–07.
[116] See id. at 605–6 (referring to Barak, 'Proportional Effect: The Israeli Experience').
[117] See *Toronto Star Newspaper v. Canada* [2010] 1 S.C.R. 721 at 752–7; *Canadian Broadcasting Corp. v. Canada (Attorney General)* [2011] 1 S.C.R. 19 at 58–61.
[118] *Toronto Star* [2010] 1 S.C.R. 721 at 752; *Canadian Broadcasting Corp.* [2011] 1 S.C.R. 19 at 58.
[119] *Toronto Star* [2010] 1 S.C.R. 721; *Canadian Broadcasting Corp.* [2011] 1 S.C.R. 19.

it invalidated a provision that authorised the police to intercept private communications in *R v. Tse*.[120] The court argued that the measure was not rationally connected to its purpose.[121] It neither engaged in balancing nor cited its decision in *Hutterian Brethren*.

However, the court took the next step in two judgments in 2013 when it predominantly relied on balancing while overturning acts of the legislature. In *Bedford*, it held that prohibiting prostitutes to offer services in brothels violated the guarantee of the security of the person in section 7 of the Canadian Charter, because endangering the safety of prostitutes was a grossly disproportionate means to prevent neighbourhood disruptions.[122] In *United Food and Commercial Workers*, the court invalidated a data protection provision preventing labour unions from posting videos on the Internet of people violating a picket line because it was a disproportionate restriction of the labour union's freedom of expression.[123]

3.4 *Quo Vadis?*

Although this development may, prima facie, look like a 'turning point' in the jurisprudence of the Canadian Supreme Court, a closer look shows that the development is probably less significant than it seems at first sight. The fundamental discussion in *Hutterian Brethren* and the subsequent frequency of balancing decisions referring to *Hutterian Brethren* are certainly indications for a new direction. Furthermore, the Canadian Supreme Court first introduced an extensive balancing analysis in decisions in which it confirmed a piece of legislation. This might remind one of the strategy of the German Constitutional Court, which also first used balancing in cases that posed less of a legitimacy issue.

However, this does not mean that the Canadian Supreme Court will suddenly turn into a balancing court. Even after *Bedford* and *United Food and Commercial Workers*, the Court has relied on the traditional approach in the vast majority of its decisions.[124] In *Whatcott*, for example,

[120] *R v. Tse* [2012] 1 S.C.R. 531.

[121] Id. at 569.

[122] *Canada (Attorney General) v. Bedford* [2013] 3 S.C.R. 1101.

[123] *Alberta (Information and Privacy Commissioner) v. United Food and Commercial Workers, Local 401* [2013] 3 S.C.R. 733 at 746–53.

[124] *Saskatchewan (H.R.C.) v. Whatcott* [2013] 1 S.C.R. 467; *Canada (Attorney General) v. Whaling* [2014] S.C.R. 392 at 428–29; *Mounted Police Association of Ontario v. Canada* [2015] S.C.R. 3 at 76–78; *Carter v. Canada (Attorney General)* [2015] 1 S.C.R. 331 at 381–88; *Canada (Attorney General) v. Federation of Law Societies of Canada* [2015] 1 S.C.R.

the Supreme Court partly invalidated a statute prohibiting hate speech.[125] Although the court acknowledged that the protection of societal groups against marginalisation and systematic discrimination was an important objective, it argued that the statute was too broad. It not only prohibited the exposure of a group to hatred, but also the "ridicul[ing], belitt[ling] or otherwise affront[ing] the dignity" of any person or class of persons. The court thought that these offences were not strong enough to expose a group to hatred, so that it held that they were not rationally connected to the purpose of the statute and thus had to be struck out.[126] Although the argument contains implicit balancing, it is framed as a rational-connection argument.

In *Whaling*, the court held that the retroactive severance of a parole scheme for young offenders violated the Canadian Charter.[127] The court did not take issue with the severance of the parole scheme in general, but argued that a prospective severance would have been sufficient to attain the legislature's goal.[128] Finally, in *Mounted Police Association of Ontario*, the court found that prohibiting police forces from organising in labour unions and from participating in collective bargaining violated the freedom of association.[129] The court acknowledged that the objective of the regulation to "enhance public confidence in the neutrality, stability and reliability of the RCMP" was pressing and substantial.[130] However, it argued that there was no rational connection between measure and purpose as the government had failed to offer persuasive evidence that allowing the police force to participate in the collective bargaining process would disrupt its stability.[131]

It is, however, noticeable that the Canadian Supreme Court sometimes uses the balancing test in the first step of its fundamental rights jurisprudence to determine whether the fundamental right has been infringed. This occurs, in particular, in relation to right to life, liberty and security of the person in section 7 and the prohibition of cruel and unusual

401 at 429, 443–7; *R. v. Nur* [2015] 1 S.C.R. 773 at 827; *Saskatchewan Federation of Labour v. Saskatchewan* [2015] 1 S.C.R. 245 at 291–8; *R. v. Smith* [2015] 2 S.C.R. 602 at 616–17; *R. v. Appulonappa* [2015] 3 S.C.R. 754 at 789–90.

125 *Saskatchewan (H.R.C.) v. Whatcott* [2013] 1 S.C.R. 467.

126 Id. at 511–14.

127 *Canada (Attorney General) v. Whaling* [2014] S.C.R. 392.

128 Id. at 428–9.

129 *Mounted Police Association of Ontario v. Canada* [2015] S.C.R. 3.

130 Id. at 74–5.

131 Id. at 76–7.

punishment in section 12 of the Charter. Nevertheless, in the limitations analysis, the court then resorts to rational-connection or less-restrictive-means arguments. In *Nur*, for example, the court found that minimum sentences of three and five years for the mere unlawful possession of a weapon constituted a cruel and unusual punishment because they were "grossly disproportionate" for certain conduct covered by the provision.[132] But in the limitation analysis, the court resorted to the minimal impairment test, arguing that a more narrowly tailored provision would have been a less restrictive means.[133]

It is thus unlikely that balancing will replace the previous approach of the Canadian Supreme Court to rely heavily on the rational-connection and the less-restrictive-means test. It remains to be seen whether balancing will play a more prominent role in cases in which the Canadian Supreme Court challenges the constitutional validity of a piece of legislation, as it did in *Bedford* and *United Food and Commercial Workers*. Nevertheless, talk of a "turning point" in the Canadian proportionality jurisprudence seems to be overblown. In the foreseeable future, balancing will not replace the minimal impairment test as the most important instrument of the Canadian fundamental-rights jurisprudence.

4. The Reluctance to Rely on Balancing in South Africa

The South African Constitutional Court developed the proportionality test in an early landmark judgment.[134] In *Makwanyane*, the court held that capital punishment violated the South African constitution.[135] The balancing of competing interests played a significant role in this decision. In its subsequent case law, however, the court was rather reluctant to use balancing when confronting the legislature. Instead, as its German counterpart, the South African Constitutional Court used balancing quite frequently in other cases, in which it did not overturn legislation. The reason for the reluctance of the South African Constitutional Court probably lies in its precarious institutional position: because the South African political system is dominated by the African National Congress (ANC), the court does not have much room to constrain political decision-making.

[132] *R. v. Nur* [2015] 1 S.C.R. 773 at 815, 823.

[133] Id. at 827.

[134] The argument in this section is partly based on an earlier publication; see Niels Petersen, 'Proportionality and the Incommensurability Challenge in the Jurisprudence of the South African Constitutional Court' (2014) 30 *South African Journal on Human Rights* 405–29.

[135] *S v. Makwanyane* 1995 (3) SA 391 (CC).

4.1 The Makwanyane Judgment as Origin of Proportionality

The decision of the South African Constitutional Court in Makwanyane was not only one of the first decisions of the newly established court – it was an early landmark judgment that significantly shaped the subsequent fundamental rights doctrine of the Court.[136] The Court held that the death penalty violated the South African Constitution.[137] In his reasoning, the president of the constitutional court, Arthur Chaskalson, developed the proportionality test as the central instrument of fundamental rights review. In a famous passage, he argued as follows:

> The limitation of constitutional rights for a purpose that is reasonable and necessary in a democratic society involves the weighing up of competing values, and ultimately an assessment based on proportionality. [. . .] Principles can be established, but the application of those principles to particular circumstances can only be done on a case-by-case basis. This is inherent in the requirement of proportionality, which calls for the balancing of different interests. In the balancing process, the relevant considerations will include the nature of the right that is limited, and its importance to an open and democratic society based on freedom and equality; the purpose for which the right is limited and the importance of that purpose to such a society; the extent of the limitation, its efficacy, and particularly where the limitation has to be necessary, whether the desired ends could reasonably be achieved through other means less damaging to the right in question.[138]

In the subsequent reasoning, the president of the court relied on a combination of less-restrictive-means, consistency, and balancing considerations. Chaskalson analysed two principal justifications of the death penalty – deterrence and retribution. Regarding deterrence, he examined whether a long prison term was a less restrictive punishment than the death penalty, albeit equally deterrent.[139] That imprisonment was a less severe means than capital punishment seemed obvious. The crucial question, however, was whether it had the same deterrent effect. Chaskalson imposed a burden of proof on the state and held that the state had not made a plausible case for the greater deterring effect of the death

[136] See Hoyt Webb, 'The Constitutional Court of South Africa: Rights Interpretation and Comparative Constitutional Law' (1998) 1 *University of Pennsylvania Journal of Constitutional Law* 205–83 at 228 (comparing Makwanyane with *Marbury v. Madison*)

[137] *S v. Makwanyane* 1995 (3) SA 391 (CC).

[138] Id. at para 104 (per Chaskalson CJ).

[139] Id. at paras. 116–24.

penalty.[140] He argued that the likelihood of being apprehended, convicted and punished had a much stronger deterring effect than the severity of the punishment.[141] Therefore, the state would have had to come up with convincing empirical arguments to justify the death penalty.

With respect to retribution, the president relied on balancing, but combined the balancing exercise with a consistency argument.[142] He argued that retribution "carries less weight than deterrence"[143] and went on to state:

> We have long outgrown the literal application of the biblical injunction of 'an eye for an eye, and a tooth for a tooth'. Punishment must to some extent be commensurate with the offence, but there is no requirement that it be equivalent or identical to it. The state does not put out the eyes of a person who has blinded another in a vicious assault, nor does it punish a rapist, by castrating him and submitting him to the utmost humiliation in gaol."[144]

By pointing out that punishment is not usually identical to the committed offence, the president highlighted that capital punishment was not the only coherent means of retribution when it comes to punishing murder. But he went one step further by stressing that giving undue weight to the principle of retribution would be inconsistent with the principle of reconciliation, which played an important role in the transition from the old apartheid system to a new constitutional democracy.[145] Reconciliation was exactly the opposite of trying to seek exact retribution for every wrong committed. For this reason, President Chaskalson came to the conclusion that "[r]etribution cannot be accorded the same weight under our Constitution as the rights to life and dignity" and that the death sentence for murder could, therefore, not be justified under the constitution.[146]

Both arguments are not free of subjective assessments. If there is uncertainty whether long prison sentences are as powerful a deterrent as capital punishment, the Court makes a risk assessment. It deemed the danger of rising crime after the abolishment of the death penalty less important than the risk of wrongly imposing the death penalty on a convicted person. The

140 Id. at para. 127. See also Patrick Lenta, 'Deterrence and capital punishment' (2007) 22 *SA Public Law* 385–404 at 389–92 (making a review of the empirical literature on this issue and arguing that the evidence in favour of capital punishment is inconclusive).

141 *S v. Makwanyane* 1995 (3) SA 391 (CC) at para. 122.

142 Id. at paras. 129–31.

143 Id. at para. 129.

144 Id.

145 Id. at para. 130.

146 Id. at para. 146.

consistency argument compared a value decision that was due to a specific situation of transitional justice with the situation of routine criminality. Even if this argument has certain persuasiveness, it is not free of a subjective assessment. The reasoning in *Makwanyane* thus shows two things. Unlike the German Constitutional Court and the Canadian Supreme Court, the South African Constitutional Court already relied on balancing in the first months of its existence. However, it tried to rationalise balancing by combining it with less-restrictive-means and consistency considerations and by imposing a burden of proof on the legislature.

4.2 Balancing and Legislative Review

Although the South African Constitutional Court relied on balancing very early in its case law, it predominantly refrained from continuing to do so in its subsequent jurisprudence. There have been only three other decisions in which the South African Constitutional Court overturned a statute and based its decision on balancing.[147] All three concern statutes in criminal law or criminal procedure matters. The case *Ex parte Minister of Safety and Security* is exemplary. It concerned a provision of the Criminal Procedure Act, which allowed persons to kill suspects if they could not arrest them or otherwise prevent them from fleeing.[148] Justice Kriegler held for the unanimous court that the provision violated the right to life.[149] In his justification analysis, the Justice pointed out that there may be circumstances in which it might be justified to kill a fleeing suspect, in particular when the fugitive poses a threat to the people on the scene or to the public at large.[150] However, the challenged provision allowed the use of lethal force even in cases of relatively petty offences, like pickpocketing.[151] Therefore, the court held that there was a "manifest disproportion between the rights infringed and the interests sought to be advanced."[152]

However, the style of argumentation in *Ex parte Minister of Safety and Security* remained the exception. In the vast majority of cases, the court relied on rational-connection, less-restrictive-means or overbreadth

[147] *S v. Niemand* 2002 (1) SA 21 (CC) at para. 19; *Ex parte Minister of Safety and Security: In Re S v. Walters* 2002 (4) SA 613 (CC) at paras. 41–6; *De Vos N.O. v. Minister of Justice and Constitutional Development* 2015 (2) SACR 217 (CC) at paras. 40–8 and 53–8.

[148] *Ex parte Minister of Safety and Security* 2002 (4) SA 613 (CC).

[149] Id. at para. 30.

[150] Id. at para. 39.

[151] Id. at para. 41.

[152] Id. at para. 46.

considerations.[153] One famous example is the court's reasoning in *Manamela*. In its judgment, the court had to decide about the constitutionality of a reverse onus clause in a provision of the penal code that dealt with the acquisition of stolen goods.[154] If somebody was found to be in possession of stolen goods, it was presumed that he believed at the time of acquisition that the person from whom he acquired the goods had no right to dispose of them. The accused thus had to prove the lack of *mens rea* in order to escape conviction. The court held that the provision infringed upon the presumption of innocence enshrined in section 35 (3)(h) of the Constitution.[155]

The state had argued that the reverse onus clause was a necessary measure to eradicate the market of stolen property, because only the accused had the relevant information about his or her internal beliefs. The court held that a reverse onus clause might be reasonable in cases in which purchasers usually keep a record of documents, with which they can prove the purchase.[156] However, in practice, the provision often concerned people who were poor, unskilled and illiterate, so that they were not likely to keep records of the informal transactions they performed every day and thus had difficulties proving their innocence.[157] The court argued that imposing an evidential burden on the accused would be a less restrictive means.[158] This evidential burden would force the accused to make plausible why he or she reasonably believed that the acquired goods were not stolen without requiring a formal proof. It would thus be less burdensome for the accused and still supply the prosecution with the necessary information about the accused's inner state of mind.

4.3 Balancing and the Review of Common Law

That the court mostly refrains from balancing when challenging the legislature does not mean that the court does not balance at all. In fact, it relies on balancing quite often, but the practice is similar to the one of the German Constitutional Court in its early case law.[159] The South African Constitutional Court uses balancing either to confirm the constitutionality

[153] See earlier Table 4.3.
[154] *S v. Manamela* 2000 (3) SA 1 (CC).
[155] *S v. Manamela* 2000 (3) SA 1 (CC) at para. 26.
[156] Id. at para. 43.
[157] Id. at para. 44.
[158] Id. at para. 49.
[159] See section 2.4.

of a statute,[160] or when invalidating common-law norms that deal with the relationship of private individuals[161] or principles of customary law.[162] If the court wants to confirm a piece of legislation, balancing is a necessary doctrinal step, so that this observation should not surprise us. Furthermore, the court does not challenge the legislature, so that the use of balancing does not undermine its own institutional position.

However, the constitutional review of common-law principles does not pose the same legitimacy challenge as the review of legislation. The constitutional court only reviews a body of law that has been developed by other courts. When overturning a common-law principle as unconstitutional, it, therefore, does not interfere with the political sphere. To be sure, it has to engage in a comparison of incommensurable values. But we have seen that this is a necessary element of our daily lives and of judicial decision-making in such cases.[163] Therefore, the court uses balancing in order to strike "a fair balance" between the private parties involved when it comes to the review of common- law principles.

This is particularly obvious in Justice O'Regan's judgment for a unanimous court in the *Khumalo* case.[164] In the judgment, the court had to deal with the conflict between the freedom of the press and human dignity in defamation cases when a newspaper published potentially defamatory facts without being able to prove them. The Justice found that imposing a full burden of proof on either side would be a zero-sum result, and that

> [s]uch a zero-sum result, whomsoever's favour, fits uneasily with the need to establish an appropriate constitutional balance between freedom of expression and human dignity."[165]

[160] See *Bernstein v. Bester NO* 1996 (2) SA 751 (CC) at paras. 54–5; *Beinash v. Ernst & Young* 1999 (2) SA 91 (CC) at paras. 17–21; *S v. Dlamini* 1999 (4) SA 623 (CC) at paras. 54–7; *Christian Education South Africa v. Minister of Education* 2000 (4) SA 757 (CC) at paras. 36–51; *De Reuck v. Director of Public Prosecutions (Witwatersrand Local Division)* 2004 (1) SA 406 (CC) at paras. 59–91; *Mohunram v. National Director of Public Prosecutions (Law Review Project as Amicus Curiae)* 2007 (4) SA 222 (CC) at paras. 76–102; *Road Accident Fund and Another v. Mdeyide* 2011 (2) SA 26 (CC) at paras. 65–94; *South African Transport and Allied Workers Union v. Garvas* [2012] ZACC 13 (CC) at paras. 61–84.

[161] See *Khumalo v. Holomisa* 2002 (5) SA 401 (CC) at paras. 41–4; *Twee Jonge Gezellen (Pty) Ltd v. Land and Agricultural Development Bank of South Africa t/a The Land Bank* 2011 (3) SA 1 (CC) at paras. 56–65.

[162] *Bhe v. Khayelitsha Magistrate* 2005 (1) SA 580 (CC) at paras. 96–7.

[163] See ch. 2, section 1.4.

[164] *Khumalo v. Holomisa* 2002 (5) SA 401 (CC).

[165] Id. at para. 42.

Instead, she required the publisher only to show that the publication was reasonable under all circumstances in order not to be held liable for defamation.[166] She went on to say that

> [t]he defence of reasonable publication avoids therefore a winner-takes-all result and establishes a proper balance between freedom of expression and the value of human dignity.[167]

This example shows that using balancing when reviewing customary or common law norms does not endanger, but rather strengthens, the legitimacy of the court because it allows the latter to strike compromises and to express respect for the position of each of the parties.[168]

4.4 The Precarious Institutional Position of the South African Constitutional Court

Even though the South African case law does not show any historical trends, the observation follows the same pattern as in Germany and Canada. We hypothesised that courts with a strong institutional position would be more likely to use balancing when confronting the legislature.[169] The institutional position of the South African Constitutional Court is rather weak. Constitutional courts usually draw their institutional strength from public acceptance. If a court enjoys a high level of legitimacy, it can make decisions that are costly for government and the legislative majority. The latter have to fear losing public approval if they try to impose sanctions on a popular court. However, in a system dominated by one political party – as in the case in South Africa with the African National Congress (ANC) – public acceptance does not work in favour of the Constitutional Court. The ANC does not have a serious political rival. Therefore, it does not have to fear public backlash if it tries to limit the competencies of the constitutional court.[170] For this reason, the South African Constitutional Court is dependent on the cooperation of the political branches to a greater extent than the Canadian Supreme Court or the German Federal Constitutional Court. Consequently, the court has to strike a difficult balance between individual rights protection and securing its own institutional position.[171]

[166] Id. at para. 43.
[167] Id.
[168] On this function of balancing, see Stone Sweet and Mathews, 'Proportionality Balancing', 90; Sadurski, 'Reasonableness', p. 140.
[169] See ch. 3, section 1.2.
[170] Roux, 'Principle and Pragmatism', 111.
[171] Klug, 'Introducing the Devil', 189.

That the court used balancing so prominently in its landmark decision in *Makwanyane* is no outlier in this respect, but rather the exception that proves the rule. In the drafting process of the new constitution after the transition from the apartheid era, there had been fierce debate between the elites of the ANC and its political support base.[172] The elite favoured the abolition of the death penalty because it had disproportionately been used against black offenders in the apartheid era.[173] In contrast, the political base supported the death penalty because of South Africa's high crime rate.[174] The question had been left open in the interim constitution and was delegated to the constitutional court. When the court thus declared that the death penalty violated the South African Constitution, it did not challenge, but instead support the dominant political elites.[175] The latter achieved the desired result, the abolishing of the death penalty, without having to bear the political responsibility in relation to the general population.

5. Conclusion

If courts introduce proportionality as the central instrument of individual rights review, they make a deliberate choice. Consequently, the exact design and application of the proportionality test may differ significantly from country to country. This difference is particularly obvious if the steps of the proportionality test differ. The South African Constitutional Court modified the proportionality test that it imported from Germany and Canada by relying only on the last step. However, the preceding analysis has shown that such a focus on the merely formal structure of the test may be misleading. Although the South African version of the proportionality test in theory only consists of the balancing stage, the court mostly abstains from balancing in practice.

But even if the prongs of the test are the same, there may be differences in their application and in the emphasis that courts put on the different steps. Whereas the German Constitutional Court mainly focuses on the balancing step in its recent jurisprudence, the Canadian Supreme

172 Theunis Roux, *The Politics of Principle. The First South African Constitutional Court, 1995–2005* (Cambridge: Cambridge University Press, 2013), pp. 238–40.

173 Richard Spitz and Matthew Chaskalson, *The Politics of Transition: A Hidden History of South Africa's Negotiated Settlement* (Oxford: Hart, 2000), p. 331. See also Roux, *Politics of Principle*, p. 239 on Nelson Mandela's strong opposition to the death penalty.

174 Roux, 'Principle and Pragmatism', 118. See also Webb, 'Constitutional Court', 233.

175 Roux, 'Principle and Pragmatism', 120.

Court and the South African Constitutional Court rather rely on rational-connection or less-restrictive-means considerations. But we do not only find differences across courts. Instead, the application of proportionality changes over time. The German Constitutional Court's reliance on balancing started in the late 1970s.[176] Before, the court had put the emphasis on less-restrictive-means considerations.[177] Similarly, we can observe that the Canadian Supreme Court has cautiously extended its use of balancing in recent years.[178] Only the South African Constitutional Court has largely abstained from balancing.[179]

These observations confirm the theoretical hypotheses that were developed in the previous chapter.[180] The principal argument was that the use of balancing when overturning legislation was related to the institutional strength of the court relying on balancing and the familiarity with the doctrinal argumentation framework. The stronger a court, the more likely it is to use balancing. Institutional strength and familiarity provide an explanation for the historical developments that we observe.

This is particularly striking in the German example. When the German Constitutional Court developed the proportionality test in the 1950s, its position was still contested by significant political actors. For this reason, it refrained from balancing when overturning legislation. When it finally increased its use of balancing in the late 1970s, its institutional position was much more stable. Furthermore, balancing had by then become a commonly accepted doctrinal argumentation framework.

The reluctance of the South African Constitutional Court to use balancing is not surprising either. Because the South African political system is dominated by the ANC, the institutional position of the court is highly dependent on the latter. It thus has to strike a precarious balance between providing effective individual rights protection against the most serious violations and not imposing too onerous costs on the executive. It is thus telling that the court relied most extensively on balancing in its famous *Makwanyane* decision, in which it supported the position of the prevailing political elites when it invalidated the death penalty.

The situation is slightly different in Canada. The reluctance to use balancing in the early jurisprudence is probably due to the influence of

176 See ch. 4, section 1.
177 See ch. 4, section 2.2.
178 See ch. 4, section 3.3.
179 See ch. 4, section 4.2.
180 See ch. 3, section 1.2.

the legal realism and the critical legal studies movements that was much stronger in North America than in continental Europe.[181] Because the balancing stage is the step that is most susceptible to realist critique, the Canadian Supreme Court was reluctant to use it in its early jurisprudence. The slight increase in the use of balancing in the late 2000s may be due to a growing familiarity of Canadian legal scholars with the proportionality test.[182] Furthermore, the Canadian Supreme Court referred to Aharon Barak in *Hutterian Brethren* not without reason. By pointing to the experience of other constitutional or supreme courts, such as the Israeli Supreme Court, with the use of the balancing stage, it could underline the doctrinal nature of the balancing test.

The differences highlighted in this chapter are primarily formal. The classification underlying our database relied to a large extent on the labels that the individual courts gave their own arguments. This approach has advantages. It tells us something about how courts perceive the legitimacy of their own arguments. But it also has one fundamental weakness: It might be that the courts are not doing what they say they do. For example, the Canadian Supreme Court is sometimes accused that its less-restrictive-means test is indeed a form of balancing in disguise.[183] For this reason, the two following chapters will analyse in more detail the argumentation within the different steps of the proportionality analysis. The next chapter deals with balancing-avoidance strategies and examines the extent to which non-balancing arguments do sometimes contain balancing elements. Chapter 6 looks at balancing in more detail and tries to identify strategies that courts use in order "rationalise" balancing.

181 See Kristoffel Grechenig and Martin Gelter, 'The Transatlantic Divergence in Legal Thought: American Law and Economics vs. German Doctrinalism' (2008) 31 *Hastings International and Comparative Law Review* 295–360.

182 The use of balancing in *Hutterian Brethren* received predominantly positive reviews in legal academia, see earlier note 108.

183 Vicki C. Jackson, 'Ambivalent Resistance and Comparative Constitutionalism: Opening up the Conversation on "Proportionality," Rights and Federalism' (1999) 1 *University of Pennsylvania Journal of Constitutional Law* 583–639 at 608; Grimm, 'Proportionality', 395.

5

The Avoidance of Balancing

In the previous chapter, we saw that courts often try to avoid balancing as far as possible. The South African Constitutional Court and the Canadian Supreme Court only rely on balancing in exceptional cases; and the German Constitutional Court waited for almost thirty years before balancing developed into the predominant argumentation framework that it is today. However, on which arguments do courts rely instead? This is the principal question that will be examined in this chapter. We will analyse the arguments that courts use as an alternative to balancing. We have already seen that the other steps of the proportionality test can also entail problematic normative valuations.[1] Non-proportionality arguments can contain implicit balancing as well. Therefore, I will analyse how these arguments work and whether they are really balancing alternatives or whether courts only hide implicit balancing behind other terms.

The following analysis will begin with the different prongs of the proportionality test: the legitimate-aim (section 1), the rational-connection, and the less-restrictive-means requirements (section 2). Then it will continue with arguments that are often used either as complements to proportionality or as auxiliary considerations within the proportionality test. These are, in particular, consistency arguments (section 3) or procedural considerations (section 4), which we find in all three jurisdictions. Furthermore, the German Constitutional Court and the Canadian Supreme Court sometimes also impose determinacy requirements on the legislature (section 5) or try to protect legitimate expectations (section 6). Finally, we will take a look at two forms of argumentation that are distinct alternatives to proportionality reasoning and that are occasionally used by the German Constitutional Court: categorical arguments and deductive reasoning (section 7). Section 8 concludes. I will argue that these alternative means of argumentation predominantly aim at controlling legislative rationality. The most problematic modes of reasoning are those that are not related to proportionality, that is, categorical forms of argumentation and deductive reasoning.

[1] See ch. 2, section 1.4.

1. Lack of a Legitimate Aim

Courts are usually reluctant to find that the legislature pursued an illegitimate aim with a measure restricting fundamental rights. Denying the legitimacy of the purpose requires courts to second-guess legislative policy goals. Nevertheless, there are a few examples in which courts held that a fundamental rights restriction did not even pursue a legitimate aim. Most of these examples stem from the jurisprudence of the South African Constitutional Court.[2] But we also find decisions denying the legitimacy of the aim of the fundamental rights restriction in the case law of the German Constitutional Court[3] and the Canadian Supreme Court.[4]

[2] See *National Coalition for Gay and Lesbian Equality v. Minister of Justice* 1999 (1) SA 6 (CC) at para. 37 (criminal liability for sodomy); *Dawood v. Minister of Home Affairs* 2000 (3) SA 936 (CC) at para. 56 (lack of factors guiding the discretion of administrative decisions concerning residence permits of spouses of South African nationals); *Minister of Home Affairs v. National Institute for Crime Prevention and the Re-Integration of Offenders (NICRO)* 2005 (3) SA 280 (CC) at paras. 65–6 (prohibition to vote for prisoners); *Bhe v. Khayelitsha Magistrate* 2005 (1) SA 580 (CC) at paras. 72–3 (specific legal provisions for the succession of black citizens that were enacted during the Apartheid era); *Minister of Home Affairs v. Fourie* 2006 (1) SA 524 (CC) at paras. 110–3 (marriage prohibition for homosexual couples); *Richter v. the Minister of Home Affairs* 2009 (3) SA 615 (CC) at para. 76 (impossibility for a certain group of South African citizens living temporarily abroad to cast their vote during national elections outside the South African territory); *Centre for Child Law v. Minister for Justice and Constitutional Development* 2009 (6) SA 632 (CC) at paras. 52, 57, 60 (introduction of a minimum prison sentence for delinquents of less than eighteen years of age for specific offences).

[3] See Entscheidungen des Bundesverfassungsgerichts [BVerfGE] vol. 19, p. 206 at 216 (state law extending the duty to pay church taxes to certain corporations); vol. 19, p. 226 at 237–9 (state law extending the duty to pay church taxes to spouses of church members even if the spouses themselves did not belong to the church); vol. 19, p. 242 at 247 (state law that requires taking the spouses' income into account for the application of the tax rate, even if the spouse was not a church member); vol. 20, p. 150 at 157, 159 (provision according to which the collection of donations was subject to administrative authorisation); vol. 36, p. 146 at 163 (marriage prohibition for a couple if one of the partners had previously lived in a sexual relationship with a parent of the other partner, even though the partners were not related to each other); vol. 38, p. 61 at 100–1 (tax exemption for a specific category of transportation from a general tax for the transport of goods without any further justification); vol. 61, p. 358 at 375–82 (impossibility to establish joint parental custody of a child after divorce, even if both parents desired such joint custody); vol. 71, p. 138 at 198–200 (prohibition to indicate more than one treatment method for a sanatorium headed by a medical doctor); vol. 84, p. 168 at 181 (prohibition to establish joint custody for children born out of wedlock); vol. 95, p. 193 at 212–3 (automatic classification of former GDR professors as teaching assistants after the German reunification, even if qualification as professor was certified). For an empirical analysis of the structure of the analysis of the legitimate aim by the German Constitutional Court, see Christoph Engel, 'Das legitime Ziel in der Praxis des Bundesverfassungsgerichts: Eine quantitative Analyse der Entscheidungen des Jahres 2011', in Matthias Jestaedt and Oliver Lepsius (eds.), *Verhältnismäßigkeit: Zur Tragfähigkeit eines verfassungsrechtlichen Schlüsselkonzepts* (Tübingen: Mohr Siebeck, 2015), pp. 97–128.

[4] See *R. v. Big Drug Mart Ltd.* [1985] 1 S.C.R. 295 at 351 (compelling someone to observe a religious duty); *Vriend v. Alberta* [1998] 1 S.C.R. 493 at 554–7 (omission of sexual orientation as a

In order to justify the illegitimacy of the aim, the courts resort to different argumentation strategies. In some cases, they declare an aim to be illegitimate if it runs directly counter to an explicit constitutional objective. An example is the decision of the South African Constitutional Court in *Bhe v. Khayelitsha Magistrate*, in which it held a provision of the Black Administration Act of 1927 to be inconsistent with the constitution.[5] The Black Administration Act only dealt with the legal succession of black citizens, whereas the legal succession of whites was subject to a separate statute. The provision that was the subject of the constitutional court's decision referred to customary law for the regulation of legal succession. According to customary rules, only male descendants could succeed into the inheritance of a deceased person. The court argued that the statute had been part of a racist ideology based on separation and submission.[6] For this reason, the statute already lacked a legitimate aim because it ran counter to the fundamental principles of the new constitutional order.[7]

Sometimes, courts qualify the aim of a fundamental rights restriction as illegitimate if it is obviously based on false stereotypes or specific considerations of morality.[8] In a judgment from November 1973, the German Constitutional Court overturned a provision according to which a couple was unable to get married if one of the partners had previously been in a sexual relationship with one of the parents or grandparents of the other partner.[9] In the specific case, the applicant had been barred from getting married to a man who had previously had a sexual relationship with her mother and who had two children from this relationship. The constitutional court held that there were no rational reasons for such a prohibition.[10] It was rather based on specific considerations of morality that could not be the basis for a fundamental rights restriction in a secular

reason for discrimination in Alberta's Individual Rights Protection Act); *R. v. Ruzic* [2001] S.C.R. 687 at 735 (state failed to justify why defence of duress is limited to a specific group of defendants); *Canada (Attorney General) v. Hislop* [2007] 1 S.C.R. 429 at 454–5, 457–8 (time restriction for benefits from a pension scheme for survivors of a homosexual relationship after the death of the partner). See also *Nova Scotia (Workers' Compensation Board) v. Martin* [2003] 2 S.C.R. 504 at 574 (arguing that "[b]udgetary considerations [...] cannot normally be invoked as a free-standing pressing and substantial objective").

5 *Bhe v. Khayelitsha Magistrate* 2005 (1) SA 580 (CC).

6 Id. at para. 72.

7 Id.

8 See also Kumm, 'Socratic Contestation', 159 (arguing that measures reflecting prejudices against specific social groups lack a legitimate aim).

9 BVerfGE 36, 146.

10 BVerfGE 36, 146 Id. at 163.

and pluralistic society. Similarly, the South African Constitutional Court struck down a criminal provision punishing sodomy.[11] The court noted that the government had not come up with a single purpose that was pursued by the statute.[12] Instead, it could be assumed that the provision aimed at the implementation of particularistic considerations of morality.[13]

It is not uncommon for courts to combine the denial of a legitimate purpose with imposing a burden of justification on the legislature. If the latter does not come up with any plausible reason, it is very likely that the specific measure was driven by particularistic interests rather than by concerns of the public good. In *Vriend v. Alberta*, the Canadian Supreme Court had to deal with Alberta's Individual Rights Protection Act (IRPA).[14] This statute allowed employees to take action against their employer if they had been discriminated based on specific grounds of discrimination. However, discrimination based on sexual orientation was not part of the grounds included in the IRPA. The respondent failed to submit reasons for the omission.[15] The court argued that mere "moral" considerations were not sufficient to meet the "pressing and substantial objective" standard required under the Canadian Charter, so that the measure already failed at the first stage of the proportionality test.[16]

The examples discussed in this section show that courts rarely rely on the first stage of the proportionality test. They usually do so either if the purpose directly contradicts an explicit requirement of the constitution or if the legislature has not come up with a plausible reason for a specific measure. The failure to give reasons suggests that the legislature was motivated by "moral" or particular concerns that cannot be sufficient to justify fundamental rights restrictions in pluralistic society.

2. Rational Connection and Less Restrictive Means

The importance of the rational-connection and the less-restrictive-means stages differs across the three analysed jurisdictions.[17] In Canada, the Supreme Court held in more than half of the decisions in which it overturned a piece of legislation that the measure lacked a rational connection

11 *National Coalition for Gay and Lesbian Equality v. Minister of Justice* 1999 (1) SA 6 (CC).
12 Id. at para. 37.
13 Id.
14 *Vriend v. Alberta* [1998] 1 S.C.R. 493.
15 Id. at 557.
16 Id. at 556–7.
17 See ch. 4, Tables 4.1–4.3.

to its purpose or that there was a less restrictive means to achieve the same purpose.[18] The situation is similar in South Africa: Here, rational-connection and less-restrictive-means arguments are the predominant considerations when the constitutional court finds a statute to be inconsistent with the fundamental rights of the constitution.[19] By contrast, these

[18] See *R. v. Oakes* [1986] 1 S.C.R. 103 at 142; *R. v. Vaillancourt* [1987] 2 S.C.R. 636 at 660; *Ford v. Quebec (Attorney General)* [1988] 2 S.C.R. 712 at 779–80; *R. v. Morgentaler* [1988] 1 S.C.R. 30 at 114–21; *Edmonton Journal v. Alberta (Attorney General)* [1989] 2 S.C.R. 1326 at 1346–7; *Andrews v. Law Society of British Columbia* [1989] 1 S.C.R. 143 at 155–7; *Black v. Law Society of Alberta* [1989] 1 S.C.R. 591 at 628–33; *R. v. Hess; R. v. Nguyen* [1990] 2 S.C.R. 906 at 921–6; *R. v. Martineau* [1990] 2 S.C.R. 633 at 647; *R. v. Swain* [1991] 1 S.C.R. 933 at 986, 1018–9; *R. v. Wholesale Travel Group Inc.* [1991] 3 S.C.R. 154 at 193–5; *Tetreault-Gadoury v. Canada (Employment and Immigration Commission)* [1991] 2 S.C.R. 22 at 43–7; *R. v. Genereux* [1992] 1 S.C.R. 259 at 313; *Sauvé v. Canada (Attorney General)* [1993] 2 S.C.R. 438 at 439–40; *R. v. Laba* [1994] 3 S.C.R. 965 at 1008–10; *RJR-MacDonald Inc. v. Canada (Attorney General)* [1995] 3 S.C.R. 199 at 342–9; *Benner v. Canada (Secretary of State)* [1997] 1 S.C.R. 358 at 404–5; *Libman v. Quebec (Attorney General)* [1997] 3 S.C.R. 569 at 617–20; *Thomson Newspapers Co. v. Canada (Attorney General)* [1998] 1 S.C.R. 877 at 963–4; *Corbiere v. Canada (Minister of Indian and Northern Affairs)* [1999] 2 S.C.R. 203 at 277; *M. v. H.* [1999] 2 S.C.R. 3 at 76; *U.F.C.W., Local 1518 v. KMart Canada Ltd.* [1999] 2 S.C.R. 1083 at 1131–3; *Dunmore v. Ontario (Attorney General)* [2001] 3 S.C.R. 1016 at 1068–77; *R. v. Guignard* [2002] 1 S.C.R. 472 at 488; *Sauvé v. Canada (Chief Electoral Officer)* [2002] 3 S.C.R. 519 at 543–53; *Lavallee, Rackel & Heintz v. Canada (Attorney General); White, Ottenheimer & Baker v. Canada (Attorney General); R. v. Fink* [2002] 3 S.C.R. 209 at 241–8; *Figueroa v. Canada (Attorney General)* [2003] 1 S.C.R. 912 at 953, 956–7, 961–3; *Nova Scotia (Workers' Compensation Board) v. Martin; Nova Scotia (Workers' Compensation Board) v. Laseur [2003]* 2 S.C.R. 504 at 575–8; *Trociuk v. British Columbia (Attorney General)* [2003] 1 S.C.R. 835 at 851–2; *Chaoulli v. Quebec (Attorney General)* [2005] 1 S.C.R. 791 at 827–36; *Charkaoui v. Canada (Citizenship and Immigration)* [2007] 1 S.C.R. 350 at 392–400; *R. v. D.B.* [2008] 2 S.C.R. 3 at 40; *Quebec (Education, Recreation and Sports) v. Nguyen* [2009] 3 S.C.R. 208 at 237–8; *Saskatchewan (Human Rights Commission) v. Whatcott* [2013] 1 SCR 467 at 511–4, 519; *Canada (Attorney General) v. Whaling* [2014] S.C.R. 392 at 428–9; *Mounted Police Association of Ontario v. Canada* [2015] S.C.R. 3 at 76–8; *Carter v. Canada (Attorney General)* [2015] 1 S.C.R. 331 at 381–8; *Canada (Attorney General) v. Federation of Law Societies of Canada* [2015] 1 S.C.R. 401 at 429, 443–7; *R. v. Nur* [2015] 1 S.C.R. 773 at 827; *Saskatchewan Federation of Labour v. Saskatchewan* [2015] 1 S.C.R. 245 at 291–8; *R. v. Smith* [2015] 2 S.C.R. 602 at 616–7; *R. v. Appulonappa* [2015] 3 S.C.R. 754 at 789–90. In other cases, the court found the legislation to be overbroad: *R. v. Smith (Edward Dewey)* [1987] 1 S.C.R. 1045 at 1080–1; *Rocket v. Royal College of Dental Surgeons of Ontario* [1990] 2 S.C.R. 232 at 250; *Osborne v. Canada (Treasury Board)* [1991] 2 S.C.R. 69 at 100–1; *R. v. Seaboyer; R. v. Gayme* [1991] 2 S.C.R. 577 at 626; *Committee for the Commonwealth of Canada v. Canada* [1991] 1 S.C.R. 139 at 215–9; *R. v. Zundel* [1992] 2 S.C.R. 731 at 768–74; *R. v. Heywood* [1994] 3 S.C.R. 761 at 790–803; *R. v. Demers* [2004] 2 S.C.R. 489 at 519.

[19] See *S v. Makwanyane* 1995 (3) SA 391 (CC) at para. 127; *Coetzee v. Government of the Republic of South Africa* 1995 (4) SA 631 (CC) at paras. 13, 22; *S v. Williams* 1995 (3) SA 632 (CC) at paras. 64–77; *Ferreira v. Levin NO* 1995 (1) SA 984 (CC) at para. 127; *S v. Bhulwana*

two stages are also significant in the jurisprudence of the German Federal Constitutional Court, but they are used less frequently than balancing.[20]

In both stages, the central question is usually an empirical one.[21] In the rational-connection test, courts have to analyse whether there

1995 (1) SA 388 (CC) at paras. 23–4; *S v. Mbatha* 1996 (2) SA 464 (CC) at paras. 21–6; *South African National Defence Union v. Minister of Defence* 1999 (4) SA 469 (CC) at para. 35; *S v. Manamela* 2000 (3) SA 1 (CC) at para. 49; *Islamic Unity Convention v. Independent Broadcasting Authority* 2002 (4) SA 294 (CC) at para. 50; *Nyathi v. Member of the Executive Council for the Department of Health Gauteng* 2008 (5) SA 94 (CC) at para. 51; *Johncom Media Investments Limited v. M* 2009 (4) SA 7 (CC) at para. 30; *Brümmer v. Minister for Social Development* 2009 (6) SA 323 (CC) at paras. 65–6; *Malachi v. Cape Dance Academy International* 2010 (6) SA 1 (CC) at para. 32; *Law Society of South Africa v. Minister for Transport* 2011 (1) SA 400 (CC) at para. 99; *National Credit Regulator v. Opperman* 2013 (2) SA 1 (CC) at para. 76; *Print Media South Africa v. Minister of Home Affairs* 2012 (6) SA 443 paras. 65–72; *Mail and Guardian Media v. Chipu* 2013 (6) SA 367 (CC) at paras. 59–93; *Teddy Bear Clinic for Abused Children v. Minister of Justice and Constitutional Development* 2014 (2) SA 168 (CC) at paras. 84–94; *J v. National Director of Public Prosecutions* [2014] ZACC 13 at para. 50; *Da Silva v. Road Accident Fund* 2014 (5) SA 573 (CC) at para. 7; *Chevron SA (Pty) Limited v. Wilson t/a Wilson's Transport* [2015] ZACC 15 at para. 33; *Sarrahwitz v. Maritz N.O.* 2015 (4) SA 491 (CC) at paras. 65–7; *De Vos N.O. v. Minister of Justice and Constitutional Development* 2015 (2) SACR 217 (CC) at para. 52. In some cases, the South African Constitutional Court also declares legislation to be overbroad; see *Case v. Minister of Safety and Security* 1996 (3) SA 617 (CC) at paras. 48–61, 93; *Mistry v. Interim National Medical and Dental Council* 1998 (4) SA 1127 (CC) at paras. 29–30; *South African National Defence Union v. Minister of Defence* 1999 (4) SA 469 (CC) at para. 13; *First National Bank of SA Limited t/a Wesbank v. Commissioner for the South African Revenue Services* 2002 (4) SA 768 (CC) at para. 108; *Phillips v. Director of Public Prosecutions* 2003 (3) SA 345 (CC) at para. 28; *Minister of Home Affairs v. National Institute for Crime Prevention and the Re-Integration of Offenders (NICRO)* 2005 (3) SA 280 (CC) at para. 67; *Jaftha v. Schoeman* 2005 (2) SA 140 (CC) at paras. 44, 48; *Magajane v. Chairperson, North West Gambling Board* 2006 (5) SA 250 at paras. 88–94; *Gaertner v. Minister of Finance* 2014 (1) SA 442 (CC) at para. 66. The overbreadth argument is usually considered to be a special case of the less-restrictive-means argument; see Currie and Waal, *Bill of Rights*, p. 184. But see also Vos and Freedman, *South African Constitutional Law*, p. 372 (arguing that less-restrictive-means inquiry and overbreadth are distinct concepts).

[20] See BVerfGE 7, 320 at 325–6; 7, 377 at 419–23, 440–1; 9, 39 at 52–5; 11, 30 at 46–7; 11, 168 at 188; 12, 144 at 148–50; 17, 269 at 277, 279–80; 17, 306 at 316; 19, 330 at 339–40; 21, 261 at 268–70; 21, 271 at 283; 30, 1 at 31–2; 30, 227 at 245–6; 30, 336 at 354–5; 34, 71 at 79–81; 36, 47 at 60, 63; 40, 371 at 383; 41, 378 at 396–7; 50, 265 at 277–8; 53, 135 at 145–6; 54, 301 at 317–22; 55, 159 at 166; 57, 361 at 387–8; 59, 302 at 322–3; 63, 88 at 116–7; 63, 131 at 146; 69, 209 at 218; 74, 297 at 337; 75, 284 at 296–7; 79, 256 at 272; 81, 242 at 263; 90, 263 at 272; 91, 1 at 35–6; 92, 158 at 181–2; 93, 362 at 371; 94, 372 at 392–3; 98, 17 at 42–3; 99, 341 at 354, 101, 54 at 85, 91; 101, 106 at 128; 102, 197 at 217–18; 103, 1 at 13–17; 104, 357 at 365; 106, 181 at 195; 107, 186 at 198–204; 108, 150 at 167–8; 115, 1 at 17; 127, 132 at 155–62; 135, 90 at 118–24.

[21] See Hogg, 'Section 1 Revisited', 18; Anne van Aaken, 'Vom Nutzen der ökonomischen Theorie für das öffentliche Recht: Methode und Anwendungsmöglichkeiten', in Marc Bungenberg et al. (eds.), *Recht und Ökonomik* (München: C. H. Beck, 2004), pp. 1–31 at

is indeed a causal link between measure and purpose, and in the less-restrictive-means test, they have to examine whether a potentially less restrictive alternative means is equally effective in pursuing the same purpose. These empirical analyses pose considerable challenges for judges.[22] In the first part of this section, we will take a closer look at how courts deal with this challenge (section 2.1). The second part will then analyse a critique that is often raised with regard to the less-restrictive-means test: Even though courts argue that an alternative means is less restrictive, they implicitly balance because they neglect certain costs of the alternative means (section 2.2). The final part evaluates the observations made in this chapter: I will argue that, despite certain deficiencies, the rational-connection and the less-restrictive-means test are generally used as instruments for controlling the legislative rationality (section 2.3).

2.1 *The Review of Legislative Prognoses*

Courts have different ways to control legislative prognoses.[23] First, they can afford the legislature a margin of appreciation. However, courts have to determine the limits of this margin of appreciation and to decide when to exercise deference to the legislature and when to impose a burden of proof on the latter. Second, they can substitute the legislative prognosis through their own prognosis. Certainly, the question is always whether courts have the appropriate tools for such a prognosis. Finally, they can turn empirical questions into analytical questions and thus sidestep the issue of how to control legislative prognoses.

2.1a. Deference vs. Burden of Proof

The court that has dealt most extensively with the question of the limits of the legislative margin of appreciation is the Canadian Supreme Court. When the court established the proportionality test in *Oakes*, the matter seemed to be relatively simple:

19; Sujit Choudhry, 'So what is the real legacy of *Oakes?* Two decades of proportionality analysis under the Canadian Charter's Section 1' (2006) 34 *Supreme Court Law Review* 501–35 at 524; Robertson, *Judge as Political Theorist*, p. 80; Moshe Cohen-Eliya and Iddo Porat, 'Proportionality and the Culture of Justification' (2011) 59 *American Journal of Comparative Law* 463–90 at 469–70.

22 See Petersen, 'Common Wisdom Fallacy'.

23 Id. at 306–17.

> The onus of proving that a limit on a right or freedom guaranteed by the Charter is reasonable and demonstrably justified in a free and democratic society rests upon the party seeking to uphold the limitation.[24]

It imposed a burden of proof on the legislature. In cases of doubt, a measure restricting a fundamental right could thus not be justified. However, this approach did not last for long.[25] Only ten months later, in *Edwards Books*, a case concerning a statute that required retail businesses to close on Sundays, the court afforded the legislature a significant margin of appreciation.[26] In its subsequent jurisprudence, the court continuously revisited the question of how to determine the limits of the legislative margin of appreciation. However, it has not found clear criteria for when to impose a burden of proof on the legislature and when to exercise deference.[27] In the most controversial decisions of the court, the dividing line between the majority of the court and the dissenting judges was often the treatment of uncertainty and the lack of sufficient evidence.

In *RJR-MacDonald*, the court held in a 5–4 decision that a ban on tobacco advertising was inconsistent with the constitution.[28] The judges agreed that the advertising ban pursued a legitimate aim.[29] However, they disagreed on whether a partial ban would have been sufficient to achieve the legislative purpose. The majority argued that a partial ban focusing on "lifestyle" advertising would have been a less restrictive means.[30] A ban on advertising of a merely informational character that did not seek to increase the overall tobacco consumption, but only to increase the market share among all tobacco producers would not have been necessary. By contrast, the dissenting judges argued that a partial advertising ban would have been less effective.[31]

[24] *R. v. Oakes* [1986] 1 S.C.R. 103 at 136–7.

[25] Pamela A. Chapman, 'The Politics of Judging: Section 1 of the Charter of Rights and Freedoms' (1986) 24 *Osgoode Hall Law Journal* 867–96 at 891; Andrew Lokan, 'The Rise and Fall of Doctrine under Section 1 of the Charter' (1992) 24 *Ottawa Law Review* 163–92 at 179–81; Choudhry, 'Legacy of *Oakes*', 506–8; Hogg, *Constitutional Law*, p. 149. See also Lorraine Eisenstat Weinrib, 'Canada's Charter of Rights: Paradigm Lost?' (2002) 6 *Review of Constitutional Studies* 119–78 at 157–8; Christopher D. Bredt and Adam M. Dodek, 'The Increasing Irrelevance of Section 1 of the Charter' (2001) 14 *Supreme Court Law Review* 175–88 at 186–8 (arguing that the court weakened its burden of proof requirement over time).

[26] *R. v. Edwards Books and Art Ltd.* [1986] 2 S.C.R. 713.

[27] Choudhry, 'Legacy of *Oakes*', 503.

[28] *RJR-MacDonald* [1995] 3 S.C.R. 199.

[29] Id. at 336 (per McLachlin J.).

[30] Id. at 343–8.

[31] Id. at 304–10 (per La Forest J.).

The decisive question was thus an empirical one:[32] Would a partial advertising ban have been as effective as a total ban? The majority imposed a burden of proof on the legislature.[33] However, the legislature neither offered proof on the necessity of a total advertising ban nor on the insufficient effectiveness of a partial ban.[34] By contrast, the four dissenting judges wanted to grant the legislature a margin of discretion in this matter.[35] The effect of advertising on tobacco consumption was not entirely understood.[36] If the court wanted to impose a burden of proof on the legislature in such a situation, it

> would place an impossible onus on Parliament by requiring it to produce definitive social scientific evidence respecting the root causes of a pressing area of social concern every time it wishes to address its effects.[37]

Furthermore, the dissenting judges made a procedural argument. They pointed out that the ban on tobacco advertising was the result of a drafting and consultation process that had lasted for twenty years.[38] Considering the extensive discussion of the topic in parliament, they argued, "it is not the role of this court to substitute its opinion for that of Parliament concerning the ideal legislative solution to this complex and wide-ranging social problem."[39] The majority countered that the legislature would have had the opportunity to clarify the empirical question of the effectiveness of a partial ban with sufficient certainty. The judges pointed out that legislature had actually performed a study on the question, but refused to disclose it to the court during the procedure.[40]

Similar discussion patterns can also be found in the *Chaoulli* decision, in which the Supreme Court held that a public monopoly for health insurances in Quebec was inconsistent with the Canadian Charter in a 6–3 decision.[41] The statute that was subject to the procedure prohibited private health insurances to offer benefits that were covered by the public scheme. Quebec feared that a parallel system of public and private health

[32] Choudhry, 'Legacy of *Oakes*', 531.
[33] *RJR-MacDonald* [1995] 3 S.C.R. 199 at 345 (per McLachlin J.).
[34] Id.
[35] Id. at 275, 306–7, 314–5 (per LaForest J.).
[36] Id. at 275.
[37] Id.
[38] Id. at 306–7.
[39] Id. at 314–15.
[40] Id. at 345 (per McLachlin J.).
[41] *Chaoulli v. Quebec* [2005] 1 S.C.R. 791.

insurances would lead to financial means, and not medical need, being the main factor for the allocation of medical care.[42]

The main point of discussion was again an empirical question:[43] To what extent would the introduction of private health insurances impair the effectiveness of the public scheme? The majority of the court imposed a burden of proof on the legislature. The judges argued that Quebec had not produced sufficient evidence that the public health insurance scheme required a monopoly to be effective.[44] By contrast, the three dissenting judges argued that the introduction of private health insurances would impair the effectiveness of the public scheme.[45] They relied on expert witnesses stating that a pure public health insurance scheme was the most cost-effective.[46]

Furthermore, the dissenting judges conceded a margin of appreciation to the legislature.[47] They justified this margin of appreciation with a procedural argument. They pointed out that the legislature had made a significant effort to evaluate the existing health insurance scheme. The consulted experts had all recommended continuing the current system with a public-health-insurance monopoly. As the court did not have any reason to doubt the credibility of the experts consulted in the legislative procedure, the legislature had a sufficient empirical basis for its decision.

In both decisions that we have discussed in this section, the majority imposed a burden of proof on the legislature, whereas the dissenting judges wanted to exercise deference. However, there are also a number of decisions in which the majority afforded a margin of appreciation to the legislature.[48] However, the criteria for determining the limits of the margin of appreciation were not always coherent. In *Irwin Toy*, the majority of the court exercised deference because the social science evidence was "somewhat inconclusive".[49] In *Malmo-Levine*, the court argued that parliament deserved deference once it had shown that the danger that was addressed

[42] See id. at 890 (per Binnie and LeBel JJ.).

[43] Christopher P. Manfredi and Antonia Maioni, 'Judicializing Health Policy: Unexpected Lessons and an Inconvenient Truth', in James B. Kelly and Christopher P. Manfredi (eds.), *Contested Constitutionalism – Reflections on the Canadian Charter of Rights and Freedoms* (Vancouver: UBC Press, 2009), pp. 129–44 at 136.

[44] *Chaoulli v. Quebec* [2005] 1 S.C.R. 791 at 828–31 (per Deschamps J.).

[45] Id. at 899 (per Binnie and LeBel JJ.).

[46] Id. at 903.

[47] Id. at 904.

[48] See, for example, *Irwin Toy Ltd v. Quebec (Attorney General)* [1989] 1 S.C.R. 927 at 990; *R. v. Sharpe* [2001] 1 S.C.R. 45 at 98; *R. v. Malmo-Levine, R. v. Cain* [2003] 3 S.C.R. 571 at 641; *Harper v. Canada* [2004] S.C.R. 827 at 888–9.

[49] *Irwin Toy v. Quebec* [1989] 1 S.C.R. 927 at 990. See also *R. v. Sharpe* [2001] 1 S.C.R. 45 at 98.

by the statute was not "insignificant or trivial".[50] Finally, in *Harper*, the judges did not want to second-guess the balance struck by the legislature if the balancing was "genuine and reasonable".[51] Furthermore, the court only relied on the margin of appreciation as an argumentation framework when it confirmed a piece of legislation.[52] When it overturned a statute, the court only referred to the margin of appreciation doctrine to explain why it was not applicable in the present case. However, it did not make the effort to define the limits of the doctrine more precisely.[53]

The situation is not better in other jurisdictions.[54] In Germany, the Federal Constitutional Court argued that the extent of the legislative margin of appreciation depended on different factors, such as the area of legislation, the amount of uncertainty and the importance of the legal values concerned.[55] However, these factors are so vague that they can justify almost any conclusion.[56] Therefore, it is not surprising that the doctrine of the legislative margin of appreciation was not developed consistently in the court's jurisprudence.[57] In some cases, the court relies on a procedural approach to determine the limits of legislative

[50] *R. v. Malmo-Levine* [2003] 3 S.C.R. 571 at 641.

[51] *Harper v. Canada* [2004] S.C.R. 827 at 888–9.

[52] Beatty, 'Canadian Charter', 493.

[53] Hogg, 'Section 1 Revisited', 22; Beatty, 'Canadian Charter', 493; Mendes, 'Crucible of the Charter', 87–96; Thomas M. J. Bateman, 'Legal Modesty and Political Boldness: The Supreme Court of Canada's Decision in Chaoulli v. Quebec' (2006) 11 *Review of Constitutional Studies* 317–43 at 323–4. See also Andrée Lajoie and Henry Quillinan, 'Emerging Constitutional Norms: Continuous Judicial Amendment of the Constitution – The Proportionality Test as a Moving Target' (1992) 55 *Law and Contemporary Problems* 285–302 (proposing a systematisation of the court's approach); Kent Roach, *The Supreme Court on Trial: Judicial Activism or Democratic Dialogue* (Toronto: Irwin Law, 2001), p. 172 (identifying a historical trend). The normative evaluation of the court's jurisprudence differs. Some authors criticise that the court exercises too much deference; see Beatty, 'Canadian Charter'; Weinrib, 'Paradigm Lost?'. Others welcome the development; see Robert E. Charney and S. Zachary Green, 'Prophets of Doom, Seers of Fortune: 20 Years of Experience under the Oakes Test' (2006) 34 *Supreme Court Law Review* 479–99.

[54] See also David Bilchitz, 'How Should Rights Be Limited?' (2011) 2011 *Tydskrif vir die suid-afrikaanse Reg* 568–79 at 573–6 (criticising that the approach of the South African Constitutional Court concerning the examination of empirical fact-finding by the legislature was underdeveloped).

[55] BVerfGE 50, 290 at 332–3.

[56] See Niels Petersen, *Verhältnismäßigkeit als Rationalitätskontrolle: Eine rechtsempirische Studie verfassungsgerichtlicher Rechtsprechung zu den Freiheitsgrundrechten* (Tübingen: Mohr Siebeck, 2015), p. 92; Indra Spiecker gen. Döhmann, *Staatliche Entscheidungen unter Unsicherheit* (Tübingen: Mohr Siebeck, forthcoming), part IV, ch. 3 B I.

[57] Klaus Meßerschmidt, *Gesetzgebungsermessen* (Berlin: Berlin Verlag, 2000), p. 845.

deference.[58] According to this approach, the legislature enjoys a margin of appreciation if it makes an appropriate effort to establish the empirical basis of its decision. In other cases, the court wants to exercise deference to the extent that the legislature has acted consistently.[59]

These observations raise the suspicion that the application of different argumentation frameworks is largely driven by the desired result.[60] However, the observed incoherence might be due to the nature of the challenge.[61] Even though there are several ways of conceptualising the margin of appreciation doctrine, none is without weaknesses.[62] It may thus be analytically impossible to determine the limits of legislative deference in the abstract. However, this does not automatically mean that judicial decisions in this respect are arbitrary. They may rather implicitly be based on the intuition whether the legislative prognosis was – as the Canadian Supreme Court expressed in *Harper* – "genuine and reasonable".[63]

When the judges impose a burden of proof on the legislature, they usually resort to additional arguments to justify the burden of proof. For example, in *RJR MacDonald*, the majority of the court referred to the study on the effectiveness of a partial advertising ban that the legislature had made, but not disclosed to the court. This raised the suspicion that the government had something to hide so that the prognosis was not genuine. The court thus controls whether the legislature had a sufficient understanding of the empirical implications of its legislation and whether the legislation was based on the available empirical evidence.[64]

2.1b. Judicial Prognoses

In some situations, courts control legislative prognoses themselves. In particular, the constitutional courts in Germany and South Africa often rely on such direct control of empirical prognoses. In a 1976 decision, the German Constitutional Court overturned a provision according to which legal representatives of conscientious objectors of military service could not appear in other courts than the one they were registered with.[65] The legislature had argued that this provision was necessary to ensure

[58] See BVerfGE 88, 203 at 263; 125, 175 at 225.
[59] BVerfGE 121, 317 at 362.
[60] See Robertson, *Judge as Political Theorist*, p. 372.
[61] Similarly Lokan, 'Rise and Fall', 192; Hogg, *Constitutional Law*, p. 152.
[62] See Petersen, 'Common Wisdom Fallacy', 311–15.
[63] *Harper v. Canada* [2004] S.C.R. 827 at 888–9.
[64] See Choudhry, 'Worse than Lochner?', p. 86; Choudhry, 'Legacy of *Oakes*', 534.
[65] BVerfGE 41, 378.

effective control of these legal representatives by the judicial administration. However, the court held that the limitation was not necessary, as the court where the legal representative was registered could be informed of any disciplinary infraction that occurred before a different court.[66]

The South African Constitutional Court used direct means to control the factual evaluation of the legislature in the *Manamela* case, in which it had to decide on the constitutionality of a reverse onus clause in a provision of the penal code.[67] If a person was found to be in possession of stolen goods, it was presumed that this person had believed at the time of acquisition that the individual from whom he had acquired the goods had no power of disposal over them. The accused person thus had to prove the lack of *mens rea* in order to escape conviction. The court held that this reversal of the burden of proof infringed upon the presumption of innocence enshrined in section 35 (3)(h) of the constitution.[68]

The state had argued that the reverse onus clause was a necessary measure to eradicate the market of stolen property, as only the accused had relevant information about his internal beliefs. The court held that a reverse onus clause might be reasonable for cases in which purchasers usually keep a record of documents they can use to prove the purchase.[69] However, in practice, the provision often concerned people who were poor, unskilled and illiterate, so that they were not likely to keep records of the informal transactions they performed every day and thus had difficulties proving their innocence.[70] The court argued that imposing an evidential burden on the accused would be a less restrictive means.[71] This evidential burden would force the accused to make plausible, without requiring formal proof, why he reasonably believed that the acquired goods were not stolen. It would thus be less burdensome for the accused and still supply the prosecution with the necessary information about the accused's inner state of mind.

Sometimes, courts use their own factual evaluation of the case to determine the extent of the legislative margin of appreciation. In *Chaoulli*, the Canadian Supreme Court relied on a comparison with health-insurance schemes in other countries to argue that the legislature should have to

[66] BVerfGE 41, 378 at 396–7.
[67] *S v. Manamela* 2000 (3) SA 1 (CC).
[68] Id. at para. 26.
[69] Id. at para. 43.
[70] Id. at para. 44.
[71] Id. at para. 49.

prove the necessity of the public monopoly.[72] The experience of countries in which public and private schemes co-existed showed that a prohibition of private health insurances was not necessary to ensure the effectiveness of the public scheme. The German Constitutional Court also relied on similar cross-country or cross-state comparisons in some of its cases.[73] In the pharmacy judgment, for example, it compared the Bavarian situation to the one in Switzerland in order to demonstrate that Bavaria did not need to fear a breakdown of its pharmacy system if it lifted the access restriction.[74]

In some cases, judicial common sense may be an appropriate instrument to control legislative prognoses. This is particularly the case when the situation is not overly complex, as it was with regard to the practice restrictions for legal representatives of conscientious objectors or the reverse onus clause in *Manamela*. However, judicial prognoses have their limits.[75] In *Chaoulli*, the dissenting judges pointed out that comparisons with the experience of other countries were difficult because they might not fit the specific circumstances of the Canadian health system.[76] We have already seen, in the previous section, that it is difficult to find a conceptual solution to the problem of reviewing legislative prognoses. Therefore, it should not surprise us that courts often try to be pragmatic in this respect. This pragmatic approach seems to be suitable as long as the empirical questions underlying the fundamental rights challenge are not overly complex.

2.1c. Turning Empirical into Analytical Questions

A different kind of pragmatism that is often found in the jurisprudence of the German and the South African Constitutional Courts is the attempt to turn empirical into analytical questions. Consistency arguments are the main instrument for this doctrinal move. They allow courts to show that the legislature has evaluated the same danger differently in other contexts. One example is a decision of the German Constitutional Court on the shipping of vaccines from 2003.[77] The challenged regulation prohibited the sale of preventive vaccines to doctors by mail order. The Constitutional Court relied on a consistency argument to hold that this prohibition was

[72] *Chaoulli v. Quebec* [2005] 1 S.C.R. 791 at 831–6 (per Deschamps J.). On *Chaoulli*, see also ch. 5, section 2.1a.

[73] See BVerfGE 7, 377 at 415–6; 94, 372 at 392; 103, 1 at 17.

[74] BVerfGE 7, 377 at 415–6. On the pharmacy judgment, see also ch. 4, section 2.1.

[75] Petersen, 'Common Wisdom Fallacy', 307–9.

[76] *Chaoulli v. Quebec* [2005] 1 S.C.R. 791 at 893 (per Binnie and LeBel JJ.)

[77] BVerfGE 107, 186.

not necessary to achieve the aim of the regulation. It pointed out that the selling of protective vaccines by mail order was allowed while the shipping of preventive vaccines was prohibited, even though there was no plausible reason for this distinction.[78]

The South African Constitutional Court also often relies on analytical arguments when it has to deal with empirical questions.[79] One example is the court's judgment in *Malachi*.[80] In its decision, the court overturned a provision according to which a magistrate could order the detention of a debtor in circumstances where a creditor reasonably believed that the debtor was about to flee the country in order to avoid paying her debts.[81] The court argued that the measure was not rationally connected to its purpose and based this argument on a consistency consideration.[82] Debtors could only be arrested before the judgment in the matter was given. However, after the judgment, they could not be detained anymore. The provision thus did not ensure that a debtor indeed remained in the country until the payment of the debt.[83]

2.2 *Implicit Balancing*

Given the difficulties courts face when evaluating empirical questions, it is not surprising that they are often criticised for balancing implicitly in the context of the less-restrictive-means test.[84] We can observe this practice of implicit balancing in the jurisprudence of all three analysed courts. Implicit balancing usually occurs when courts control an empirical prognosis of the legislature. One example is a decision of the German Constitutional Court from March 1960, in which the court had to deal with an access restriction for doctors who wanted to register for the treatment of publicly insured patients.[85] According to the provision, only one doctor per 500 participants in the public-health-insurance scheme could be registered in each region. At the time of the decision, 80 percent of the population was

[78] Id. at 198.
[79] Petersen, 'Incommensurability Challenge', 420.
[80] *Malachi v. Cape Dance Academy International* 2010 (6) SA 1 (CC) at para. 32.
[81] See id. at para. 2.
[82] Id. at para. 32.
[83] Id.
[84] See Joseph H.H. Weiler, 'Epilogue: Towards a Common Law of International Trade', in Joseph H.H. Weiler (ed.), *The EU, the WTO, and the NAFTA. Towards a Common Law of International Trade?* (Oxford: Oxford University Press, 2000), pp. 201–32 at 222; Grimm, 'Proportionality', 394; Stone Sweet and Mathews, 'Proportionality Balancing', 164.
[85] BVerfGE 11, 30.

insured under the public-health-insurance scheme. Registration was thus of central economic importance, as it was a prerequisite to treat patients insured in the public scheme.

The government had argued that the access restriction should avoid an oversupply of medical services that could have endangered the existence of the public-health insurances.[86] After an analysis of the empirical evidence, the court concluded that the public-health insurances would not be strained excessively if the access restriction were lifted.[87] Therefore, it held that the access restriction was not necessary to achieve the legislative aim.[88] This argumentation pattern was not singular. Instead, we can also find it in several other decisions of the court dealing with market access restrictions.[89]

However, the argument of the court rests on the assumption that the decision was taken under certainty. If we are certain that liberalisation does not harm the system, the access restrictions are indeed not necessary. However, as soon as we add uncertainty to the equation, the less-restrictive-means argument turns into implicit balancing. Even if there are only slight doubts that liberalisation does not cause any harm to the system, the question becomes a question of societal risk preferences.[90] The court thus implicitly balanced the costs of the market access restrictions for doctors against the utility to avoid even minor residual risks for the public-health-insurance scheme.

But implicit balancing is not necessarily related to empirical uncertainty. Rather, normative considerations may also implicitly play a role in the less-restrictive-means test. In *Wholesale Travel*, the Canadian Supreme Court had to deal with a provision that imposed strict liability for false or misleading advertising.[91] According to the provision, the representatives of a company could only avoid a criminal sanction if they could prove that they exercised due diligence in designing the advertisement and if they took reasonable measures to correct the misleading content in a timely

[86] See Id. at 37.
[87] Id. at 45–7.
[88] Id. at 47.
[89] See BVerfGE 7, 377 at 419–41 (licence requirement for the establishment of new pharmacies); 9, 39 at 52–5 (minimum trade volume requirement for receiving a licence to sell milk); 11, 168 at 188 (taxi concessions); 12, 144 at 148–50 (registration requirement for dentists for treating participants in the public health insurance scheme); 17, 269 at 277–80 (itinerant sale of medical drugs); 19, 330 at 339–40 (certification requirement for retailers); 21, 261 at 268–70 (public monopoly for professional work placement).
[90] See Ulrich Haltern, *Europarecht* (Tübingen: Mohr Siebeck, 2nd edn, 2007), para. 1646.
[91] *R. v. Wholesale Travel Group Inc.* [1991] 3 S.C.R. 154.

manner. The applicant had advertised travel packages at wholesale prices. The Canadian competition agency argued that the advertising was misleading because wholesale prices could only refer to the prices that the company paid for the individual packages. The applicant argued that the criminal provision violated his freedom of speech. The competition agency responded that the strict liability requirement and the obligation to correct misleading information immediately was necessary in order to avoid companies taking advantage of grey areas where it was not immediately obvious that information was misleading.

The Canadian Supreme Court held that the scope of the provision was unnecessarily broad because it also applied to companies that did not correct their advertisements because they had not realised that the advertisements were misleading.[92] The judges found that a requirement to correct the advertisement once its misleading character was known was a less-restrictive means.[93] They acknowledged that the deterrent effect of this alternative might be weaker than the strict liability prescribed by the challenged provision.[94] However, the court deemed it inadmissible to base the potential sanction of imprisonment on mere strict liability.[95] If the legislature wanted to stick to the strict liability standard, it would have to exclude imprisonment as a potential sanction.[96] Even though the court used the terminology of "not necessary" and "less intrusive means", the court implicitly balanced by referring to the intensity of the criminal sanction as a reason for the unsuitability of the strict liability standard.

2.3 *The Empirical Stages of Proportionality and the Review of Legislative Rationality*

The preceding analysis has shown that the less-restrictive-means test is more problematic in practice than it appears to be in theory. Two difficulties stand out. First, the core of the less-restrictive-means test implies an empirical evaluation of the effectiveness of the challenged measure and potentially less-restrictive alternatives. However, courts have not yet found a consistent framework to deal with these issues. When they want to grant a margin of appreciation to the legislature, they have to determine

[92] Id. at 194.
[93] Id.
[94] Id. at 195.
[95] Id.
[96] Id.

the limits of the margin of appreciation in the abstract. However, a consistent concept regarding these limits has yet to be developed. Furthermore, they may control legislative prognoses directly in simple cases. However, they are often ill equipped to do so if the empirical questions become more complex. Sometimes, courts may be able to turn empirical questions into analytical ones, but even this approach is only applicable in a limited number of cases.

This first problem directly leads to a second one. If courts are unable to determine the effectiveness of competing measures with certainty, they often have to turn to implicit balancing at the less-restrictive-means stage. Certainly, implicit balancing becomes more urgent when a court refrains from making use of the balancing stage of the proportionality test.[97] It is thus not surprising that the examples of the German Constitutional Court using implicit balancing in the less-restrictive-means test predominantly stem from the early jurisprudence when the court still largely abstained from openly using the balancing test.[98]

When courts rely on implicit balancing in the less-restrictive-means test, they are primarily driven by the worry that turning to open balancing could weaken their institutional position.[99] Nevertheless, this does not automatically mean that implicit balancing is an instrument of judicial activism. Rather, if courts avoid balancing openly, it is a necessary tool in order not to turn the proportionality test into a blunt instrument.[100] Furthermore, the scope of implicit balancing is usually limited. Courts do not second-guess the core of legislative policy goals, but only compare different measures to achieve these goals. This may imply that courts evaluate trade-offs differently than the legislature. However, courts cannot refrain from evaluating such trade-offs because a bad fit of measure and purpose may be an indication that the legislature pursued different purposes from the ones it relied on explicitly to justify the measure, that is, that it tried to discriminate against minorities or was influenced by strong lobby groups.[101]

[97] See ch. 2, section 1.4. See also Jackson, 'Constitutional Law in an Age of Proportionality', 3118–9 (arguing that the U.S. Supreme Court sometimes does not distinguish between less restrictive means which are equally effective and those that are not, because the Court lacks an analysis of proportionality *stricto sensu*).

[98] See ch. 4, section 2.2.

[99] See Grimm, 'Proportionality', 394; Charles-Maxime Panaccio, 'In Defence of Two-Step Balancing and Proportionality in Rights Adjudication' (2011) 24 *Canadian Journal of Law and Jurisprudence* 109–28 at 114.

[100] See ch. 2, section 1.4.

[101] Petersen, 'Capture', 659.

It goes too far, however, to argue – as some authors do – that the proportionality test is a neutral instrument that allows judges to focus on empirical questions and to abstain from normative evaluations.[102] On the contrary, courts sometimes make highly problematic normative valuations in the context of the less-restrictive-means test that should rather be left to the legislature. The most striking example is the *Chaoulli* decision of the Canadian Supreme Court.[103] In *Chaoulli*, the court controlled, at first sight, only the empirical prognosis of the legislature. However, by framing the empirical analysis, the court already made a significant normative statement.[104] It asked whether a public-health-insurance scheme could still be effective if individuals were allowed to opt out of the public scheme and to enter into private health insurances. However, this framing of the empirical analysis disregards certain important normative aspects of the problem.[105] The prohibition of private health insurances does not necessarily only aim at ensuring the effectiveness of the public scheme. It may also prevent privately insured patients from being privileged over publicly insured individuals, thus helping to allocate medical services according to medical needs rather than financial means. Through framing the empirical analysis, courts can thus hide important political considerations.

However, this observation does not automatically turn the less-restrictive-means test into a tool for judicial activism. The practice of the three analysed courts shows that decisions like *Chaoulli* are rather the exception. In most cases, courts evaluate the fit between measure and purpose to control whether the legislature took minority interests insufficiently into account or was disproportionately influenced by certain interest groups. Consequently, they use the rational-connection and the less-restrictive-means test predominantly not as an instrument of judicial activism but, rather, as a tool to review legislative rationality.

3. Consistency and Coherency Arguments

Consistency or coherency arguments are a popular mode of reasoning in all three jurisdictions.[106] They can either be used as auxiliary considerations in

[102] See Beatty, 'Human Rights', p. 51; Beatty, *Ultimate Rule of Law*, pp. 169–71.
[103] *Chaoulli v. Quebec* [2005] 1 S.C.R. 791.
[104] Marmor, 'Canada's Supreme Court', 316–17.
[105] Id.
[106] See *R. v. Morgentaler* [1988] 1 S.C.R. 30 at 125; *Black v. Law Society of Alberta* [1989], 1 S.C.R. 591 at 632–3; *M. v. H.* [1999] 2 S.C.R. 3 at 66; *R. v. Guignard* [2002] 1 S.C.R. 472 at 487–8; *Charkaoui v. Canada (Citizenship and Immigration)* [2007] 1 S.C.R. 350 at

the proportionality test or substitute for proportionality arguments. In the following section, I will analyse consistency arguments in three steps. First, I will describe the different types of consistency arguments that we encounter: internal, external and historical consistency. Second, I will argue that the main purpose of consistency arguments is the smoking out of illicit motives and thus the control of the rationality of the legislative procedure. However, consistency arguments have certain limits that will be examined in the third part of this section.

3.1. *Internal, External and Historical Consistency*

Consistency arguments can come in three different forms.[107] First, courts may impose an internal consistency requirement on the legislature. A measure usually lacks internal consistency if it is evidently over- or under inclusive, that is, if the legislature intended to react to a specific problem, but only addressed part of the problem. An example for a decision partly based on an internal consistency argument is the *Charkaoui* judgment of the Canadian Supreme Court.[108] After the attacks on the Twin Towers in New York in September 2001, the Canadian legislature adopted the Immigration and Refugee Protection Act (IRPA). This statute authorised the Minister for Citizenship and Immigration to order the detention of foreign citizens who were suspected to be a danger to public security. The detainee could only ask for a review of the detention by an independent court after 120 days had elapsed.

The court held that the period of detention without the possibility of a review was excessive. It based its reasoning on a consistency consideration. The detention of a Canadian citizen or a permanent resident had

392–7; *Canada (Attorney General) v. Hislop* [2007] 1 S.C.R. 429 at 457–8; *Mounted Police Association of Ontario v. Canada* [2015] S.C.R. 3 at 78 (for Canada); *S v. Makwanyane* 1995 (3) SA 391 (CC) at paras. 129–31; *Minister of Home Affairs v. National Institute for Crime Prevention and the Re-Integration of Offenders (NICRO)* 2005 (3) SA 280 (CC) at para. 67; *Brümmer v. Minister for Social Development* 2009 (6) SA 323 (CC) at paras. 67, 69; *Richter v. the Minister of Home Affairs* 2009 (3) SA 615 (CC) at para. 76; *Malachi v. Cape Dance Academy International* 2010 (6) SA 1 (CC) at paras. 32, 34; *De Vos N.O. v. Minister of Justice and Constitutional Development* 2015 (2) SACR 217 (CC) at para. 54 (for South Africa); BVerfGE 8, 1 at 26–7; 25, 236 at 251–2; 107, 150 at 180–2; 115, 276 at 309–16; 125, 175 at 238, 242–4; 127, 132 at 156–7; 130, 151 at 208–9; 132, 134 at 166–70 (for Germany). See also ch. 6, section 2.3, for the use of consistency considerations as auxiliary arguments on the balancing stage in the case law of the German Constitutional Court.

[107] Petersen, 'Legislative Inconsistency', 510.

[108] *Charkaoui v. Canada* [2007] 1 S.C.R. 350.

to be reviewed within forty-eight hours. When it was possible to review the detention within two days for a certain group of suspects, it seemed implausible why the review period amounted to almost four months for foreign citizens.[109] For this reason, the long time period without the possibility of reviewing the detention was not considered to be necessary to achieve the legislative purpose.

Second, a measure can be unjustifiable because it is externally inconsistent, that is, if the legislature pursues the same aim with less intensity in different circumstances. The *Brümmer* case of the South African Constitutional Court illustrates how external consistency arguments work.[110] The South African Promotion of Access to Information Act prescribed a thirty-day limit for lodging applications against denials of information by public agencies to court. The applicant argued that this short time limit violated her constitutional rights of access to information (Art. 32 of the South African Constitution) and of access to court (Art. 34 of the South African Constitution).

The court found that the time limit was very short if one considered that the applicant had to get legal advice and organise financing of the procedure.[111] At the same time, it acknowledged that bar provisions of time limits had an important function in promoting legal certainty.[112] However, it pointed out that time limits in other statutes contained much more generous time limits than the Promotion of Access to Information Act, even though there was no reason that legal certainty was more important in the context of seeking information.[113] Because of this inconsistency, it held that the time limit was disproportionately short.[114]

Historical consistency, finally, comes into play when the legislature changes an already existing legal regime. If the legislature changes legislation in a way that restricts an individual right more severely, the court imposes a burden of justification on the legislature. The latter has to justify why the previous regulation had not been sufficient to pursue the intended purpose. The argument can be nicely illustrated by the *Casino* decision of the German Federal Constitutional Court.[115] The dispute arose after the state of Baden-Württemberg had changed its statute governing the operation and

[109] Id. at 403.
[110] *Brümmer v. Minister for Social Development* 2009 (6) SA 323 (CC).
[111] Id. at paras. 54–6.
[112] Id. at para. 64.
[113] Id. at paras. 67, 69.
[114] Id. at para. 70.
[115] BVerfGE 102, 197.

supervision of casinos. Under the old regime, a licence to operate a casino could also be awarded to private operators. After the change of the statute, casinos could only be operated by the state. The two existing private operators in Baden-Württemberg challenged this change of legislation.

The legislature had justified the change of the legislation, *inter alia*, with the intention to increase the efficiency of the control, monitoring and supervision of casinos. However, the court rejected this argumentation.[116] It observed that there had not been any occasions in the past where the supervision and monitoring of the casinos run by private operators had proven to be insufficient.[117] On the contrary, the parliamentarians themselves had acknowledged during the debate on the new law that the operation of the private casinos had not encountered a single complaint.[118] Consequently, the court argued that there was no indication that an increase of the supervision and monitoring powers had been necessary to guarantee a smooth operation of the existing casinos. For this reason, it found the restriction of casino licences to public operators to be disproportionate.[119]

3.2 Consistency and the Rationality of the Legislative Procedure

Consistency requirements are often seen as an intrusion into the legislative margin of appreciation.[120] Critics argue that the political process with its compromises and political bargains is inherently confusing.[121] Consistency is thus not considered to be a proper standard of review. This argument has a certain force if consistency is seen as an end in itself, as an inherent expression of the reasonable,[122] or even as a doctrinal

116 BVerfGE 102, 197 at 218–20.

117 Id. at 219.

118 Id.

119 Id. at 221.

120 Lepsius, 'Anmerkung', 262; Dann, 'Verfassungsgerichtliche Kontrolle gesetzgeberischer Rationalität', (2010) 49 *Der Staat* 634–5; Möllers, 'Legalität', p. 397–9; Payandeh, 'Folgerichtigkeit', 612–3.

121 Christoph Engel, 'Inconsistency in the Law: In Search of a Balanced Norm', in Christoph Engel and Lorraine Daston (eds.), *Is there Value in Inconsistency?* (Baden-Baden: Nomos, 2006), pp. 221–81 at 225; Lepsius, 'Anmerkung', 262; Dann, 'Verfassungsgerichtliche Kontrolle gesetzgeberischer Rationalität', 640; Möllers, 'Legalität', p. 399.

122 See Paul Kirchhof, 'Allgemeiner Gleichheitssatz', in Josef Isensee and Paul Kirchhof (eds.), *Handbuch des Staatsrechts der Bundesrepublik Deutschland. Band VIII: Grundrechte: Wirtschaft, Verfahren, Gleichheit* (Heidelberg: C. F. Müller, 3rd edn, 2010), ch. 181 at paras. 209–10.

translation of coherence theories of truth.[123] However, this is not the only possible interpretation of consistency arguments. Instead, consistency can also be seen as an indication for legislative motivation.[124] If a legislative measure is inconsistent, we have reason to believe that the legislature has pursued other purposes than the ones explicitly mentioned to justify the legislation. It may have been influenced by particular interest groups, may have had a discriminatory intention or simply promoted their own interests.

The design of the detention scheme in *Charkaoui* is an example of symbolic legislation in criminal matters, to the detriment of specific disadvantaged social groups, and meant to appease the general public. As foreign citizens do not have a right to vote, the political elites did not have to fear any backlash from the affected individuals in the upcoming elections. In *Brümmer*, the government did not have a particular interest in submitting administrative decisions to deny information to a review by independent courts. For this reason, it prescribed a time limit to lodge an application against the decision that was so short that it effectively denied the applicants access to courts. Finally, in the case concerning gambling casinos in Baden-Württemberg, the state intended to open up new sources of revenue for the chronically tight public budget, even though budgetary considerations could not be a sufficient reason to establish a state-run monopoly. Consequently, if consistency arguments are understood as instruments to control legislative motivation, they are much less problematic than the critique assumes. Instead of compromising the legislative margin of appreciation, they are tools to police political market failure and thus to increase the rationality of the political process.

3.3 The Limits of Consistency

However, the rationalising potential of consistency arguments has limits. It becomes increasingly problematic, the more consistency is seen as an end in itself and not just an instrument to control legislative motivation. This is particularly evident in the smoking ban judgment of the German Federal

[123] See Neil MacCormick, *Legal Reasoning and Legal Theory* (Oxford: Oxford University Press, 1978), pp. 152–228; Klaus Günther, 'Ein normativer Begriff der Kohärenz für eine Theorie der juristischen Argumentation' (1989) 20 *Rechtstheorie* 163–90. See also Joel Feinberg, 'Justice, Fairness and Rationality' (1972) 81 *Yale Law Journal* 1004–31 at 1019–20 on the coherence theory of truth.

[124] Petersen, 'Legislative Inconsistency', 521–2.

Constitutional Court from July 2008.[125] In this decision, the court overturned smoking ban laws in two states, Baden-Württemberg and Berlin, because they had not been designed in a consistent manner. Both states had included exceptions in their smoking ban legislation. Restaurants, bars and nightclubs could offer special smoking areas if these were sufficiently separated from the main rooms. Furthermore, Baden-Württemberg had excluded tents and outdoor restaurants from the smoking ban. The court argued that these exceptions showed that the underlying estimation of the health risks of passive smoking was not consistent.[126] Instead they indicated that the legislature did not deem the health risks to be severe enough to merit absolute supremacy over the freedom of profession.[127] Because of this inconsistency, the court held that the smoking ban was disproportionate.

However, the reasoning is not convincing.[128] The challenged legislation at least contributes to increasing the protection for passive smokers, even if the level of protection might not be optimal. By introducing the exceptions, the legislature tried to strike a balance between the interests of the respective establishments and the protection of public health. The inconsistency detected by the Constitutional Court was no indication that the smoking ban pursued any other purposes than health protection. Instead, Justice Brun-Otto Bryde remarked astutely in his separate opinion that

> A legislative reform like the protection of passive smokers [. . .] requires a strenuous political effort, where the legislature faces massive resistance of powerful lobby organizations. The fact that the Federal Republic of Germany is a straggler in Western Europe when it comes to the protection of passive smokers already shows the extent of the resistance. Under such circumstances, it will often not be possible to attain anything but a more or less perforated compromise at first attempt – and compromise is virtually an essential characteristic of democratic politics."[129]

Consequently, the inconsistency may not have been an indication for an illicit legislative purpose, but rather for the opposite: It is a plausible explanation that the exceptions are, as Justice Bryde suggests, the result

[125] BVerfGE 121, 317.

[126] Id. at 362–3.

[127] Id. at 362.

[128] Matthias Cornils, 'Folgerichtiger Nichtraucherschutz: Von Verfassungs wegen keine halben Sachen?' (2008) 1 *Zeitschrift für das Juristische Studium* 660–3 at 662; Rolf Gröschner, 'Vom Ersatzgesetzgeber zum Ersatzerzieher' (2008) 23 *Zeitschrift für Gesetzgebung* 400–12 at 406; Dann, 'Verfassungsgerichtliche Kontrolle gesetzgeberischer Rationalität', 635.

[129] BVerfGE 121, 317 at 380 (per Bryde J. dissenting) (translation by the author).

of lobbying efforts by the gastronomic industry. However, the problem would then not be the legislation itself, but the exceptions. Therefore, by overturning the legislation, the court threw out the baby with the bath water.[130] It gave the lobbyists a victory that they could not achieve in the political process.

Nevertheless, the mere fact that a specific doctrinal instrument is not free of occasional errors and misapplications does not automatically discredit the instrument as such. Instead, the analysis of the case law shows that consistency considerations predominantly serve the purpose of "smoking out" illicit motives.[131] Consequently, they are rather a means of reviewing the rationality of the legislative process than an activist intrusion upon the legislative margin of appreciation.

4. Procedural Arguments

The rationale underlying procedural arguments in the context of fundamental rights review is the insight that the process of norm application is never free of mistakes. If a statute authorises the executive to restrict fundamental rights, the substantial conditions contained in the statute are supposed to ensure that the affected constitutional rights are not limited disproportionately. However, these substantial elements have to be interpreted and applied by the administration. Procedural guarantees aim at compensating for potential mistakes in this process of norm application. Therefore, they have a rationalising function.[132]

This procedural compensation is, in part, already rooted in the constitutional texts. All three of the analysed constitutions contain not only substantive, but also procedural rights. However, courts also impose procedural requirements on the legislature outside the scope of procedural rights.[133] These procedural arguments in the context of substantial rights are predominantly part of the proportionality test. In these cases, the courts accept the substantial value decision of the legislature. However,

130 Petersen, 'Capture', 663.

131 See also Petersen, 'Legislative Inconsistency'.

132 Axel Tschentscher, *Prozedurale Theorien der Gerechtigkeit* (Baden-Baden: Nomos, 2000), p. 346.

133 See Susan Rose-Ackerman, Stefanie Egidy and James Fowkes, *Due Process of Lawmaking: The United States, South Africa, Germany, and the European Union* (New York: Cambridge University Press, 2015), p. 158 (arguing for the South African context that "procedural requirements are [often] driven by substantive concerns related to the protection of rights").

they require the latter to introduce additional procedural guarantees for the protection of the fundamental rights of the affected individuals. In the following, we will look at three points in more detail: procedural arguments play a significant role in the review of criminal law and criminal procedure provisions (section 4.1). However, they have also been used to strengthen the impartiality of the decision-making process (section 4.2). In some cases, procedural arguments do not refer to the regime of norm application established by a statute but, rather, to the legislative procedure in which a statute was established (section 4.3).

4.1 Procedural Arguments Referring to Criminal Law and Criminal Procedure Provisions

In the context of criminal law and criminal procedure law, all three courts have used procedural arguments to protect the rights of individuals being subject to a criminal procedure or a criminal investigation.[134] The German approach can be illustrated by a 1999 decision on a telecommunications surveillance statute.[135] In the judgment, the court reviewed a statute authorising the German intelligence agency to monitor international calls and to pass on the obtained data to other administrative agencies. The judges acknowledged that the aim to prevent and to prosecute criminal actions was a legitimate goal. However, it held that the statute was inconsistent with the constitution in several respects. In its reasoning, the court relied to a great extent on procedural arguments. First, it required modifications of the provisions allowing the transfer of data to other administrative agencies.[136] *Inter alia*, it demanded that the involved agencies make a record of the data transfer in order to enable a subsequent judicial review of the measure for the affected individual.[137]

[134] See BVerfGE 100, 313 at 395–402; 109, 279 at 366–79; 110, 33 at 75; 113, 273 at 309–15; 113, 348 at 390; 120, 274 at 331–9; 120, 378 at 431–2; 125, 260 at 325–58; 128, 282 at 320–1; 129, 269 at 283; 133, 112 at 139–42; 133, 277 at 370–5 (for Germany); *Corporation professionnelle des médecins du Québec v. Thibault* [1988] 1 S.C.R. 1033 at 1044–5; *R. v. Bain* [1992] 1 S.C.R. 91 at 102–4; *Baron v. Canada* [1993] 1 S.C.R. 416 at 435–6; *R. v. Heywood* [1994] 3 S.C.R. 761 at 796–800; *Charkaoui v. Canada* [2007] 1 S.C.R. 350 at 392–400, 403; *R. v. Tse* [2012] 1 S.C.R. 531 at 563–7; *Goodwin v. British Columbia (Superintendent of Motor Vehicles)* [2015] 3 S.C.R. 250 at 288–90 (for Canada); *S v. Steyn* 2001 (1) SA 1146 at para. 32; *S v. Niemand* 2002 (1) SA 21 (CC) at para. 19 (for South Africa).

[135] BVerfGE 100, 313 at 395–402.

[136] Id. at 391–6.

[137] Id. at 395–6.

Furthermore, the court extended the obligation to inform the affected individual that his or her communication had been subject to surveillance measures. The statute only required such information if the data was stored for at least three months. This requirement led to a practice according to which data was regularly deleted before the expiration of the three-month period. The court argued that this provision impaired the ability of the affected individual to obtain a subsequent judicial review of the measure because an application could only be lodged if the applicant was aware of the measures.[138] Consequently, it held that informing the affected individual was only unnecessary if the data was deemed irrelevant and destroyed immediately after being recorded without any further processing.[139]

The *Tse* case of the Canadian Supreme Court concerned a similar constellation.[140] The court had to deal with a criminal procedure provision allowing the police to monitor private communication without prior judicial authorisation. The competent agent could order such a monitoring if she believed that it was necessary to avoid serious harm and if a judicial authorisation could not be attained in time. The Supreme Court acknowledged the need for such an emergency competence in principle. However, it required additional procedural safeguards: First, the affected individual had to be informed about the measure after its termination.[141] Second, the police had to report regularly to parliament about its monitoring activity.[142] Third, the monitoring activities had to be recorded to allow for an effective subsequent judicial control.[143] Finally, the purposes for which the data could be used had to be explicitly contained in the authorising statute.[144]

The approaches of the two courts, with regard to police and intelligence surveillance measures, illustrated by the discussed cases, display a striking similarity. Both courts accept the reviewed measures in principle, but impose procedural requirements on the legislature. These aim at increasing the accountability of the monitoring agencies and enable the affected individual to achieve a subsequent judicial review of the measure.

In South Africa, the cases usually concern the lack of judicial control mechanisms for individual rights restrictions. In *Steyn*, for example, the court had to deal with a provision that significantly restricted the possibility

138 Id. at 397–9.
139 Id. at 399.
140 *R. v. Tse* [2012] 1 S.C.R. 531.
141 Id. at 563–6.
142 Id. at 566–7.
143 Id. at 567.
144 Id. at 568.

to appeal convictions by criminal courts.[145] The government had argued that this restriction was necessary to prevent the clogging of appeal rolls. However, the court held that the measure violated the constitutional right of appeal contained in section 35 of the constitution. Although the court acknowledged that procedural efficiency was, in principle, a valid concern,[146] it argued that the government had failed to produce any evidence on the "clogging of appeal rolls" or the "existence of any resource-related problems".[147]

The existence of procedural control mechanisms is also a central concern in some other decisions that do not concern criminal or criminal procedure provisions in the strict sense, but refer to norms related to public security.[148] In *Lawyers for Human Rights v. Minister of Home Affairs*, the South African Constitutional Court held that an immigration provision allowing for the detention of illegal immigrants was inconsistent with the constitution.[149] The provision in question authorised the South African immigration agency to order the detention of illegal immigrants trying to reach South Africa by ship on the vessel on which they had tried to enter the country or to remove them from South African territory. Alternatively, the agency could also imprison the immigrants. The Constitutional Court acknowledged that the agency was, in principle, justified in detaining illegal immigrants until their extradition.[150] However, it argued that the statute did not establish sufficient procedural safeguards. In particular, the provision did not require the detention to be reviewed by a court.[151] Therefore, the court held that the statute had to provide for an automatic judicial review procedure at least for cases in which the detention exceeded thirty days.[152]

4.2 Procedural Arguments and the Impartiality of the Decision-making Process

Procedural arguments are not limited to the context of criminal law and criminal procedure. In some cases, they aim at preserving the impartiality

145 See *S v. Steyn* 2001 (1) SA 1146.
146 Id. at para. 31.
147 Id. at para. 32.
148 See *Lawyers for Human Rights v. Minister of Home Affairs* 2004 (4) SA 125 (CC); *C v. Department of Health and Social Development, Gauteng* 2012 (2) SA 208 (CC) at paras. 68–73; *Gaertner v. Minister of Finance* 2014 (1) SA 442 (CC) at paras. 68–73.
149 *Lawyers for Human Rights v. Minister of Home Affairs* 2004 (4) SA 125 (CC).
150 Id. at para. 42.
151 Id. at para. 43.
152 Id. at para. 45.

of the decision-making process.[153] One example is the *Provincial Court Judges* case, in which the Canadian Supreme Court had to deal with the guarantee of judicial independence.[154] Several Canadian provinces had implemented austerity measures, which also included the reduction of judges' salaries. The court argued that such a reduction of judges' salaries was not *per se* inconsistent with the constitution.[155] However, it required the measure to be reviewed by an independent commission in order to avoid the impression of politics interfering with the judiciary.[156] As all three provinces in question had not submitted their plans to such an independent commission, the court qualified the salary cuts as violations of the guarantee of judicial independence.[157]

The German Constitutional Court sometimes uses procedural arguments to avoid conflicts of interest.[158] In a 2009 judgment, it overturned a statute of the state of Brandenburg, according to which financial subsidies to Jewish religious communities had to be allocated by the state association of Jewish congregations.[159] The applicant was a Jewish congregation, which had a competitive relationship with the state association and had been consistently ignored in the process of allocating the subsidies. The Constitutional Court argued that the regulation led to a conflict of interest.[160] Because the state association had a significant self-interest in the allocation of the subsidies, the procedure led to an unequal distribution. For this reason, the court asked the state legislature to find a different allocation procedure.

4.3 *Arguments Relating to the Legislative Procedure*

In some cases, procedural arguments do not target the administrative procedure implementing the statute, but rather the drafting process. In *Health Services Bargaining Association*, the Canadian Supreme Court dealt with a

153 See *R. v. Campbell, R. v. Ekmecic; R. v. Wickman* [1997] 3 S.C.R. 3 at 102–15; *R. v. Bain* [1992] 1 S.C.R. 91 at 102–4; *Mackin v. New Brunswick (Minister of Finance); Rice v. New Brunswick* [2002] 1 S.C.R. 405 at 437–8; *Health Services and Support – Facilities Subsector Bargaining Assn. v. British Columbia* [2007] 2 S.C.R. 391 at 466–8; *Saskatchewan Federation of Labour v. Saskatchewan* [2015] 1 S.C.R. 245 at 291–2, 296–7.

154 *R. v. Campbell* [1997] 3 S.C.R. 3.

155 Id. at 88.

156 Id. at 102–11.

157 Id. at 154.

158 See BVerfGE 39, 1 at 61–3; 65, 1 at 60; 101, 106 at 126; 109, 279 at 370–1; 123, 148 at 183–4.

159 BVerfGE 123, 148.

160 Id. at 183–4.

statute of British Columbia that enabled employers in the health sector to invalidate certain provisions of the collective agreements with the labour unions unilaterally.[161] The court acknowledged that the measure was a reaction to an existential crisis in the health sector.[162] However, the legislature should have made a stronger effort to look for alternative means to resolve the crisis. In particular, it should have consulted the labour unions to seek a consensual solution.[163] Furthermore, the legislative history did not show why the legislature decided to establish a unilateral right to dissolve collective agreements. There were no indications that the legislature discussed potential alternative means that would have respected the bargaining autonomy of the labour unions to a greater extent.[164] Therefore, the court did not base its verdict on substantial considerations, but rather on arguments relating to the legislative process. Failures in the legislative procedure were thus the principal reason for the violation of the Canadian Charter.

A similar argumentation pattern can be found in a recent decision of the German Federal Constitutional Court from February 2010.[165] In a judgment regarding the suitable amount of social benefits for people whose income cannot secure a minimum standard of living, the court heavily relied on procedural considerations regarding the legislative procedure.[166] The applicants had argued that the social benefits were not sufficient to guarantee a minimum standard of living. In its reasoning, the court refrained from establishing substantive requirements concerning the extent of the social benefits. Instead, it imposed an obligation on the legislature to determine the suitable amount of social benefits in a "transparent and rational procedure".[167]

The court argued that the legislature had not fulfilled this obligation in all respects. In principle, the legislature had determined the suitable amount of social benefits according to a specific statistical model. However, it had made deductions from certain items of the basket of commodities without justifying these deductions. In particular, the

161 *Health Services and Support – Facilities Subsector Bargaining Assn. v. British Columbia* [2007] 2 S.C.R. 391.

162 Id. at 463.

163 Id. at 466–8.

164 Id. at 467.

165 *See* Rose-Ackerman, Egidy and Fowkes, *Due Process of Lawmaking*, pp. 178–82.

166 BVerfGE 125, 175. See also BVerfGE 132, 134 at 170–3 (where the Court also relies on considerations relating to the legislative procedure with regard to a decision on social benefits for asylum seekers).

167 BVerfGE 125, 175 at 225 (translation by the author).

court criticised that the deductions did not have any empirical basis.[168] Furthermore, it argued that the establishment of the standard for determining the extent of social benefits for children was equally flawed. According to the court, the determination was "devoid of any empirical or methodological foundation".[169]

As in the Canadian case, the procedural considerations were the central part of the court's reasoning. This is, in part, due to the subject matter. It would have been impossible for the court to derive concrete monetary standards for measuring the extent of social benefits from the constitution. However, the court imposed certain procedural requirements on the legislature. The legislature had to determine the standards in an adequate procedure. The procedural standard is thus a compensatory element for the lack of adequate substantial standards.

4.4 *Conclusion*

Procedural arguments have two different foci. On the one hand, they concern the implementation procedure. In these cases, courts accept the substantial purpose of the legislation. However, they require additional procedural guarantees to ensure a proportionate implementation of the statute. Such procedural arguments occur primarily in the context of criminal and criminal procedure laws. However, in some cases, they are also used to avoid conflicts of interest. On the other hand, courts control the legislative procedure of norm formation. In this context, they usually try to ensure that the legislation is based on an adequate empirical basis and that the legislature took all relevant interests into account.

Both types of procedural arguments have the same purpose. They aim at avoiding political market failures. If procedural arguments concern the legislative procedure, they should ensure a balanced deliberation of the appropriate legislative measures. In both discussed cases, there was a particular danger that the legislature would put budgetary considerations over the interests of specific stakeholders. To the extent that procedural considerations concern the implementation procedure, they are supposed to ensure that the legislature does not disproportionately favour concerns of procedural efficiency in cases where the affected individuals do not have a strong lobby in the political process.

[168] BVerfGE 125, 175 at 239.

[169] BVerfGE 125, 175 at 246 (translation by the author).

5. Determinacy

A further argument on which courts rely to declare a statute to be inconsistent with the constitution is the lack of determinacy. This argument is found most often in the jurisprudence of the German Constitutional Court.[170] But there are also a few Canadian cases in which the Supreme Court relied on the lack of determinacy.[171] The determinacy requirement has two purposes: On the one hand, more determinate norms increase the transparency, predictability and comparability of administrative decisions.[172] On the other hand, a court that demands norms to be more determinate also implies that the principal decision should be determined by the legislature during the drafting process of the norm, not by the executive during the norm implementation.[173] The latter interpretation of determinacy arguments sees them as instruments to strengthen the accountability and the control of democratic decision-making.

In its jurisprudence, the Canadian Supreme Court focuses primarily on safeguarding legal certainty when it deems a statute to be indeterminate. In *Morales*, the court overturned a criminal procedure provision that prohibited bail and allowed pre-trial detention if it was required by the "public interest".[174] The court argued that the term *public interest* was too vague and imprecise and thus incapable of structuring administrative discretion appropriately.[175] Because of this vagueness, the court held that the provision was overbroad.[176]

[170] See BVerfGE 8, 71 at 77; 9, 83 at 87; 20, 150 at 157; 22, 42 at 47–8; 27, 355 at 362–3; 33, 303 at 346–7; 45, 393 at 398–9; 47, 46 at 81–3; 65, 1 at 65–6; 73, 118 at 182–4; 78, 179 at 197–8; 78, 374 at 383–8; 100, 313 at 387–8; 105, 135 at 158–71; 107, 104 at 122–9; 110, 33 at 57–73; 111, 191 at 214–24; 113, 348 at 378–81, 385, 389; 118, 168 at 186–91; 120, 274 at 316–8; 120, 378 at 407–19; 125, 260 at 355–6; 128, 282 at 318–9; 128, 326 at 383–4; 129, 269 at 283; 130, 151 at 202–5; 133, 112 at 132–7; 133, 277 at 336–341, 348–50; 135, 48 at 78–9; BVerfG, 1 BvR 1501/13 (12 May 2015) at para. 75.

[171] See *R. v. Swain* [1991] 1 S.C.R. 933 at 1016–7; *Committee for the Commonwealth of Canada v. Canada* [1991] 1 S.C.R. 139 at 209–15; *R. v. Morales* [1992] 3 S.C.R. 711 at 733–4.

[172] See Ulrich M. Gassner, 'Gesetzgebung und Bestimmtheitsgrundsatz' (1996) 11 *Zeitschrift für Gesetzgebung* 37–56 at 38–9; Papier and Möller, 'Das Bestimmtheitsgebot und seine Durchsetzung', 179; Sobota, *Rechtsstaatsprinzip*, p. 497–8.

[173] See Hesse, 'Bestand und Bedeutung der Grundrechte', 435; Papier and Möller, 'Das Bestimmtheitsgebot', 179–80; von Bogdandy, *Gubernative Rechtsetzung*, p. 191; Towfigh, 'Komplexität und Normenklarheit', 63–5.

[174] Morales, *supra* note 171.

[175] Id. at 726.

[176] Id. at 733–4.

In the German case law, we find both functions of the determinacy argument. The protection of legal certainty through determinacy plays a pivotal role in decisions concerning criminal and criminal procedure law.[177] In other decisions, institutional considerations are prevalent. For example, in a decision on the selection process for university students, the court argued that the selection criteria for access to public universities should be determined by the legislature and not by the universities.[178] In the area of data protection, the determinacy requirement plays a similar role. According to Federal Constitutional Court, data can only be collected and passed on to other administrative agencies if the purpose of using the data is sufficiently determinate.[179] In this context, the determinacy requirement also aims at limiting the competencies of the administration. The administrative agency should not be free to determine the use of stored data, but should only use such data for purposes clearly determined by the legislature.

6. The Protection of Legitimate Expectations

In some of its judgments, the German Constitutional Courts overturns statutes if they do not sufficiently protect legitimate expectations.[180] These concern legislative changes, that is, the replacement of an old legal regime by a new one. In these decisions, the court usually requires the legislature to introduce transitional provisions for people who had made arrangements under the old regime and suffered significant losses through the change of the law. In the context of legitimate expectations, the court often explicitly resorts to balancing.[181] It compares the interest of the legislature to implement the new legal regime as quickly and extensively as possible to

177 See BVerfGE 78, 374 at 383–8; 105, 135 at 158–71.

178 BVerfGE 33, 303 at 346–7; similarly BVerfGE 45, 393 at 398–9.

179 BVerfGE 65, 1 at 65–6; 100, 313 at 387–8; 110, 33 at 70–3; 118, 168 at 186–91; 120, 378 at 407–16; 125, 260 at 355–6.

180 See BVerfGE 2, 380 at 403; 13, 206 at 213; 13, 261 at 270–1; 15, 167 at 209; 18, 429 at 439; 24, 75 at 97–103; 30, 367 at 385–91; 31, 94 at 99; 51, 356 at 362–8; 72, 200 at 255–63; 116, 96 at 133–4; 127, 1 at 21–5; 127, 31 at 49–56; 127, 61 at 78–85; 132, 302 at 329–33; 133, 143 at 158–61; 135, 1 at 13–28.

181 Stefan Muckel, *Kriterien des verfassungsrechtlichen Vertrauensschutzes bei Gesetzesänderungen* (Berlin: Duncker & Humblot, 1989), p. 104; Karl Albrecht Schachtschneider, 'Das Vertrauensschutzprinzip im Verfassungs- und Verwaltungsrecht', in Max-Emanuel Geis and Dieter C. Umbach (eds.), *Planung – Steuerung – Kontrolle: Festschrift für Richard Bartlsperger* (Berlin: Duncker & Humblot, 2006), pp. 133–47 at 139.

the interest of the affected individuals in the protection of their legitimate expectations.

However, the scope of balancing in the context of the protection of legitimate expectations is limited. The Constitutional Court does not second-guess the legislative purpose as such. It only corrects the date at which the new legal regime is introduced. Furthermore, this correction mostly concerns only a small group of people who have been affected most significantly by the change. The functioning of balancing in this context can be illustrated by a decision of the Constitutional Court from 1971, which concerned pension cuts for widows of public servants in the Saar region.[182] To the extent that these pension cuts also applied to widows whose husband had already deceased, the court argued that the provision violated the principle of legitimate expectations.[183] The widows could have legitimately expected their pensions to be preserved at the existing level.[184] When comparing the legitimate expectations of the widows to the financial interest of the state, the latter was sufficiently achieved if the new regulation only applied to widows whose husbands deceased after the pension cut had entered into force.[185] In its reasoning, the court took into account that only a small fraction of the potentially affected individuals already received pensions, so that the financial consequences of the court's decision were limited.[186]

When protecting legitimate expectations of the applicants, the German Constitutional Court thus tries to strike a compromise between the interests of the applicants and the interests of the legislature. On the one hand, it protects legitimate expectations of the applicants. However, it does not second-guess the legislative aim in principle but only requires the introduction of transitional provisions. Furthermore, these transitional provisions usually only benefit a small fraction of all individuals who are potentially affected by the new regulation.

7. Categorical Arguments and Deductive Reasoning

Two further modes of reasoning of the German Constitutional Court may not be of high significance in quantitative terms; however, they concern

182 BVerfGE 31, 94.
183 Id. at 99.
184 Id.
185 Id.
186 Id.

decisions of high political importance, so that they deserve a more detailed analysis. These modes of reasoning are categorical arguments, on the one hand, and deductive reasoning, on the other.

7.1 Categorical Arguments

Many of the authors criticising the proportionality test propose categorical arguments as an alternative.[187] Whereas the proportionality test tries to avoid absolute value judgments and rather focuses on the circumstances of each individual case, categorical arguments aim at making such absolute value judgments. Categorical reasoning is thus supposed to increase legal certainty. The doctrinal anchor of categorical arguments is the guarantee of human dignity in Art. 1 of the German Constitution. Unlike other fundamental rights, human dignity is predominantly perceived to be an absolute guarantee, that is, a restriction of human dignity cannot be justified.[188] In the jurisprudence of the German Constitutional

[187] See ch. 2, section 2.

[188] Michael Kloepfer, 'Leben und Würde des Menschen', in Peter Badura and Horst Dreier (eds.), *Festschrift 50 Jahre Bundesverfassungsgericht. Zweiter Band: Klärung und Fortbildung des Verfassungsrechts* (Tübingen: Mohr Siebeck, 2001), pp. 77–104 at 98; Ernst-Wolfgang Böckenförde, 'Menschenwürde als normatives Prinzip' (2003) 58 *Juristenzeitung* 809–15 at 809–10; Ralf Poscher, '"Die Würde des Menschen ist unantastbar"' (2004) 59 *Juristenzeitung* 756–62; Hans-Jürgen Papier, 'Die Würde des Menschen ist unantastbar', in Rainer Grote *et al.* (eds.), *Die Ordnung der Freiheit: Festschrift für Christian Starck* (Tübingen: Mohr Siebeck, 2007), pp. 371–82 at 374; Karl-Heinz Ladeur and Ino Augsberg, *Die Funktion der Menschenwürde im Verfassungsstaat* (Tübingen: Mohr Siebeck, 2008), pp. 27–30; Jochen von Bernstorff, 'Pflichtenkollision und Menschenwürdegarantie' (2008) 47 *Der Staat* 21–40 at 29–33; Wolfram Höfling, 'Unantastbare Grundrechte – ein normlogischer Widerspruch?', in Rolf Gröschner and Oliver W. Lembcke (eds.), *Das Dogma der Unantastbarkeit* (Tübingen: Mohr Siebeck, 2009), pp. 111–20 at 114; Philip Kunig, 'Zum Dogma der unantastbaren Menschenwürde', in Rolf Gröschner and Oliver W. Lembcke (eds.), *Das Dogma der Unantastbarkeit* (Tübingen: Mohr Siebeck, 2009), pp. 121–32; Siegfried Broß, 'Die Würde des Menschen bleibt unantastbar', in Caroline Y. Robertson-von Trotha (ed.), *60 Jahre Grundgesetz: Interdisziplinäre Perspektiven* (Baden-Baden: Nomos, 2009), pp. 41–50; Ralf Poscher, 'Menschenwürde und Kernbereichsschutz' (2009) 64 *Juristenzeitung* 269–77; Jochen von Bernstorff, 'Der Streit um die Menschenwürde im Grund- und Menschenrechtsschutz: Eine Verteidigung des Absoluten als Grenze und Auftrag' (2013) 68 *Juristenzeitung* 905–15. However, an increasing number of voices in German constitutional law scholarship advocate that human dignity should be subject to balancing in certain cases; see Karl-Eberhard Hain, 'Konkretisierung der Menschenwürde durch Abwägung?' (2006) 45 *Der Staat* 189–214; Thomas Elsner and Klara Schobert, 'Gedanken zur Abwägungsresistenz der Menschenwürde' (2007) 122 *Deutsches Verwaltungsblatt* 278–87; Winfried Brugger, 'Menschenwürde im anthropologischen Kreuz der Entscheidung' (2008) 56 *Jahrbuch des öffentlichen Rechts der Gegenwart* 95–124 at 123; Hans-Georg Dederer, 'Die Garantie der Menschenwürde (Art. 1 Abs. 1 GG)' (2009)

Court, categorical arguments have, for a long time, not played a significant role. However, this has changed in recent years. In quantitative terms, categorical arguments are still a rather peripheral phenomenon. However, the judgments that applied such arguments were of fundamental importance. One decision concerned the eavesdropping on apartments in order to fight organised crime,[189] and the other concerned the authorisation to shoot down commercial aircraft in cases of an emergency.[190]

In the latter case, the German Constitutional Court held that the authorisation to shoot down commercial aircraft in emergency situations violated the guarantee of human dignity.[191] The obligation to protect human dignity prohibited treating human beings as "mere objects" of sovereign power.[192] If a commercial airliner has been hijacked, the passengers are usually in a position that prevent them from escaping the exercise of sovereign force.[193] Consequently, by shooting down the airplane, the state would treat them as "mere objects" in its attempt to save the lives of others.[194]

Doctrinally, the court's reliance on human dignity is not convincing.[195] The government does not treat the passengers as instruments when it orders shooting down the airplane; instead, the death of the passengers is only a necessary, but unintended, consequence of shooting down the aircraft.[196] Instead, the court should have asked whether the statute violated the right to life of the German Constitution. However, such an analysis would have raised difficult questions about how to balance human

57 *Jahrbuch des öffentlichen Rechts der Gegenwart* 89–124 at 112–24; Nils Teifke, *Das Prinzip Menschenwürde: Zur Abwägungsfähigkeit des Höchstrangigen* (Tübingen: Mohr Siebeck, 2011); Christoph Goos, *Innere Freiheit: Eine Rekonstruktion des grundgesetzlichen Würdebegriffs* (Göttingen: V&R unipress, 2011), pp. 164–6; Manfred Baldus, 'Menschenwürde und Absolutheitsthese – Zwischenbericht zu einer zukunftsweisenden Debatte' (2011) 136 *Archiv des öffentlichen Rechts* 529–52.

189 BVerfGE 109, 279.

190 BVerfGE 115, 118.

191 Id.

192 Id. at 153.

193 Id. at 154.

194 Id.

195 Mattias Kumm, 'Jenseits des Verhältnismäßigkeitsgrundsatzes: Grundrechtlicher Strukturpluralismus im Verfassungsrecht der Vereinigten Staaten', in Jan-Reinard Sieckmann (ed.), *Die Prinzipientheorie der Grundrechte* (Baden-Baden: Nomos, 2007), pp. 241–62 at 257–8; Christian Hillgruber, 'Der Staat des Grundgesetzes – nur "bedingt abwehrbereit"?' (2007) 62 *Juristenzeitung* 209–18 at 215–6; Paul Tiedemann, 'Vom inflationären Gebrauch der Menschenwürde in der Rechtsprechung des Bundesverfassungsgerichts' (2009) 62 *Die Öffentliche Verwaltung* 606–15 at 610.

196 Kumm, 'Jenseits des Verhältnismäßigkeitsgrundsatzes', p. 257–8.

lives against each other. By resorting to human dignity, the court avoided touching this issue.[197] The shooting down of airliners was prohibited without the need to analyse the consequences in more detail.

Implicitly, however, the court relied on balancing.[198] In one passage of the judgment, the court argued that it could often not be determined with sufficient reliability whether the conditions for shooting down an aircraft were fulfilled.[199] The judges deemed it unimaginable to kill passengers who were not able to escape their fate, taking into account that there might not be absolute certainty that the aircraft indeed posed a danger for society.[200] However, such a consequentialist analysis should be irrelevant if the dignity of the passengers is concerned, no matter how likely it is that the targeted airplane indeed poses a threat to public security.

The judges were thus aware of the sensitivity of the problem. They realised that they could not evaluate the statute without taking into account its negative and positive social consequences. The reliance on human dignity was thus rather a means to legitimise the decision. Had they based their decision on balancing considerations in the context of the right to life, they would have attracted a lot of criticism: How does the court justify replacing the value decision of the legislature with a judicial value decision in such a controversial issue? By basing their decision on human dignity, the judges make it appear to be an exclusively legal issue about the scope of the definition of human dignity. Consequently, it is a move to increase the acceptance of a controversial decision.[201]

The eavesdropping judgment follows similar argumentation patterns.[202] The court argued that the authorisation to monitor judgments through eavesdropping measures violated, in part, the guarantee of human dignity.[203] Implicitly, however, the court again relied on balancing different

197 Jochen von Bernstorff, 'Die Wesensgehalte der Grundrechte und das Verhältnis von Freiheit und Sicherheit unter dem Grundgesetz', in Felix Arndt *et al.* (eds.), *Freiheit – Sicherheit – Öffentlichkeit* (Baden-Baden: Nomos, 2009), pp. 40–60 at 48–9.

198 Teifke, *Menschenwürde*, pp. 131–4; Borowski, 'Abwehrrechte', p. 102–4; Baldus, 'Menschenwürde und Absolutheitsthese', 539.

199 BVerfGE 115, 118 at 155–7.

200 BVerfGE 115, 118 at 157.

201 See also Winfried Hassemer, 'Über den argumentativen Umgang mit der Würde des Menschen', in Gerhard Robbers, Dieter C. Umbach and Klaus-Eckart Gebauer (eds.), *Innere Sicherheit, Menschenwürde, Gentechnologie* (Frankfurt a.M.: Peter Lang, 2005), pp. 65–79 at 70 (arguing that human dignity is a means to make weak arguments appear strong).

202 For a detailed analysis, see Petersen, *Verhältnismäßigkeit*, pp. 187–9.

203 BVerfGE 109, 279.

affected interests.[204] In both judgments, the court thus only seemed to rely on absolute legal standards of review. Implicitly, however, it resorted to balancing. The conflict between individual liberty and collective security was thus not discussed openly, but hidden behind categorical arguments. The main reasons for this strategy are legitimacy concerns. The judges had the impression that they enjoy greater legitimacy to base politically controversial decisions on categorical arguments, rather than on balancing.[205]

7.2 Deductive Reasoning

A second alternative to proportionality considerations that is often used in the jurisprudence of the German Constitutional Court is deductive reasoning. This mode of reasoning is particularly prevalent when it comes to the status of public servants and the review of tax law.[206] One example is a decision from March 1977 on special child benefits for public servants.[207] When the government coalition cut these, the public servants still benefited from the, albeit less generous, general child-benefit payments that were addressed to all citizens. The court held that this legislative reform violated the alimentation principle for public servants contained in the German Constitution. It derived the alimentation principle from Art. 33 para. 5 of the constitution. This provision protects the institution of the public service "with due regard to the traditional principles". In particular, the court argued that the salary public servants could claim according to this constitutional standard depended "evidently" on the size of the family and the higher costs entailed by having to care for a bigger family.[208]

[204] Niels Petersen, 'Auf dem Weg zur zweckrationalen Relativität des Menschenwürdeschutzes' (2004) 37 *Kritische Justiz* 316–26 at 324; Dederer, 'Garantie der Menschenwürde', 114–5; Rolf Gröschner and Oliver W. Lembcke, 'Dignitas absoluta. Ein kritischer Kommentar zum Absolutheitsanspruch der Würde', in Rolf Gröschner and Oliver W. Lembcke (eds.), *Das Dogma der Unantastbarkeit* (Tübingen: Mohr Siebeck, 2009), pp. 1–24 at 19; Teifke, *Menschenwürde*, p. 121; Möllers, 'Legalität', p. 394; Baldus, 'Menschenwürde und Absolutheitsthese', 538.

[205] See also Stephen Gardbaum, 'The Myth and the Reality of American Constitutional Exceptionalism' (2008) 107 *Michigan Law Review* 391–466 at 426 (observing a similar tendency in the jurisprudence of the US Supreme Court).

[206] See BVerfGE 11, 203 at 210–4; 44, 249; 72, 155 at 172–3; 81, 363 at 376; 82, 60; 87, 153; 99, 216; 99, 246; 99, 300; 117, 372 at 382–3; 119, 247; 120, 125 at 156–7; 130, 263; BVerfG, 2 BvL 17/09 (5 May 2015); 2 BvL 19/09 (17 November 2015).

[207] BVerfGE 44, 249.

[208] Id. at 267.

Consequently, the alimentation principle required that public servants should benefit from the same standard of living independent of the size of their family.[209] The court then analysed the historical development of salaries for public servants and concluded that the general child benefits were not sufficient to compensate for income disadvantages of families with many children.[210] However, it is not clear how the Constitutional Court derives its normative standard. The constitution does not contain an explicit requirement that the salary of public servants should be "family neutral".[211] Instead, it seems that the decision on the size of the family is a private decision of every couple that is unrelated to the specific profession. One might argue that higher child benefits create incentives to have more babies. However, even though such incentives might be socially desirable in an aging society, the decision on financial incentives in family policy should be left to parliament and not to the courts. The German Constitutional Court also used the alimentation principle in further decisions in order to justify the inadequacy of the basic salary for associate professors at German public universities[212] or the remuneration of certain judges[213] and public servants.[214] These decisions also raise the question of whether the matter of professorial remuneration is not rather a matter that should be left to political decision-making.

In several decisions concerning matters of tax law, the Constitutional Court developed the principle that the salary should be tax-free to the extent that it ensured the minimum standard of living.[215] The principle dates back to a decision of the German Constitutional Court from May 1990.[216] The decision concerned an application lodged against a statute that had reduced child benefits for individuals with high incomes. The Constitutional Court held that this reduction of child benefits violated the guarantee of human dignity contained in Art. 1 of the constitution. From this guarantee, the court derived the normative requirement that the financial amount necessary to allow a minimum standard of living had to be tax-exempt for each family member.[217] This requirement was

209 Id. This standard was confirmed in later judgments; see BVerfGE 81, 363 at 376; 99, 300, 314–16.

210 BVerfGE 44, 249 at 276–8.

211 BVerfGE 99, 300 at 316.

212 BVerfGE 130, 263.

213 BVerfG, 2 BvL 17/09 (5 May 2015).

214 BVerfG, 2 BvL 19/09 (17 November 2015).

215 BVerfGE 82, 60 at 84; 87, 153 at 169; 99, 216 at 233; 99, 246 at 264–5; 120, 125 at 156–7.

216 BVerfGE 82, 60.

217 Id. at 85.

independent of the level of the total salary of the taxpayer.[218] Based on this requirement, the court argued, the legislature had an obligation to compensate for costs caused by children either through social benefits or through tax exemptions.[219] When the court applied these requirements to the child benefits paid to individuals with high incomes, it found that the benefits were insufficient.[220]

It is remarkable that the court based its reasoning on the guarantee of human dignity and the requirement to ensure a minimum standard of living for every individual. Although these concerns seem to be intuitively plausible, it seems odd that the decision exclusively benefited people with high incomes. However, the court did not justify why the amount covering the minimum standard of living had to be tax-exempt, even though the salary in question transgressed this minimum standard of living by far. When we try to explain these decisions, the theories of political economy might give us certain insights: Almost all judges of the Constitutional Court are public servants; after serving for the Constitutional Court, they usually return to their previous jobs as university professors or career judges; and most of them are family fathers. This shows us that judges are not always neutral. When their own interests are concerned, decisions will be biased. However, it is interesting to note that the court did not base its decisions on proportionality considerations, but rather on deductive reasoning.

7.3 *Conclusions*

In this section, we have considered two alternatives to proportionality reasoning that are at times employed by the German Federal Constitutional Court. On the one hand, the court used categorical forms of argumentation in a couple of landmark cases. On the other hand, it used deductive reasoning to extend certain welfare benefits for the middle and upper middle class. It is remarkable that the court refrained from proportionality reasoning in both categories of cases. In the two cases based on categorical reasoning, the court had to deal with politically highly controversial questions. By referring to human dignity, it wanted to give its argument a certain normative strength justifying why the court interfered in these sensitive matters. However, by relying on categorical arguments, the court

218 BVerfGE 82, 60 at 86.
219 BVerfGE 82, 60 at 84.
220 BVerfGE 82, 60 at 91–7.

veiled the difficult normative implications of the argument that would have been transparent if the court had relied on balancing instead.

The extension of welfare benefits through deductive reasoning is normatively highly problematic because it primarily benefits the middle and upper-middle class, that is, social groups whose interests are fairly well represented in the political process. Again, the Constitutional Court did not rely on proportionality considerations but, rather, on deductive reasoning. This suggests that, contrary to what some critics argue, proportionality is not the primary instrument of judicial activism for apex courts. Instead, if they want to hide political intentions, courts rather resort to modes of reasoning that are less transparent than proportionality, such as categorical argumentation or deductive reasoning.

8. The Review of Legislative Rationality

In the previous chapter, we saw that courts avoid open balancing. The German Constitutional Court was the only one of the three analysed courts that used balancing extensively, but even the German court was initially reluctant. This chapter sought to examine whether courts use alternatives to balancing as means to introduce implicit balancing. The analysis has shown that none of the alternative arguments is totally free from implicit balancing. This is particularly obvious in the rational-connection and less-restrictive-means stage of the proportionality test. If these prongs of the test are supposed to have some teeth, courts cannot avoid implicit balancing.

However, this does not mean that courts use these tests as instruments of judicial activism. Instead, we have seen that they can be perceived as frameworks for reviewing legislative rationality. The different arguments were used to correct political market failures. Courts found that a measure lacked a legitimate aim if it was based on problematic stereotypes. The lack of a rational connection, the existence of a less-restrictive alternative measure or the inconsistency of a legislative measure usually indicate that the legislature pursued additional purposes to the ones that were explicitly mentioned to justify the measure. Procedural requirements and determinacy considerations are supposed to increase the accountability of the legislature and the administration implementing the legislation. Finally, the protection of legitimate interests usually protects the interests of a small group that is strongly affected by a change in legislation and whose interests were often not taken into account in the legislative procedure.

However, not all modes of reasoning aim at a review of legislative rationality. Instead, we saw that the German Constitutional Court sometimes uses categorical arguments or bases its decisions on deductive reasoning. Both argumentation categories hide normative problems, rather than discuss them extensively. In particular, deductive reasoning allows the constitutional court to engage in active social policymaking. Our analysis thus leads to a nuanced picture. Constitutional courts do not totally refrain from judicial activism. However, it is noteworthy that these tendencies of judicial activism in the German constitutional jurisprudence are not based on proportionality considerations, but rather on alternative forms of reasoning, in particular traditional norm interpretation.

6

Rationalising Balancing

In Chapter 4, we saw that none of the three analysed courts totally avoids balancing. However, the frequency of using balancing is different. Whereas balancing has become the predominant argumentation framework for overturning legislation in the German fundamental rights adjudication since the late 1970s, the other two courts have been more reluctant to rely on balancing. Both in Canada and South Africa, balancing decisions have remained the exception. This chapter will take a closer look at the content of these balancing decisions. When courts use balancing, do they use it as an instrument of judicial self-empowerment? Or can we characterise the balancing jurisprudence in a different way?

The chapter will proceed in three steps: In all three jurisdictions we find balancing decisions that deal with criminal law or criminal procedure provisions (section 1). Outside the field of criminal law, the Canadian Supreme Court and the South African Constitutional Court rely on balancing only very exceptionally. The German Constitutional Court uses balancing more often. However, the vast majority of cases fit into one of four categories, which have, as I will argue, the function to rationalise balancing (section 2). Finally, there are only a few judgments in Germany and Canada that do not fit into one of these two groups – they neither try to rationalise balancing, nor do they deal with a criminal law or criminal procedure provisions. However, these latter cases are outliers (section 3). Overall, balancing is much less problematic than the normative critique suggests. Courts do not use balancing as a means to second-guess legislative value decisions. Instead, it is an instrument for reviewing the rationality of the legislative procedure (section 4).

1. Balancing and the Review of Criminal Law and Criminal Procedure Measures

All three analysed courts occasionally use balancing as an instrument to invalidate criminal-law and criminal-procedure measures. As we have seen, the South African landmark decision in *Makwanyane*, in which the constitutional court developed the proportionality test and heavily relied on balancing, concerned the abolition of the death penalty. Most of the Canadian cases, in which the Supreme Court resorted to balancing in order to overturn a piece of legislation, also concerned criminal law or criminal procedure. Finally, the German Constitutional Court has issued several decisions concerning criminal procedure based on balancing considerations over the last one-and-a-half decades. I argue that balancing is used so frequently in the criminal-law and criminal-procedure context because there are probably few other fields where the danger of the legislature acting disproportionately is as pronounced. The addressees of these measures are usually underrepresented in the political process, so the political incentives are systematically skewed.

1.1 South Africa

All four judgments in which the South African Constitutional Court relied on balancing in order to overturn a piece of legislation both concerned provisions of criminal law and criminal procedure.[1] In *Makwanyane*, the court held that the death penalty violated the South African Constitution. The court based its decision on two arguments.[2] On the one hand, it argued that long prison sentences were a less restrictive means regarding deterrence because the government had failed to produce any evidence that capital punishment had a higher deterring effect than long prison sentences.[3] On the other hand, the court held that the death penalty was a disproportionate means to achieve retribution. As we have seen, *Makwanyane* was in certain respects an atypical case.[4] Even though the court seemed to challenge the legislature by overturning a piece of legislation, the decision was very much in the interest of the political elites.

The decision in *Niemand* concerned a provision of the criminal procedure act that allowed designating even minor offenders as "habitual criminals" if the Court found that the person in question "habitually commits offences".[5] A person designated as a habitual criminal had to remain in

[1] See *S v. Makwanyane* 1995 (3) SA 391 (CC); *S v. Niemand* 2002 (1) SA 21 (CC); *Ex parte Minister of Safety and Security: In Re S v. Walters* 2002 (4) SA 613 (CC); *De Vos N.O. v. Minister of Justice and Constitutional Development* 2015 (2) SACR 217 (CC).

[2] See for more details, ch. 4, section 4.1.

[3] *S v. Makwanyane* 1995 (3) SA 391 (CC) at para. 127.

[4] See ch. 4, section 4.4.

[5] *S v. Niemand* 2002 (1) SA 21 (CC).

prison for at least seven years, without a maximum period being provided by the legislation. The court held that the absence of a maximum sentence was "grossly disproportionate", considering that the crimes leading to the designation did not necessarily need to be violent or pose a danger to society.[6]

In *Ex parte Minister of Safety and Security*, the court invalidated a statute that allowed everybody to kill a suspect if they could not arrest him or otherwise prevent him from fleeing.[7] This authorisation to kill a fleeing suspect was not limited to major crimes. Instead, it also applied to relatively minor offences, like pickpocketing.[8] For this reason, the court held that the provision was manifestly disproportionate.[9] However, it did not totally disallow the killing of fleeing suspects. Rather, Justice Kriegler, writing the judgment for a unanimous court, pointed out that there may be circumstances in which it might be justified to kill a fleeing suspect, in particular when the fugitive poses a threat to the people on the scene or to the public at large.[10] The court thus struck a compromise. It generally accepted the legislative purpose, but limited the scope of the measure in order to correct the grossly disproportionate effects.

Finally, the court partly invalidated a provision dealing with offenders who were not criminally responsible because of a mental illness in *De Vos*.[11] According to the legislation, mentally ill individuals had to be detained in a psychiatric hospital or in a prison. However, the court found that imprisonment was disproportionate even as a "stop-gap" measure if the accused was unlikely to cause severe harm to himself or others.[12] The court also held that a further provision according to which mentally ill accused persons necessarily had to be detained in a psychiatric institution even if they only committed no act or a minor offence was disproportionate.[13] Certainly, such a detention might in some cases be justified.[14] However, the existence of a mental disability alone could not lead to detention just because the concerned person came into contact with the criminal justice system.[15]

6 Id. at para. 19.
7 *Ex parte Minister of Safety and Security* 2002 (4) SA 613 (CC).
8 See id. at para. 41.
9 Id. at para. 46.
10 Id. at para. 39.
11 *De Vos N.O. v. Minister of Justice and Constitutional Development* 2015 (2) SACR 217 (CC).
12 Id. at paras. 44–8.
13 Id. at paras. 53–9.
14 Id. at para. 57.
15 Id. at para. 58.

1.2 Canada

In Canada, the majority of cases in which the Supreme Court relied on balancing also concern criminal law provisions.[16] The decision in *Logan* dealt with a norm attributing criminal responsibility to individuals who had not committed the criminal act.[17] According to section 21 (2) of the Canadian Criminal Code, persons who agree to commit a criminal act are criminally liable for an offence committed by one of their partners if they "ought to have known that the commission of the offence would be a probable consequence" of the commonly planned offence. The court held that this provision unduly impaired section 7 of the Canadian Charter because it only required negligent conduct for the conviction of an intentional act.[18] The court argued that this measure "renders the infringement too serious and outweighs the legislative objective".[19]

In *Sharpe*, the court dealt with a provision criminalising the possession of child pornography.[20] It acknowledged that child pornography posed a "reasoned harm to children", so that the criminalisation of its possession was a pressing and substantial objective[21] and that the law was proportionate for the vast majority of its applications.[22] However, it held that the provision was disproportionate with regard to two rather peripheral categories of cases. On the one hand, the court argued that self-created works of child pornography that were only used for private purposes did not endanger children in any way.[23] It thus concluded that the criminalisation of the possession of such material "falls perilously close to criminalising the mere articulation of thought."[24] On the other hand, the criminalisation was also regarded as disproportionate with regard to visual recordings that the person made of him- or herself alone and that were only intended for personal use.[25]

Finally, in *Bedford*, the court invalidated parts of three provisions of the Canadian Criminal Code prohibiting, *inter alia*, to keep a "bawdy-house".[26]

16 See *R. v. Logan* [1990] 2 S.C.R. 731; *R. v. Sharpe* [2001] 1 S.C.R. 45; *Canada (Attorney General) v. Bedford* [2013] 3 S.C.R. 1101.
17 *R. v. Logan* [1990] 2 S.C.R. 731.
18 Id. at 747.
19 Id. at 747.
20 *R. v. Sharpe* [2001] 1 S.C.R. 45.
21 Id. at para. 82.
22 Id. at para. 103.
23 Id. at paras. 107–8.
24 Id. at para. 108.
25 Id. at para. 109.
26 *Canada (Attorney General) v. Bedford* [2013] 3 S.C.R. 1101.

These provisions only regulated the working conditions of prostitutes. However, selling sex for money was not unlawful. The prohibition of brothels had the effect that prostitution could only be offered in two ways: Either as street prostitution or through "out-calls", where the prostitute meets the client at a designated location, such as the client's home.[27] The court held that the criminal provisions negatively affected the safety of prostitutes and thus restricted their right to life, liberty and security, as guaranteed by section 7 of the Charter.[28] The purpose of the bawdy-house provision was to prevent nuisances caused by brothels to neighbours.[29] The judges argued that the identified harm was "grossly disproportionate to the deterrence of community disruption" so that they held that the provision was unconstitutional.[30]

In both, *Logan* and *Sharpe*, the Canadian Supreme Court only invalidated a part of the challenged criminal provision. In *Logan*, the judges found the attribution provision only to be unconstitutional as far as it concerned negligent conduct. In *Sharpe*, the court confirmed the criminalisation of possessing child pornography in general and only overturned the statute with regard to two rather "peripheral applications".[31] Furthermore, the reasoning in *Sharpe* is very close to what the court did in other cases when it held provisions to be overbroad.[32] In *Bedford*, by contrast, the court did not strike a compromise overturning the "bawdy-house" provision. However, the decision concerned the protection of prostitutes, arguably one of the most underrepresented groups of society.

1.3 Germany

In the last fifteen years, the Constitutional Court issued several judgments concerning criminal procedure provisions that were, at least in part, based on balancing.[33] These decisions primarily concerned conditions for police or intelligence surveillance measures. One example is

[27] Id. at 1134.
[28] Id. at 1133–7.
[29] Id. at 1154–5.
[30] Id. at 1156.
[31] See *R. v. Sharpe* [2001] 1 S.C.R. 45 at para. 2.
[32] See ch. 5, section 2.
[33] See Entscheidungen des Bundesverfassungsgerichts [BVerfGE] vol. 100, p. 313 at 384–5; vol. 109, p. 279 at 347–9; vol. 120, p. 274 at 326–31; vol. 125, p. 260 at 329–30; vol. 133, p. 277 at 347–50, 363–4. See also BVerfGE 128, 282; 129, 269, which dealt with the implementation of care orders.

the telecommunications surveillance judgment.[34] The judgment dealt with a provision that authorised the German intelligence service to monitor international phone calls. Surveillance could be authorised for the prevention or detection of certain explicitly designated crimes. The list included, inter alia, the prevention of international terrorist attacks, and the proliferation of weapons of war.[35] One of the listed crimes was also money forgery. The court argued that money forgery did not have the same weight as the other offences contained in the list.[36] Consequently, the judges found that the inclusion of money forgery was disproportionate.[37]

In the eavesdropping judgment, the Constitutional Court corrected the list of offences that allowed for a bugging operation.[38] It held that the eavesdropping of an apartment was inconsistent with the constitution if it was authorised for an offence that merited a maximum prison sentence of less than five years.[39] In its decisions on the surveillance of electronic communication, the court argued that the surveillance measure was only consistent with the constitution if it sought to protect an extremely important public interest.[40] Finally, the court held in its judgment concerning the storage of telecommunication data that data could only be stored if there was reasonable suspicion that the affected person was involved in a severe crime.[41]

In all these judgments, the court relied on balancing. It evaluated the legitimacy of the public purpose and found that a part of the pursued purpose did not have sufficient weight to justify the restriction of the affected individual rights of the potential suspects. However, it is important to note that the court in all cases only overturned a small part of the legislation, while upholding the major portion of the statute and thus sanctioning the fundamental purpose in principle. The corrections were rather at the margins. In a couple of cases, the Court discarded a few offences from the list of crimes that authorise a surveillance measure. In other cases, it slightly intensified the conditions for a police intervention. But it never prohibited the intervention as a whole.

[34] BVerfGE 100, 313.
[35] See id. at 318.
[36] Id. at 384–5.
[37] Id. at 385.
[38] BVerfGE 109, 279.
[39] Id. at 347–9.
[40] BVerfGE 120, 274 at 326–31.
[41] BVerfGE 125, 260 at 329–30.

1.4 *Criminal Law and Underrepresentation in the Political Process*

In Chapter 1, we have seen that it is one task of constitutional courts to correct pathologies of the political process. Such pathologies occur, in particular, when the political elite has only a limited responsiveness to the interests of the affected individuals.[42] This is often the case in matters of criminal and criminal procedure law. Suspects of criminal offences usually come from a socio-economic group that lacks voice in the political process. The majority of the population rather fears to be the victim of a crime than to be subject of a criminal investigation. Being "soft on crime" will not bring parties any additional votes. In contrast, a tough stance on crime can sometimes win elections.

The South African government implicitly admitted this concern in the procedure of *Minister of Home Affairs v. National Institute of Crime Prevention*.[43] The case dealt with the question of whether prisoners could be deprived of their right to vote. In its argument, the government claimed that "if prisoners are allowed to vote that will send a message to the public that the government is soft on crime."[44] In some cases, there are additional factors contributing to the vulnerability of the targeted group. This is particularly obvious in the *Bedford* decision of the Canadian Supreme Court, in which the challenged regulations deemed preventing nuisances for neighbours more important than the protection of prostitutes.[45]

Certainly, criminal sanctions are an essential part of every legal order. However, this does not disburden the legislature from striking an appropriate balance with regard to the severity of the sanctions and the intrusiveness of police measures. Courts exercising constitutional review thus have a vital function to counterbalance excesses of the legislature in this respect. It is exactly this function that the analysed courts assume when they overturn criminal law and criminal procedure legislation. In most cases, however, the courts refrained from imposing significant costs on the political branches. They usually did not prohibit the criminal measures in principle, but only required corrections at the margins.

[42] See ch. 1, section 2.

[43] *Minister of Home Affairs v. National Institute for Crime Prevention and the Re-Integration of Offenders (NICRO)* 2005 (3) SA 280 (CC).

[44] See id. at para. 55.

[45] *Canada (Attorney General) v. Bedford* [2013] 3 S.C.R. 1101.

2. Rationalising Balancing in German Constitutional Jurisprudence

Although the focus on criminal law and criminal procedure explains almost all of the explicit balancing decisions of the Canadian Supreme Court and the South African Constitutional Court, it only covers a minor fraction of the balancing cases in Germany. When developing the hypotheses for this study, I assumed that courts try to rationalise balancing when they rely on it to challenge a piece of legislation.[46] Accordingly, they signal that they do not use balancing as a cover for political decision-making, but as an instrument to review the rationality of the legislative process.

If we examine the balancing decisions of the German Constitutional Court, we can see patterns of such a rationalisation of balancing. More than 85 percent can be put into one of the following four categories. First, in some decisions, the court corrects the attribution of financial burdens. In these cases, the court acknowledges the legitimacy of the legislative goal, but shifts the financial burden from the affected group to the principal beneficiaries of the measure. Second, the court finds measures to be disproportionate if they are not sufficiently tailored to achieve the purpose they are supposed to achieve. There is usually an insufficient fit between measure and purpose if the effectiveness of the measure is doubtful or if there is an alternative, less restrictive means to achieve the same purpose that is – if at all – only slightly less effective.

Third, the court resorts to consistency arguments in the balancing test. It holds that a measure is disproportionate because it is inconsistent. The final category consists of cases in which the court corrects individual hardship. In these cases, the court does not put the overall purpose of the individual rights restriction in doubt. It rather requires the legislature to introduce an exception for specific groups on which the measure has a particularly severe impact. It is important to note that these four groups are not exclusive. Rather, some judgments may fall into two or even more categories.

2.1 *Shifting Financial Burdens*

In several cases, the Federal Constitutional Court has used the balancing step of the proportionality test to shift the financial burden of a measure.[47]

[46] See ch. 3, section 1.2.

[47] See BVerfGE 31, 229 at 243–4; 47, 285 at 322–5; 49, 382 at 400–2; 53, 336 at 349–50; 58, 137 at 149–50; 68, 155 at 173–5; 77, 308 at 337; 81, 156 at 197–9; 85, 226 at 235–7; 97, 228 at 262–3; 99, 202 at 212–14; 100, 226 at 243; 101, 54 at 99–100.

The court acknowledged the legislative goal in principle, but demanded the legislature to shift the financial burden from the affected individuals to the principal beneficiaries. In this category of cases, the court does not compare incommensurable values. Instead, it tries to find a common currency by granting the affected individuals financial compensation for their loss of freedom.[48]

The most famous decision in this respect is the repository copy decision from July 1981.[49] In this case, the Federal Constitutional Court dealt with a statute of the state Hesse, according to which a publisher had to cede a free copy of every printed matter to specifically designated state libraries. The court acknowledged the purpose of the regulation to give every citizen free access to the printed matters published in the state of Hesse.[50] Nevertheless, it argued that the obligation could in some cases be disproportionate if the publisher did not receive financial compensation.[51] The legislature did not need to provide for any compensation if the value of one single copy was negligible compared to the total number of printed copies. However, the complainant had published very expensive books with art designs. There were only a few copies of each edition. Some of the editions had less fewer than 100 copies. The Constitutional Court argued that in such a case the obligation to cede several copies to state libraries without financial compensation imposed severe hardship on the complainant.[52] Consequently, it asked the legislature to pay compensation to publishers if the repository requirement constituted a particular financial burden.[53]

There are also other decisions in which the court granted financial compensation to affected individuals if the legislature had restricted their individual rights for the benefit of the general public. In one case, the court overturned a regulation of notary fees, which had exempted certain notarial acts from being chargeable.[54] It held that the notaries had to be accorded proper compensation that at least covered their costs. In other decisions, the court found obligations of employers to grant paid leave to their employees for activities in the public interest to be inconsistent with the constitution.[55] It argued that the legislature could order employers to

[48] See Engel, 'Delineating the Proper Scope of Government', 194.
[49] BVerfGE 58, 137.
[50] Id. at 149.
[51] Id. at 149–51.
[52] Id. at 150.
[53] See id. at 152.
[54] BVerfGE 47, 285 at 322–5.
[55] BVerfGE 77, 308 at 337; 85, 226 at 235–7.

grant leave to their employees in the public interest. However, as the main beneficiary of this obligation was the general public, it was disproportionate to make the leave a paid one. The task to pay financial compensation to the employees should rather be attributed to the state.

In the analysed decisions, the Federal Constitutional Court did not perform a cost-benefit analysis in which it compared the importance of competing aims and the extent to which they were affected by a specific measure. Instead, it shifted the financial burden of a measure to the group that drew the most benefit from it. If the general public wants to have access to all printed matters that are published in a state, it seems only fair if it also bears a part of the financial burden of this measure. Likewise, if the state wants to exempt certain notarial acts from being charged for social reasons, the main beneficiary is equally the general public. For this reason, it seems appropriate that the state at least compensates the notaries for the costs that occur to them.

However, this line of jurisprudence does not require the state to compensate all costs incurred by individuals for public-regarding regulation. On the contrary, this question raises complex normative issues.[56] It should only be mentioned that the German Constitutional Court has not developed any standards about when to shift costs from one group to another. It seems that the decisive criteria are the intensity of the financial burden for the affected individual and the connection between burden and purpose.[57] The structure of the proportionality principle allows the court a flexible approach to this question, according to which it can take into account the circumstances of each individual case without having to elaborate general standards.

The decisions that have been analysed so far only concerned a vertical shifting of financial burdens to the state. However, there are also a few cases in which the court re-allocated the costs to a different societal group.[58] One example of such horizontal burden shifting is a ruling on the

[56] See Mark Kelman, *Strategy or Principle? – The Choice between Regulation and Taxation* (Ann Arbor: University of Michigan Press, 1999); Samuel Issacharoff, 'Bearing the Costs' (2000) 53 *Stanford Law Review* 519–37.

[57] However, a closer examination of this issue would require an analysis of the decisions, in which the court had refused to grant financial compensation, which has not been done comprehensively for the purpose of this study.

[58] See BVerfGE 31, 229 at 243–4 (exception for textbooks in intellectual property protection); 49, 382 at 400–2 (exception for churches in intellectual property protection); 101, 54 at 99–100 (compensation for the use of real estate that had been expropriated in the German Democratic Republic).

so-called textbook privilege from July 1971.[59] The statute that gave rise to the dispute allowed publishers of textbooks to reprint texts and sheet music free of charge and without permission of the authors, even if the reprinted passages were, in principle, protected by intellectual property rules. The judges acknowledged that the reprinting of the texts and music without the permission of the authors was justified in order to familiarise students with the cultural heritage.[60] However, they argued that the authors were, in principle, entitled to the economic benefit of their work.[61] They could not identify a particular public interest that could justify a restriction of the authors' compensation.[62] Consequently, the court held that the exclusion of the authors' claim for compensation was inconsistent with the property clause of the German Constitution.

2.2 *Lacking Fit between Measure and Purpose*

The second category concerns cases in which the Federal Constitutional Court finds an insufficient fit between measure and purpose.[63] In many of these cases, the court bases its decision on arguments resembling rational connection or less-restrictive-means considerations. The effectiveness of both the less-restrictive-means and the rational connection test has limits. According to the German interpretation, a measure is already rationally connected to a purpose if it marginally contributes to the promotion of the latter.[64] A severe restriction of an individual right would thus pass the rational connection stage even if it has only a minimal positive impact. However, the low effectiveness has to be taken into account at the balancing stage.

There are several cases in which the court overturned legislation because it had doubts with regard to the effectiveness of the measure.[65] In a ruling

[59] BVerfGE 31, 229.

[60] Id. at 242.

[61] Id. at 243.

[62] Id. at 244–6.

[63] See BVerfGE 34, 165 at 198–9; 55, 134 at 143; 61, 291 at 318; 74, 203 at 216–7; 79, 256 at 272–3; 87, 114 at 148–9; 92, 26 at 45; 108, 82 at 109–11; 112, 255 at 266–8; 113, 348 at 387–8; 115, 1 at 20–24; 117, 202 at 229–39; 119, 59 at 87–9; 121, 30 at 64–7; 121, 175 at 194–202; 128, 109 at 130–6; 135, 48 at 68–76, 84.

[64] See Grabitz, 'Grundsatz der Verhältnismäßigkeit', 572; Detlef Merten, 'Verhältnismäßigkeitsgrundsatz', in Detlef Merten and Hans-Jürgen Papier (eds.), *Handbuch der Grundrechte. Band III. Grundrechte in Deutschland: Allgemeine Lehren II* (Heidelberg: C. F. Müller, 2009), ch. 68 at para. 65; Horst Dreier, 'Vorbemerkungen vor Artikel 1 GG', in Horst Dreier (ed.), *Grundgesetz-Kommentar. Band I* (Tübingen: Mohr Siebeck, 3 edn. 2013), Vorb. at para. 147.

[65] See BVerfGE 87, 114 at 148–50; 92, 26 at 45; 112, 255 at 266–8; 121, 30 at 64–7.

from September 1992, the court held that the rent control for allotment gardens was inconsistent with the property clause of the constitution.[66] The provision under review determined a controlled rent for allotments, which was far below market rates for comparable recreational facilities.[67] The legislature had justified the rent control with the protection of socially disadvantaged groups. However, the court found that the allotments were predominantly used by the middle class.[68] Consequently, the judges had doubts regarding the effectiveness of the measure. If the legislature had intended to support socially disadvantaged people, it could have targeted them directly.[69] However, the measure was not filtered out at the rational connection stage of the proportionality test. Instead, the court held that it was disproportionate at the balancing stage.[70]

At the less-restrictive-means stage, the problem is comparable. In theory, judges can only qualify those measures as potentially less restrictive means that are at least as effective in promoting the pursued purpose as the measure under review. Consequently, a measure restricting individual rights will pass the less-restrictive-means stage if it is at least questionable whether less-restrictive alternatives are indeed equally effective. However, the existence of a slightly less effective alternative measure is again a factor at the balancing stage. In several cases, the court found a measure to be disproportionate if a less restrictive alternative was available even though the alternative measure was slightly less effective.[71]

An illustrative example is the hoof-care decision of July 2007.[72] The decision dealt with a statute that required hoof caretakers and hoof technicians to have the same qualifications as a farrier. The legislature intended to confide the hoof care to the profession of the farrier because farriers had enjoyed a broad education and mastered the whole spectrum of hoof-care techniques so that they were able to choose the indicated method. However, the court argued that theoretical knowledge in the different hoof-care techniques was sufficient to achieve the legislative purpose.[73] Such theoretical knowledge enabled hoof caretakers and hoof technicians

66 BVerfGE 87, 114 at 148–50.
67 Id. at 148.
68 Id. at 149.
69 Id. at 150.
70 Id. at 148, 150.
71 See BVerfGE 34, 165 at 198–9; 117, 348 at 388; 119, 59 at 87–9; 121, 175 at 194–202; 128, 109 at 130–6.
72 BVerfGE 119, 59.
73 Id. at 88.

to refer an animal to a farrier if they lacked the sufficient practical knowledge for the indicated treatment.

Asking the hoof caretakers and hoof technicians to pass through the full practical education of farriers did not, in the eyes of the court, have any additional advantages. The court thus disputed the assumption of the legislature that requiring the full education of a farrier would increase the quality of the hoof care services in Germany. The judges supported their considerations through an analogy with the status of nonmedical practitioners. These nonmedical practitioners were not required to have medical training. Nevertheless, they were expected to refer patients to medical doctors if the treatment of the patient required medical training.[74] Consequently, the court judged the challenged training requirement to be disproportionate because there was a less restrictive alternative available even if this alternative was possibly not quite as effective.

In other decisions, the court overturned overbroad legislation.[75] In these cases, the court raised doubts concerning the accuracy of legislative standardisation. An illustrative example is a decision from February 1987.[76] The decision dealt with a statute that excluded unemployment benefits for two weeks if the affected individual had not filed an application in time after losing his or her job. The legislature had intended to prevent abusive filings for unemployment benefits. However, the court was not convinced that missing the application deadline was a sufficient indication for abusive behaviour.[77] The judges argued that people could miss deadlines for a broad variety of reasons. Consequently, they found that there was no sufficient connection between the fact of missing the deadline and the danger of abusive conduct. Therefore, they held that the exclusion from unemployment benefits was disproportionate.[78]

If a regulation is overbroad, the legislature can usually repair it by framing the statutory criteria more precisely or by carving out exceptions. Sometimes, however, erroneous assumptions may put a whole regulatory scheme into doubt.[79] This can be illustrated by a challenge of a provision of the statute on transsexuals leading to a decision of the Constitutional Court in December 2005.[80] The statute on transsexuals made a differentiation

[74] Id. at 88–9.

[75] See BVerfGE 55, 134 at 143; 74, 203 at 216–7; 79, 256 at 272–3; 108, 82 at 109–11.

[76] BVerfGE 74, 203.

[77] Id. at 216.

[78] Id. at 216–7.

[79] See BVerfGE 115, 1 at 20–4; 117, 202 at 234–9.

[80] BVerfGE 115, 1.

between a "major" and a "minor" solution for sex reassignment. The "minor" solution basically consisted of a simple change of the first name. In contrast, the "major" solution included sex reassignment surgery, as well as a hormone replacement therapy. In the official records, the sex was only changed if the individual opted for the sex reassignment surgery. Therefore, a male-to-female transsexual who adopted a female first name under the "minor" solution remained a man according to the official records.

Consequently, such a male-to-female transsexual could only enter into a (mixed-gender) marriage with a woman even though both partners perceived the partnership to be a same-sex partnership. Furthermore, the marriage had the automatic consequence that the change of the transsexual's first name was automatically revoked. The complainant was a male-to-female transsexual who had adopted a female first name. When she married a woman, she was notified by the authorities that her female first name was revoked and that she had to return to her original male first name.

In its decision, the constitutional court overturned the provision that led to an automatic revocation of the changed first name after marriage. It argued that the legislative conception was based on erroneous empirical premises. The legislature had assumed that the change of the first name under the "minor" solution was only a transitional phase that finally led to sex reassignment therapy. Under this conception, entering into a marriage was consequently perceived as an indication that the transsexual had returned to his or her original sexual identity.

The judges argued that the assumption that the change of the first name was just a transitional stage was not confirmed by recent scientific studies.[81] Many transsexuals felt that they belonged to the opposite sex without necessarily seeking to change their biological sex through a reassignment surgery. Furthermore, the court found the assumption that marriage was an indication for a return to the original sexual identity unconvincing. Many of the transsexuals had a homosexual orientation. Consequently, entering into a mixed-gender marriage was the only way to confirm the partnership officially according to the legal situation.[82] The revocation of the change of the first name thus imposed a disproportionate burden on the complainant.[83]

81 Id. at 21–2.
82 Id. at 17.
83 Id. at 20.

2.3 Consistency Arguments in the Balancing Test

In some judgments, the Federal Constitutional Court bases the result of the balancing test on consistency arguments, or uses consistency at least as an auxiliary consideration.[84] Consequently, a measure is considered to be disproportionate either because it is inconsistent, or because inconsistency is at least seen as an important indication for the lack of proportionality. One of these decisions dealt with a provision establishing conditions for the termination of rental contracts about allotment gardens.[85] The lessor could only cancel a rental agreement under two conditions: either if the lessee had grossly violated his or her contractual obligations, or if the piece of land was absolutely essential for the fulfilment of public purposes.[86] The court held that this provision disproportionately restricted the property of the lessors of such allotments.[87]

In the balancing test, the court referred to a consistency argument. Originally, the strong protection of lessees had been supposed to secure the alimentation of the general population during the Second World War.[88] Allotments were predominantly used for food production. However, by the time the complaint reached the court, allotments had had a different purpose for a long time already: Most lessees used them for recreational purposes.[89] Although the court acknowledged that this recreational use was of significant public interest, it argued that the recreational purpose did not justify stronger protection for lessees of allotments than for lessees of flats.[90] Without doubt, the rental of flats had a higher social significance than the rental of allotments.[91] Consequently, the judges held that the reviewed provision totally neglected the interests of the owners of the allotments so that it was disproportionate.[92]

Consistency considerations also played a pivotal role in a March 1988 decision, which overturned a provision of the German Civil Procedure Code.[93] The provision required the public announcement of an

[84] See BVerfGE 52, 1 at 36; 52, 357 at 366; 69, 209 at 219; 78, 77 at 86–7; 84, 133 at 156; 90, 263 at 273; 104, 357 at 368; 108, 82 at 120; 121, 317 at 360–8; 128, 157 at 177–83.
[85] BVerfGE 52, 1.
[86] See id. at 4.
[87] Id. at 30–6.
[88] See id. at 34.
[89] See id. at 35.
[90] Id. at 36.
[91] Id.
[92] Id.
[93] BVerfGE 78, 77.

incapacitation if the reason for this incapacitation was either dissipation or alcoholism. The court held that the announcement requirement was disproportionate because of its stigmatising effect on the affected individual.[94] The legislature had justified the provision because it was necessary to protect the trust of the general public into legal relations.[95] However, the court countered this justification with a consistency consideration.[96] Dissipation and alcoholism were the reasons for less than 10 percent of all incapacitations. However, for the majority of incapacitations, the legislature had deemed a public announcement to be expendable. This suggests that the legislature itself did not believe that a public announcement was necessary to protect the trust of the general public.

2.4 *Correcting Cases of Individual Hardship*

The final category consists of decisions in which the constitutional court corrects cases of individual hardship.[97] In these cases, the court makes a comparison between the importance of the individual right and of the public purpose. However, it acknowledges the legitimacy of the pursued purpose in principle and only overturns part of the regulation. It usually requires the legislature to introduce an exception for a group upon which the regulation imposes a particular burden. In some cases, the court also corrected occasions of individual hardship that occurred because of a change in the law.[98] Here, the court approves the general aim of the new legislation, but requires an interim regulation for individuals who are particularly affected by the transition.

The correction of cases of individual hardship is a residual category. Many of the cases that were discussed under one of the previous categories can also be classified as a correction of a case of individual hardship. An example is the repository copy decision that was classified as a decision in which the court shifted the financial burden from the addressed individual to the state.[99] However, it is also a case of correcting individual hardship. The court did not require the state to compensate for any repository copy that had to be given to the state libraries. Instead, it only asked

94 Id. at 86–7.
95 Id. at 85.
96 Id. at 86–7.
97 See BVerfGE 14, 19 at 23–4; 21, 173 at 183; 47, 285 at 322; 53, 257 at 302–4; 62, 117 at 152; 68, 155 at 173–5; 72, 51 at 63–4; 78, 58 at 75; 130, 372 at 395–7; 135, 48, 80–3.
98 See, for example, BVerfGE 21, 173 at 183.
99 See earlier notes 49–53 and accompanying text.

the legislature to provide for financial compensation when the obligation to provide a repository copy imposed a particular financial burden on the publisher.[100]

The decisions of this category do not usually involve significant costs for the legislature. The verdict of the court only overturns a small part of the overall legislation. In some cases, the correction may even be in the genuine interest of the legislature. According to James Rogers, constitutional court cases have an informational value for politics.[101] Legislative prognoses are never completely accurate. Furthermore, it is often difficult for the legislature to foresee the precise effect of a new regulation on each social group. Consequently, the court procedure can be seen as a feedback loop for politics: The court can correct inaccurate prognoses and reduce the error costs of political decisions.

This theory is supported by a decision from October 1984, in which the Constitutional Court had to deal with a compensation scheme for private providers of public transport.[102] These companies were obliged to transport disabled individuals free of charge. In return, they received a lump-sum compensation from the state. However, in certain municipalities, the number of disabled passengers using public transportation was significantly above average. In particular, there was a strong increase of disabled passengers in bathing resorts and holiday regions. The compensation scheme only referred to the state average and did not take these deviations into account. The constitutional court argued that there was no legitimate reason for the difference between the paid compensation and the actual decrease of the fare revenue.[103] Consequently, it held that the under-compensation of the public transport providers in bathing resorts and holiday regions was disproportionate.[104] The deficiency of the regulation is probably due to insufficient information of the legislature. When drafting the law, the legislature simply did not see that there could be a great systematic variance in the number of disabled passengers per municipality. This interpretation is confirmed by the fact that the legislature reacted even before the court reached its verdict.[105] It changed the legislation and

[100] BVerfGE 58, 137 at 149–50.

[101] James R. Rogers, 'Information and Judicial Review: A Signaling Game of Legislative-Judicial Interaction' (2001) 45 *American Journal of Political Science* 84–99 at 86–8; similarly Engel, 'Constitutional Court', pp. 300–1.

[102] BVerfGE 68, 155.

[103] Id. at 174.

[104] Id. at 175.

[105] See id. at 174.

introduced an exceptions clause providing additional compensation for transport providers with a significantly above-average number of disabled passengers.

However, Rogers' theory cannot explain all judgments in this category. In some cases, the legislature knew very well that regulation would impose particular hardship on a certain group and accepted the consequence deliberately. In February 1986, the constitutional court overturned a provision of a federal regulation governing the conduct of attorneys.[106] According to this provision, an attorney could be excluded from the bar association for life for specific infractions. The court held that it was inacceptable for the affected attorneys not to have any chance to rehabilitate themselves. Instead, the attorneys should have the opportunity for a fresh start if they could be expected not to pose any danger for administration of justice anymore.[107] It can be assumed that the ministry of justice knew fairly well what it did when it introduced the lifetime ban. Nevertheless, the decision only produces minimal political costs. The court did not deny that it was in principle legitimate to exclude attorneys from the bar association for certain infractions. It did not even generally preclude lifetime exclusions. It only required a review of each individual case in order to determine whether the attorney still constituted a danger for the administration of justice.

2.5 *Conclusion*

The preceding analysis has shown that, in most cases, the German Federal Constitutional Court does not use balancing to correct fundamental value decisions of the legislature. Instead, the jurisprudence can rather be characterised as an attempt to review the rationality of the legislative process. This rationality review comes in four different forms: The constitutional court corrects the allocation of financial burdens; it reviews the consistency of legislative value decisions; it controls the fit between measure and purpose; and it corrects cases of individual hardship.

Legislative measures are usually costly. These costs can be of immaterial nature if a measure imposes restrictions on individual liberty. In most cases, however, there are also material costs. The state can either absorb the material costs of a measure, or it can impose them on specific social groups or individuals. The constitutional court often corrects the

[106] BVerfGE 72, 51.
[107] Id. at 63–4.

allocation of the financial burden of a measure if it is particularly onerous for a specific social group and if the general public is the main benefactor of the measure. In such cases, there is no conflict between incommensurable values. The main rationale of the balancing decisions of the Federal Constitutional Court in these cases is rather that the main benefactor of a specific measure should also bear its financial burden.

The second group of cases concerns the fit between measure and purpose. The German Constitutional Court has a very strict interpretation of the less-restrictive-means test. The mere possibility that an alternative measure is not as effective as the measure under review already excludes the less-restrictive-means stage. However, in such constellations, the court may use the balancing stage to second-guess the empirical evaluations of the legislature. The court qualifies a measure as disproportionate if an alternative measure is far less restrictive but only marginally less effective, if it is doubtful that there is a rational connection between measure and purpose, or if the reviewed measure is overbroad. The argumentation in this second group of balancing decisions is thus very similar to the reasoning of the Canadian Supreme Court in the rational-connection of the less-restrictive-means stage of the proportionality test.[108]

The third group of cases combines balancing with consistency considerations. However, achieving consistency is not an end in itself. Rather, consistency may be an indication that the legislature pursued different aims than it explicitly claimed to pursue.[109] If a statute requires the public announcement only for certain kinds of incapacitations – namely, if the reason for this incapacitation was either dissipation or alcoholism – then it is unlikely that the "true" reason for this public announcement was the protection of the trust of the general public in legal relations. If this were the case, the reason for an incapacitation should not make a difference. Because it does, it seems that the public announcement was rather intended as a stigmatisation of the concerned individuals.

Finally, the court corrects cases of individual hardship. In most of these cases, the court only invalidated one part of a more extensive legal regulation that imposed a significant burden on a specific social group. Such decisions do not usually involve particularly onerous costs to the legislature, as they only require the introduction of limited exceptions provisions. In some cases, the court arguably even acts in the interest of politics,

[108] See ch. 5, section 2.2.

[109] See Petersen, 'Legislative Inconsistency'.

as it provides information about the effect of legislation that the legislature did not possess when passing the law.

Certainly, many of these judgments involve value decisions. However, that does not automatically make them examples of judicial activism. Judicial discretion is a necessary part of any form of judicial review. The main issue is rather how this judicial discretion is used. In this respect, the German Constitutional Court shows a high degree of self-restraint. Instead of second-guessing fundamental value decisions of the legislature, it rather uses balancing in order to correct systematic failures of the political process, which may be due to insufficient information, false stereotypes or misguided incentives.[110]

This is most obvious in the financial-burden-shifting cases. In these cases, politicians have incentives to impose the financial burden of a regulatory measure on private actors instead of charging the public budget. The lacking fit between measure and purpose or the inconsistency of a legislative measure are often indications for political capture.[111] One example is the hoof-care decision, where farriers were protected against competition from hoof caretakers and hoof technicians for minor caretaking services, even though this was not necessary to protect the animals concerned.[112] However, misguided incentives do not have to be caused by legislative capture. In the Baden-Württemberg casino case, where the state legislature required casinos to be run by the state, the regulation was based on incentives to generate new revenue for the state at the expense of private entrepreneurs.

In other cases, inconsistency and lacking fit may be an indication for false stereotypes. Arguably, the regulations requiring the publication of incapacitations or assuming that transsexuals entering into – what in the view of the concerned individuals were – homosexual partnerships had "found back" to their original sex were based on false stereotypes. Finally, most of the individual hardship cases can be traced back to insufficient information in the legislative procedure. The legislature was simply not aware of the effects the measure had on the specific group in question.

Furthermore, in most of the balancing cases, the court tried to achieve compromises. It rarely invalidated a measure as a whole, but usually demanded corrections at the margin. For these reasons, balancing decisions of the German Constitutional Court are an instrument to review the rationality of the legislature rather than a tool of judicial activism.

110 See ch. 1, section 2.
111 Petersen, 'Capture', 660.
112 See ch. 6, section 2.2.

3. The Outliers

There are a few decisions that overturn a piece of legislation based on balancing considerations, but none of these deal with criminal law or criminal procedure provisions, nor do they fit into one of the four categories discussed in the previous section. In Germany, the most famous case is the crucifix decision.[113] The decision overturned an ordinance of the Bavarian government that instructed all Bavarian schools to display crucifixes in their classrooms. In its core, the decision was based on a balancing of the negative religious freedom of the complainants and the positive religious freedom of the majority of society, as well as the educational mandate of the state.[114] The court acknowledged that the resolution of the conflict of the competing values was, in principle, the task of the legislature.[115] Yet, the legislature was obliged to reconcile the two competing principles.[116]

The court tried to minimalise the conflict through a corresponding interpretation of Christian values: "The idea of tolerance for believers of a different faith is a central part of Christianity as a cultural factor."[117] According to this interpretation, the display of the crucifix only marginally affects the positive freedom of religion. At the same time, the court argued that the crucifix affected the core of the negative freedom of religion of non-Christians because it symbolised the core of Christianity.[118]

The crucifix decision evaluates concrete policy goals. It argued that the visual expression of the beliefs of the societal majority was not important enough to justify a restriction of the negative freedom of religion of non-Christians. However, this evaluation is not mandatory. The European Court of Human Rights came to the opposite result in its *Lautsi* decision, in which it had to deal with a similar set of facts.[119] Religious symbols are not only religious symbols, but often also an expression of the cultural identity of a community.[120] Consequently, when the court believes that tolerance is a core element of Christian belief, it may be asked to what extent

[113] BVerfGE 93, 1.
[114] Id. at 21–4.
[115] Id. at 22.
[116] Id. at 21.
[117] Id. at 23.
[118] Id. at 24.
[119] *Lautsi v. Italy* [2011] ECHR 2412.
[120] Heckel, 'Das Kreuz im öffentlichen Raum', 482; Höffe, 'Wieviel Politik?', 191; similarly Otwin Massing, *Politik als Recht – Recht als Politik* (Baden-Baden: Nomos, 2005), pp. 233–4.

religious minorities have to tolerate religious symbols of the majority as long as these do not seek to exclude believers of a different faith.[121]

The only other decision of the German Constitutional Court that has a similar argumentation structure in the balancing stage is a 2009 decision on the business hours during the Sundays in Advent.[122] In principle, all German states have legislation that prohibits shops to open on Sundays. In 2007, the state of Berlin changed its statute on business hours and allowed shops to open on all four Sundays in Advent. This regulation was challenged by the Protestant and the Catholic churches in Berlin. In its decision, the court balanced the protection of Sundays and holidays, which it saw as enshrined in the German constitution,[123] against the economic interest to open shops on the Sundays before Christmas.[124] The judges concluded that the entrepreneurial interest to make profit could not justify a significant drop of the protection of Sundays and holidays.[125]

As in the crucifix decision, the court again made a comparison of competing interests and held that the public purpose was not sufficiently legitimate to justify such an extensive interference with the protection of Sun- and holidays. However, we find many of the elements of compromise that also characterised other balancing decisions. The question of business hours on Sundays was not a vital part of the economic policy of the state of Berlin. Furthermore, the court does not prohibit the opening on Sundays in general. Instead, it only turned against the authorization to open the shops on all four Sundays in Advent. In contrast, it did not prevent the legislature from allowing shops to open at individual Sundays in Advent.[126] Consequently, the costs that the court imposed on the political branches were rather limited.

In Canada, the one balancing decision that does not fit into the framework developed in this chapter is the judgment in *United Food and Commercial Workers.*[127] In *United Food and Commercial Workers*, the Canadian Supreme Court overturned a provision of the Personal Information Protection Act (PIPA) that prohibits the collection or disclosure of personal information

[121] Klaus Stern, *Verfassungsgerichtsbarkeit und Gesetzgeber* (Opladen: Westdeutscher Verlag, 1997), p. 29.

[122] BVerfGE 125, 39.

[123] See Art. 4 Basic Law in combination with Art. 139 of the Weimar constitution.

[124] BVerfGE 125, 39 at 90–5.

[125] Id. at 93–4.

[126] Id. at 96.

[127] *Alberta (Information and Privacy Commissioner) v. United Food an Commercial Workers, Local 401* [2013] 3 S.C.R. 733.

without consent because it violated the freedom of expression of a labour union. The respondent, a labour union, represented employees of a casino during a lawful strike. The union had established a picket line near the entrance of a casino. It videotaped and photographed all persons crossing the line and posted a sign that it would place these videos and photos on a website.

Several individuals complained that they had been videotaped or photographed by the union and claimed that these recordings contravened the PIPA. The union argued that the PIPA violated its freedom of expression guaranteed by section 2(b) of the Canadian Charter. The Canadian Supreme Court confirmed the position of the union. It held that the PIPA infringed the guarantee of freedom of expression and that this infringement could not be justified under section 1 of the Canadian Charter. The court argued that the PIPA pursued its aims with disproportionate means.[128] On the one hand, the court found that PIPA was very broad in nature. It protected all kinds of personal information, regardless of the context.[129] In the present case, the published information did not include intimate biographical details, and the individuals crossing the picket line could reasonably expect that their image could be caught and disseminated.[130] On the other hand, the court qualified the restriction imposed by PIPA to touch the core of the expressive activity of the labour union.[131] It argued that the effectiveness of the picket line was dependent on convincing the public not to do business with the employer. For this reason, PIPA imposed a restriction on one of the core strategies of a labour union during a lawful strike.[132]

The decision displays some of the classical characteristics of a balancing decision. It compares the value of the competing aims and determines to what extent the different values have been affected. Whereas the court argued that the effect for the use of personal information was not particularly severe, it deemed the PIPA prohibition to affect the core of the freedom of expression of the labour union. However, the case concerns the delimitation of competing spheres of freedom between different private parties. The evaluation of the case depends on the importance attributed to personal privacy and the effectiveness of the union's strike. There can be reasonable disagreement about the evaluation of these competing

[128] Id. at 749–53.
[129] Id. at 749.
[130] Id. at 749–50.
[131] Id. at 750.
[132] Id. at 753.

positions, and it seems that the decision should rather be taken by the legislature than by courts.

Nevertheless, none of the three decisions discussed in this section affect the overall finding of this chapter. A few activist decisions do not demonstrate that the jurisprudence of a court is generally activist in nature.[133] Instead, we have to look at the case law as a whole and try to identify general trends. We have seen that the general reasoning of balancing decisions in German and the Canadian jurisprudence differs significantly from the reasoning in the three decisions discussed in this section. The latter are mere outliers that do not change the general pattern.

4. Balancing and the Review of Legislative Rationality

Balancing is often seen as an entry gate for judicial activism. The discussion in this chapter suggests otherwise. In the first chapter, I argued that the main function of constitutional courts is the correction of political market failures. Such market failures may affect the rationality of the legislative process if the legislature does not take into account all interests at stake. There may be three types of systematic misrepresentations of the general interest.[134] First, political actors sometimes have incentives to over- or understate certain stakeholder interests. This happens, in particular, if minorities are not sufficiently represented in the political process or if certain interests are overemphasised because of strong interest group influence. Second, a misrepresentation of interests may be due to false stereotypes. Finally, the legislature may be insufficiently informed about the interests at stake.

All three courts occasionally resort to balancing when they are invalidating criminal law or criminal procedure norms.[135] The German Constitutional Court often relied on balancing when it had to deal with police or intelligence surveillance measures. The South African Constitutional Court used balancing to strike down the death penalty, a criminal procedure norm that allowed killing a fleeing suspect even for minor offences, excessive punishment of so-called "habitual criminals" or the unsuitable detention of mentally ill persons. Finally, the Canadian Supreme Court resorted to balancing in order to protect prostitutes, to

[133] James Bernard Kelly, *Governing with the Charter: Legislative and Judicial Activism and Framers' Intent* (Vancouver: UBC Press, 2005), p. 139.

[134] See ch. 1, section 2.6.

[135] See ch. 6, section 1.

correct the overbroad criminalisation of child pornography or to prevent suspects for being convicted of an intentional act when they were only culpable of negligent conduct. In all instances, the court used balancing in order to protect social groups that are not sufficiently represented in the political process. For an environment in which being "tough on crime" can help win elections, politicians have incentives to impose sanctions that are too strict, rather than too lenient. Under such circumstances, Constitutional Courts have the function to correct disproportionate political responses to the threats of crime and terrorism.

Only the German Constitutional Court also frequently used balancing outside of the criminal-law context. However, it showed a significant degree of self-restraint. Almost all the remaining cases can be placed in one of the following four categories: financial burden shifting, invalidating legislation because of the lack of fit between measure and purpose or inconsistencies, and correcting cases of individual hardship. As I showed, these four categories can also be proxies for political market failures.[136] For these reasons, balancing cannot be characterised as a Trojan horse for judicial self-empowerment. Rather, it is an instrument for reviewing the rationality of the legislature.

[136] See ch. 6, section 2.5.

Conclusion

Proportionality and the Review of Legislative Rationality

Judicial review always has a political dimension. It requires normative valuations, and these normative valuations are not exclusively determined by the constitution. However, this does not mean that judges are necessarily policymakers in disguise. On the contrary, they face constraints that differ significantly from the constraints of the political process. Legal scholarship outside the United States often focuses on the constraints that are imposed on the judiciary by legal doctrine. This is certainly an important aspect. However, it is not the only constraint that judges face. They are also subject to institutional constraints, which are often neglected in the legal debate. Courts exercising judicial review cannot implement their judgments. Instead, their strongest implementation mechanism is their institutional legitimacy. This legitimacy depends on being perceived as neutral arbiters in legal conflicts. A court that appears to be politically activist undermines its own legitimacy.

The proportionality test provides an example of how these two types of constraints play together. The last step of the proportionality test is often criticised because it is supposed to lack rational standards of decision-making. For this reason, some critics consider balancing to be a Trojan horse for political activism of apex courts. However, this reasoning neglects the institutional constraints that apex courts face. We have seen in Chapter 2 that the analytical critique has lots of merit: Balancing requires the compared values to be transformable into one single normative currency. In many cases, such a transformation is not possible. For this reason, balancing gives judges a large amount of discretion.[1]

However, this does not necessarily make balancing an ideal instrument to mask judicial activism.[2] Rather, we have observed the opposite in this study. The three analysed courts exercised considerable self-restraint when balancing. This is, in particular, illustrated by the jurisprudence of

[1] See ch. 2, section 1.1.
[2] See ch. 3, section 1.

the South African Constitutional Court and the Canadian Supreme Court. Both courts have been very reluctant to rely on balancing when they overturned pieces of legislation. In both jurisdictions, balancing decisions are rather the exception than the rule.[3] In both jurisdictions, balancing is predominantly used in the domain of criminal and criminal procedure law where the danger that the legislature acts disproportionately is particularly pronounced.[4]

By contrast, the German Federal Constitutional Court relies to a greater extent on balancing when it corrects the legislature. Nevertheless, two observations are remarkable. First, the court was initially reluctant to use balancing when it declared statutes to be inconsistent with fundamental rights of the German Constitution. It took the court more than two decades to develop balancing into the central instrument of fundamental rights review that it is today.[5] Second, when the court uses balancing to correct the legislature, the structure of the balancing test differs significantly from Alexy's reconstruction of balancing as a weighting of different competing factors that we discussed in Chapter 2.[6] Instead, most of the court's balancing decisions can be put into one of the following four categories:[7] The court shifts the financial burden of a measure from its addressee to its main benefactor; it controls the fit between measure and purpose; it takes the consistency of the measure as an indication that the legislature had potentially illicit motives; finally, it corrects cases of individual hardship.

Therefore, I have developed the counter-thesis that the proportionality test serves the function of reviewing legislative rationality. In the following, I will first specify this finding. I will argue that the review of legislative rationality is the negative correlate of judicial activism. Subsequently, I will demonstrate that the observations of this study confirm the thesis that proportionality is an instrument to review legislative rationality and, therefore, not a tool of judicial activism. The third section will deal with judicial activism in apex courts that has been observed in this study. Interestingly, however, such judicial activism is not based on proportionality arguments, but rather on alternative modes of reasoning.

[3] See ch. 4, sections 3 and 4.
[4] See ch. 6, section 1.
[5] See ch. 4, section 1.
[6] See ch. 2, section 1.2.
[7] See ch. 6, section 2.

1. Judicial Activism vs. Review of Legislative Rationality

The concept of judicial activism is not easy to define. In principle, it is supposed to capture situations in which judges are guided by political instead of legal considerations. However, judicial decisions are never exclusively determined by legal norms and legal doctrine. In the first chapter, we have seen that judicial review is inherently political.[8] Language is, to a certain extent, indeterminate, so that judges have a significant amount of discretion when interpreting and applying constitutional norms. Consequently, the distinction between political and legal considerations is no adequate factor for determining judicial activism.

In this book, I have, therefore, followed a different approach that relies on external standards to evaluate the legitimacy of judicial review. I have defined the role that judicial review is supposed to play in a liberal democracy. According to the conception developed here, judicial review has the function to correct political market failures.[9] In representative democracies, elected representatives take collective decisions mirroring the preferences of the represented citizens.[10] Sometimes, these representatives have systematic incentives to pay less attention to the preferences of certain citizens while taking into account the preferences of well-organised and influential social groups to a disproportionate degree. The citizens who tend to be rather neglected are insulated minorities, social groups that suffer from prejudices or citizens who do not have a vote, like foreigners or future generations. Citizens who have a disproportionate influence are usually interest groups with significant financial means and/or social power.

According to the conception underlying this book, courts do not act in an activist manner if they try to correct these imbalances of the political process. Mitigating a disproportionate burden of a politically disadvantaged group or policing legislative capture are legitimate exercises of judicial power. In such cases, courts merely control whether the legislature took all relevant interests into account in the legislative process, that is, they review the rationality of the legislative process. By contrast, an apex court acts in an activist manner if it extends rights or benefits for social groups that are sufficiently represented in the political process.

[8] See ch. 1.
[9] See ch. 1, section 2.
[10] See ch. 1, section 1.

2. Judicial Review and the Review of Legislative Rationality

If we apply the conceptual standards developed in the previous section to the fundamental rights jurisprudence of the three analysed courts, the proportionality test can be qualified as an instrument of reviewing legislative rationality rather than as a tool of judicial activism. This characterisation fits the case law of all three courts, despite the differences in the concrete application of the proportionality test.

The Canadian Supreme Court predominantly relies on the rational-connection and the less-restrictive-means stage of the proportionality test when it corrects the legislature.[11] These two stages focus on the fit of the measure and the pursued purpose. A lack of fit between measure and purpose is usually an indication that the legislature either did not take into account the interests of the individual rights-bearers or that it pursued illegitimate interests. Certainly, the Canadian Supreme Court often balances implicitly in the context of the less-restrictive-means test.[12] However, the extent of this implicit balancing is limited, as it usually only concerns the fit between measure and purpose.

Prima facie, the South African Constitutional Court predominantly seems to rely on balancing in its fundamental rights jurisprudence. However, a closer analysis shows that the court primarily relies on rational-connection and less-restrictive-means considerations when overturning a piece of legislation, whereas balancing remains the rare exception.[13] Like the Canadian Supreme Court, the South African Constitutional Court equally qualifies arguments as less-restrictive-means arguments, while balancing implicitly in some cases. Nevertheless, the extent of this implicit balancing is also limited.

The court that relies strongest on balancing when correcting the legislature is the German Federal Constitutional Court. However, the court exercises self-restraint when it balances. First, it uses balancing as a means to control the fit of measure and purpose. In this context, the German balancing resembles closely what the Canadian Supreme Court does in the rational-connection and less-restrictive-means test. Second, it relies on consistency considerations: A measure is considered disproportionate if it is inconsistent. Like the lack of fit, inconsistency is an indicator for the legislative intention. Third, it corrects cases of individual hardship where

[11] See ch. 4, section 1.
[12] See ch. 5, section 2.2.
[13] See ch. 4, section 1.

the legislature did not usually realise in advance that a particular group might be burdened disproportionately by a particular measure. Finally, the court shifts the financial burden of a measure from its addressee to its main benefactor.

In all three jurisdictions, the review of legislative rationality is thus the primary aim of the proportionality test. The courts usually do not use proportionality to second-guess the political goal of the legislature. Instead, they try to correct incentives of the political decision-makers not to act in the public interest. However, proportionality is not the only doctrinal instrument that courts use to review the rationality of the legislative process. Instead, coherency and consistency considerations also play an important role.[14] Furthermore, the courts sometimes rely on procedural arguments.[15] The legislature often has incentives to reduce checks and balances in the administrative procedure in order to make the procedure more cost-effective. However, this tendency is problematic if it leads to a decreased protection of individual rights. Consequently, procedural arguments aim at safeguarding individual rights through procedural means by requiring additional checks and balances in the administrative procedure.

3. Traces of Judicial Activism

Certainly, this does not mean that the analysed courts do not engage in judicial activism. There are cases in which courts undertake more than just a mere review of legislative rationality. We have already seen two such cases in the introduction. In the Crucifix case, the German Federal Constitutional Court relied on an open balancing of the positive religious freedom of the Catholic majority and the negative religious freedom of the atheists.[16] In *Chaoulli*, the court relied on controversial normative valuations in framing the empirical inquiry without making them explicit.[17]

This shows that the proportionality test is not immune to being used for activist decision-making. However, such cases are exceptions. If we look at the broad picture, the courts engage predominantly in a review of legislative rationality. The scrutiny by the public and the academic discourse ensure that the apex courts do not systematically transgress the boundaries of their own competencies.[18] The crucifix decision of the German

[14] See ch. 5, section 3.
[15] See ch. 5, section 4.
[16] See ch. 6, section 3.
[17] See ch. 5, section 2.3.
[18] See ch. 3, section 1.

Constitutional Court illustrates well how this mechanism works. After it was issued, the decision faced fierce criticism in the legal academy.[19] There was much resistance against the decision among the public and in politics.[20] Some authors diagnosed a legitimacy crisis of the court.[21]

This critique did not escape the judges' attention.[22] For this reason, it is remarkable that the judgment remained an exception. There is only one further decision in which we find an open balancing – the decision on business hours during Sundays in Advent.[23] It is impossible to determine whether the development would have been different if the Crucifix decision had been less controversial. However, the example shows that courts are not free of constraints when they rely on balancing if they do not want to jeopardise their institutional legitimacy.[24]

Similar observations have been made for the Canadian Supreme Court: Kent Roach has argued that the court reacted to criticism that it was too activist by granting the Canadian legislature a larger margin of appreciation.[25] This conclusion is in line with an analysis by Barry Friedman regarding the US Supreme Court.[26] According to Friedman, the relationship between the US Supreme Court and the public has not always been

[19] See, for example, Jörg Müller-Volbehr, 'Positive und negative Religionsfreiheit – Zum Kruzifix-Beschluß des BVerfG' (1995) 50 *Juristenzeitung* 996–1000; Christoph Link, 'Stat Crux? – Die "Kruzifix"-Entscheidung des Bundesverfassungsgerichts' (1995) 48 *Neue Juristische Wochenschrift* 3353–7; Max-Emanuel Geis, 'Geheime Offenbarung oder Offenbarungseid? – Anmerkungen zum "Kruzifix-Beschluß" des Bundesverfassungsgerichts' (1995) 43 *Recht der Jugend und des Bildungswesens* 373–86; Heckel, 'Das Kreuz im öffentlichen Raum'; Josef Isensee, 'Bildersturm durch Grundrechtsinterpretation – Der Kruzifix-Beschluss des BVerfG' (1996) 29 *Zeitschrift für Rechtspolitik* 10–5; Michael Brenner, 'Der Kruzifix-Beschluß des Bundesverfassungsgerichts' (1996) 5 *Thüringer Verwaltungsblätter* 145–52; Detlef Merten, 'Der "Kruzifix-Beschluß" des Bundesverfassungsgerichts aus grundrechtsdogmatischer Sicht', in Joachim Burmeister (ed.), *Verfassungsstaatlichkeit – Festschrift für Klaus Stern* (München: C. H. Beck, 1997), pp. 987–1009.

[20] Vanberg, *Politics of Constitutional Review*, pp. 3–4.

[21] See Isensee, 'Bundesverfassungsgericht'; Schulze-Fielitz, 'Das Bundesverfassungsgericht in der Krise des Zeitgeists', 2–3; Knies, 'Auf dem Weg', pp. 1156–7; Di Fabio, *Recht offener Staaten*, p. 66; Höffe, 'Wieviel Politik?', 171. See also Haltern, 'Demokratische Verantwortlichkeit', 552–3 (arguing that the court's "expert semantics" had been "demystified" by the decision).

[22] Helmuth Schulze-Fielitz, 'Das Bundesverfassungsgericht und die öffentliche Meinung', in Gunnar Folke Schuppert and Christian Bumke (eds.), *Bundesverfassungsgericht und gesellschaftlicher Grundkonsens* (Baden-Baden: Nomos, 2000), pp. 111–44 at 128–9.

[23] See ch. 6, section 3.

[24] See Vanberg, *Politics of Constitutional Review*, pp. 124–30.

[25] Roach, *Supreme Court on Trial*, p. 172.

[26] Friedman, *Will of the People*, p. 376.

linear. Instead, the court has on several occasions made mistakes and lost public acceptance. What is important, however, is that the court learnt from these mistakes and corrected them. Public scrutiny is thus no guarantee that courts never engage in political activism. It only predicts that such instances of activism will rather be the exception than the norm.

However, the jurisprudence of the German Federal Constitutional Court also shows traces of systematic activism. We have seen that the court extended welfare benefits to public servants and families while the reasoning often remained obscure.[27] As these decisions arguably also benefited the social groups that the judges themselves belonged to, it is likely that they were primarily driven by political considerations. Remarkably, however, the court did not resort to the proportionality test in these decisions. Instead, the reasoning rested on deductive norm interpretation. The court thus relied on a pattern of reasoning that pertains to the core competency of lawyers. In such areas, lawyers can claim a special expertise, which makes it easier for them to mask political decision-making.

4. Analytical Openness and Institutional Constraints

This observation helps us to explain what seems to be a paradox at first sight: The analytical openness of a doctrinal instrument does not automatically lead to judicial activism. Instead, the relationship may be exactly the reverse. Even if balancing gives judges a large amount of discretion, such judicial discretion is not limited to balancing. Instead, as constitutions contain many open-textured provisions, judges exercising judicial review also have considerable discretion when they engage in norm interpretation. In such a situation, it is precisely the analytical openness of proportionality that prevents judicial activism. As the political potential of proportionality is evident, political considerations are more difficult to hide than behind traditional instruments of norm interpretation.[28] Consequently, the transparency of the structure of the proportionality test has a disciplining effect.[29]

The criticism of constitutional courts often comes from two sides. On the one hand, courts are accused of being too activist, of invading the core

[27] See ch. 5, section 7.2.

[28] Similarly Gardbaum, 'A Democratic Defense of Constitutional Balancing', 88–93.

[29] See also Josef Esser, *Vorverständnis und Methodenwahl in der Rechtsfindung* (Frankfurt a.M.: Athenäum Verlag, 1970), p. 36 (advocating the discussion of normative considerations openly instead of hiding them behind traditional methods of norm interpretation).

domain of the legislature. On the other hand, they are criticised for being too cautious, for failing to provide a strong protection of individual rights. In Germany, both strands of the critique focus on the proportionality test. Some authors see proportionality as an expression of judicial activism,[30] whereas others advocate considering rights as "trumps" and argue that the proportionality approach weakens the level of protection afforded by individual rights.[31]

We can make a similar observation in the Canadian legal literature. Here, some authors consider the court to be paying too much deference to the legislature under the *Oakes* test,[32] whereas others argue that the court should be more deferential[33] or discard the proportionality test as a device of judicial activism.[34] In South Africa, finally, the prevailing opinion is that the Constitutional Court fails to protect individual rights sufficiently. The jurisprudence of the court has been called "rainbow jurisprudence" because it supposedly found consensus where there was none.[35] Other authors have argued that the doctrinal approach was under-theorised,[36] or that it failed to guarantee a strong protection of individual rights.[37] But our analysis has shown that the South African Constitutional Court has continuously stood up against the government and tried to hold the latter accountable even with regard to under-represented groups. Considering its significant dependence on the ANC, a more active approach would probably have endangered its institutional position.[38]

That the critique of proportionality comes from two opposing sides confirms the argument made in this book and shows that courts seem to find a good middle ground. This is sometimes even acknowledged by the critics. Bernhard Schlink, one of the most preeminent opponents of the balancing test, has observed that the German Constitutional Court has not surpassed the politically and socially acceptable and tolerable degree

30 Haltern, 'Integration als Mythos', 69; Leisner, *Abwägungsstaat*, pp. 170–3; Christensen and Lerch, 'Dass das Ganze das Wahre ist', 440; Classen, 'Verhältnismäßigkeit', p. 653.

31 See, for example, Rusteberg, *Gewährleistungsgehalt*.

32 See Beatty, 'Canadian Charter'; Weinrib, 'Paradigm Lost?'.

33 See Charney and Green, 'Prophets of Doom'.

34 See Webber, *Negotiable Constitution*.

35 Alfred Cockrell, 'Rainbow Jurisprudence' (1996) 12 *South African Journal on Human Rights* 1–38 at 12.

36 Christopher J. Roederer, 'Judicious Engagement: Theory, Attitude and Community' (1999) 15 *South African Journal on Human Rights* 486–506.

37 Patrick Lenta, 'Judicial Restraint and Overreach' (2004) 20 *South African Journal on Human Rights* 544–76 at 576.

38 See Roux, 'Principle and Pragmatism'.

of interference with politics when relying on balancing.[39] Schlink assumes that this self-restraint is due to a particular political sensitivity of the judges of the German Constitutional Court.[40] However, the comparison in this book has shown that the German Court is no exception in this respect. This suggests that the moderation of the judges when applying the proportionality test does not result from a particular integrity and professional ethos of the individual judges. Instead, in all three courts, it is the consequence of a healthy amount of institutional self-interest.

[39] Schlink, 'Verhältnismäßigkeit', p. 465.
[40] Schlink, 'Verhältnismäßigkeit', p. 465.

Appendix A

Coding of the Jurisprudence of the Canadian Supreme Court

Decision	Year	LEG	LRM	OVB	BAL	PRC	DET	CON	BUJ
R v Big Drug Mart	1985	1							
R v Oakes	1986		1						
R v Smith	1987			1					
R v Vallaincourt	1987		1						
Ford v Quebec	1988		1						1
R v Morgenthaler	1988		1					1	
CPMQ v. Thibault	1988					1			1
Edmonton Journal v Alberta	1989		1	1					
Andrews v Law Society of Brit Col	1989		1						
Black v Law Society of Alberta	1989		1					1	
R v Hess; R v Nguyen	1990		1						
R v Logan	1990				1				
R v Martineau	1990		1						
Rocket v Royal Coll Dental Surg	1990			1					
PSC v. Osborne	1991			1					

(*continued*)

Decision	Year	LEG	LRM	OVB	BAL	PRC	DET	CON	BUJ
R v Seaboyer; R v Gayme	1991			1					
R v Swaine	1991		1				1		
R v Wholesale Travel	1991		1						1
Tetreault-Gadoury v Canada	1991		1						
Comm Commonwealth Can v Canada	1991			1			1		
R v Genereux	1992		1						
R v Morales	1992						1		
R v Zundel	1992	1		1					1
R v Bain	1992					1			
Sauvé v Canada	1993		1						
Baron v Canada	1993					1			
R v Heywood	1994			1		1			
R v Laba	1994		1						
RJR-MacDonald v. Canada	1995		1						1
Benner v Canada	1997		1						
Libman v Quebec	1997		1						
R v Campbell	1997					1			1
Thomson Newspaper v Canada	1998		1						
Vriend v Alberta	1998	1							1
Corbiere v Canada	1999		1						1
M v H	1999		1					1	

UFCW v Kmart Canada	1999		1						1
Dunmore v Ontario	2001		1						
R v Sharp	2001				1				
R v Ruzic	2001	1							1
R v Guignard	2002		1					1	
Sauvé v Canada	2002		1						
Lavallee, Rackel & Heintz v. Canada	2002		1						
Mackin v New Brunswick	2002					1			1
Figueroa v Canada	2003		1						
Nova Scotia v Martin	2003		1						
Trociuk v British Columbia	2003		1						
R v Demers	2004			1					
Chaoulli v Quebec	2005		1						1
Charkaoui v Canada	2007		1			1		1	
Canada v Hislop	2007	1						1	1
Health Services Barg Assn v Brit Col	2007					1			
R v DB	2008		1						
Nguyen v Quebec	2009		1						
R v Tse	2012					1			
Alberta v UFWC	2013				1				
Canada v Bedford	2013				1				
Saskatchewan v Whatcott	2013		1						
Canada v Whaling	2014		1						

(*continued*)

Decision	Year	LEG	LRM	OVB	BAL	PRC	DET	CON	BUJ
Mounted Police Assn v. Canada	2015		1					1	
R v Appulonappa	2015		1	1					1
Carter v Canada	2015		1						
Canada v Federation Law Scoieties	2015		1						
Goodwin v Bristish Columbia	2015					1			
R v Nur	2015		1						
Saskatchewan Fed Lab v. Saskatchewan	2015		1			1			
R v Smith	2015		1						1

Appendix B

Coding of the Jurisprudence of the German Federal Constitutional Court

Decision	Year	LEG	LRM	BAL	EQU	PRC	DET	CON	TRU	CAT	DED
2, 380	1953								1		
4, 331	1955					1					
6, 55	1957				1						
7, 320	1958		1								
7, 377	1958		1					1			
8, 1	1958							1			
8, 71	1958						1				
9, 39	1958		1								
9, 83	1959						1				
9, 268	1959					1					
10, 118	1959					1					
10, 200	1959					1					
11, 30	1960		1								
11, 168	1960		1								
11, 203	1960										1
12, 81	1961					1					
12, 144	1961		1								

(continued)

Decision	Year	LEG	LRM	BAL	EQU	PRC	DET	CON	TRU	CAT	DED
13, 206	1961								1		
13, 261	1961								1		
13, 290	1962				1						
14, 19	1962			1							
14, 174	1962					1					
14, 254	1962					1					
15, 167	1962								1		
15, 275	1963					1					
15, 328	1963				1						
16, 94	1963										1
16, 203	1963				1						
17, 148	1963				1						
17, 269	1964		1								
17, 306	1964		1								
18, 97	1964				1						
18, 429	1965								1		
19, 206	1965	1									
19, 226	1965	1									
19, 242	1965	1									
19, 268	1965					1					
19, 330	1965		1								
20, 150	1966	1					1				
21, 139	1967					1					
21, 173	1967			1							

21, 261	1967	1							
21, 271	1967	1							
22, 42	1967					1			
22, 49	1967				1				
22, 163	1967			1					
22, 180	1967								1
24, 75	1968							1	
24, 104	1968			1					
25, 236	1969						1		
26, 79	1969				1				
27, 355	1970					1			
28, 324	1970			1					
29, 57	1970			1					
30, 1	1970	1							
30, 227	1970	1							
30, 292	1971			1					
30, 336	1971	1							
30, 367	1971							1	
31, 94	1971							1	
31, 229	1971		1						
31, 275	1971							1	
32, 1	1971							1	
33, 303	1972			1	1	1			
34, 71	1972	1							
34, 165	1972		1						
35, 79	1973				1				

(continued)

Decision	Year	LEG	LRM	BAL	EQU	PRC	DET	CON	TRU	CAT	DED
36, 47	1973		1								
36, 146	1973	1									
38, 1	1974				1						
38, 61	1974	1									
39, 1	1975					1					
40, 371	1975		1								
41, 378	1976		1								
43, 242	1977								1		
43, 291	1977								1		
44, 249	1977										1
45, 393	1977						1				
47, 46	1977						1				
47, 285	1978			1							
48, 127	1978										1
48, 376	1978				1						
49, 382	1978			1							
50, 265	1979		1								
51, 193	1979								1		
51, 356	1979								1		
52, 1	1979			1				1			
52, 357	1979			1				1			
53, 135	1980		1								
53, 257	1980			1							
53, 366	1980			1							

54, 159	1980					1			
54, 301	1980		1						
55, 134	1980			1					
55, 159	1980		1						
56, 192	1981					1			
57, 295	1981					1			
57, 361	1981		1						
58, 137	1981			1					
59, 302	1982		1						
61, 210	1982					1			
61, 291	1982			1					
61, 358	1982	1							
62, 117	1982			1					
62, 374	1982				1				
63, 88	1983		1						
63, 131	1983		1						
64, 323	1983				1				
64, 367	1983				1				
65, 1	1983					1	1		
68, 155	1984			1					
68, 272	1984								1
69, 209	1985			1				1	
71, 1	1985								1
71, 183	1985	1							
71, 255	1985								1
72, 9	1986								1

(*continued*)

Decision	Year	LEG	LRM	BAL	EQU	PRC	DET	CON	TRU	CAT	DED
72, 51	1986			1							
72, 155	1986										1
72, 200	1986								1		
72, 278	1986			1							
73, 118	1986					1	1				
74, 33	1986				1			1			
74, 203	1987			1							
74, 297	1987		1								
75, 40	1987				1						
75, 166	1987				1						
75, 284	1987		1					1			
77, 308	1987			1							
78, 58	1988			1							
78, 77	1988			1				1			
78, 179	1988						1				
78, 364	1988				1						1
78, 374	1988						1				
79, 256	1989		1	1							
81, 156	1990			1				1			
81, 242	1990		1								
81, 363	1990										1
82, 60	1990				1						1
83, 238	1991					1					
84, 133	1991			1				1			

84, 168	1991	1									
85, 226	1992			1							
85, 360	1992								1		
86, 81	1992								1		
87, 114	1992			1							
87, 153	1992										1
88, 203	1993					1					
90, 60	1993					1					
90, 128	1994				1						
90, 263	1994		1	1				1			
91, 1	1994		1								
92, 26	1995			1							
92, 158	1995		1								
93, 1	1995			1							
93, 362	1995		1								
94, 372	1996		1								
95, 193	1997	1									
97, 228	1998			1							
98, 17	1998		1								
98, 169	1998										1
98, 265	1998								1		
99, 202	1998			1							
99, 216	1998				1						1
99, 246	1998										1
99, 300	1998										1
99, 341	1999		1								

(continued)

Decision	Year	LEG	LRM	BAL	EQU	PRC	DET	CON	TRU	CAT	DED
100, 1	1999								1		
100, 226	1999			1							
100, 313	1999			1		1	1	1			
101, 54	1999		1	1				1			
101, 106	1999		1			1					
101, 397	2000					1					
102, 197	2000		1	1				1			
103, 1	2000		1					1			
104, 357	2002		1	1				1			
105, 135	2002						1				
106, 181	2002		1					1			
107, 104	2003						1				
107, 150	2003							1			
107, 186	2003		1					1			
107, 395	2003					1					
108, 82	2003			1				1			
108, 150	2003		1								
109, 64	2003				1						
109, 256	2004			1							
109, 279	2004			1		1				1	
110, 33	2004					1	1				
111, 191	2004						1				
112, 255	2005			1							
113, 273	2005					1			1		

113, 348	2005		1		1	1				
114, 1	2005				1					1
114, 73	2005									1
114, 371	2005				1					
115, 1	2005	1	1							
115, 118	2006								1	
115, 259	2006									1
115, 276	2006						1			
116, 96	2006							1		
117, 163	2006		1				1			
117, 202	2007		1							
117, 372	2007						1			1
118, 45	2007			1						
118, 168	2007					1				
119, 59	2007		1				1			
119, 181	2007				1					
119, 247	2007									1
120, 125	2008									1
120, 274	2008		1		1	1				
120, 378	2008				1	1				
121, 30	2008		1							
121, 175	2008		1							
121, 205	2008				1					
121, 317	2008		1				1			
123, 148	2009				1					
123, 267	2009				1					

(*continued*)

Decision	Year	LEG	LRM	BAL	EQU	PRC	DET	CON	TRU	CAT	DED
125, 39	2009			1							
125, 175	2010							1			
125, 260	2010			1		1	1			1	
127, 1	2010								1		
127, 31	2010								1		
127, 61	2010								1		
127, 87	2010					1					
127, 132	2010		1					1			
128, 109	2011			1				1			
128, 157	2011			1				1			
128, 282	2011			1		1	1				
128, 326	2011						1	1	1		
129, 269	2011			1		1	1				
130, 131	2012				1						
130, 151	2012						1	1			
130, 263	2012										1
130, 318	2012					1					
130, 372	2012			1							
132, 134	2012							1			

132, 302	2012							1		
133, 112	2013				1	1				
133, 143	2013							1		
133, 277	2013		1		1	1				
134, 1	2013			1						
135, 1	2013							1		
135, 48	2013		1			1				
135, 90	2014	1								
136, 9	2014				1					
136, 338	2014				1					
2 BvL 17/09	2015									1
1 BvR 1501/13	2015					1				
2 BvL 19/09	2015									1

Appendix C

Coding of the Jurisprudence of the South African Constitutional Court

Decision	Year	LEG	LRM	OVB	BAL	CON	PRC	BUJ
S v Makwanyane	1995		1		1	1		
Coetzee v Government of RSA	1995		1	1				
S v Williams	1995		1					1
S v Bhulwana	1995		1					
Ferreira v Levin	1995		1					
Case v Minister of Safety	1996			1				1
S v Mbatha	1996		1	1				
S v Ntsele	1997		1	1				
Mistry v Nat Med & Dental Counc	1998			1				
S v Mello	1998			1				
Gay & Lesbian Equ v Min Justice	1998	1						1
Lesapo v N W Agric Bank	1999						1	
SANDU v Min Defence	1999		1	1				
S v Steyn	2000						1	1
S v Manamela	2000		1	1				
Dawood v Min Home Aff	2000	1						
S v Niemand	2001				1		1	
Islamic Unity Convention v IBA	2002		1	1				

Ex parte Minister of Safety	2002				1			
Philips v Dir Publ Prosecution	2003			1				
Jaftha v Schoeman	2004			1				
Bhe v Khayelitsha Magistrate	2004	1						
Min Home Aff v NICRO	2004	1		1		1		1
Lawyers Hum Rts v Min Home Aff	2004						1	
Min Home Aff v Fourie	2005	1						
Magajane v N W Gambling Board	2006			1				
Nyathi v Dep Health Gauteng	2008		1					
Brümmer v Min Social Devel	2009		1			1		
Ctr Child Law v Min Justice	2009	1						1
Richter v Min Home Aff	2009	1				1		
Johncom Media v M	2009		1					
Law Society of SA v Min Transp	2010		1					
Malachi v Cape Dance Acad	2010		1	1		1		
C, M and Ctr Child Law v Dep Health	2012						1	
Nat Cred Reg v Opperman	2012		1					
Print Media SA v Min Home Aff	2012		1					
Mail and Guardian v Chipu	2013		1					
Teddy Bear Clinic v Min Justice	2013		1					1
Gaertner v Minister of Finance	2013			1			1	
J v. Nat. Director of Prosecutions	2014		1					
Da Silva v. Road Accident Fund	2014		1					
Chevron v. Wilson	2015		1					
Sarrahwitz v. Maritz	2015		1					
De Vos v. Minister of Justice	2015		1		1	1		

BIBLIOGRAPHY

Aaken, Anne van, *'Rational Choice' in der Rechtswissenschaft. Zum Stellenwert der ökonomischen Theorie im Recht* (Baden-Baden: Nomos, 2003).

'Vom Nutzen der ökonomischen Theorie für das öffentliche Recht: Methode und Anwendungsmöglichkeiten', in Marc Bungenberg et al. (eds.), *Recht und Ökonomik* (München: C.H. Beck, 2004), pp. 1–31.

Ackerman, Bruce, 'The Storrs Lectures: Discovering the Constitution' (1984) 93 *Yale Law Journal* 1013–72.

'Constitutional Politics/Constitutional Law' (1989) 99 *Yale Law Journal* 453–547.

We the People: Foundations (Cambridge, MA: Harvard University Press, 1991).

Afonso da Silva, Virgílio, 'Comparing the Incommensurable: Constitutional Principles, Balancing and Rational Decision' (2011) 31 *Oxford Journal of Legal Studies* 273–301.

Aleinikoff, T. Alexander, 'Constitutional Law in the Age of Balancing' (1987) 96 *Yale Law Journal* 943–1005.

Alexy, Robert, 'Zum Begriff des Rechtspinzips', in Werner Krawietz, Opalek Kazimierz, Aleksander Peczenik and Alfred Schramm (eds.), *Argumentation und Hermeneutik in der Jurisprudenz* (Berlin: Duncker & Humblot, 1979), pp. 59–87.

A Theory of Constitutional Rights (Oxford: Oxford University Press, 2002).

'Constitutional Rights, Balancing, and Rationality' (2003) 16 *Ratio Juris* 131–40.

'On Balancing and Subsumption: A Structural Comparison' (2003) 16 *Ratio Juris* 433–49.

'Balancing, Constitutional Review, and Representation' (2005) 3 *International Journal of Constitutional Law* 572–81.

Arnauld, Andreas von, *Die Freiheitsrechte und ihre Schranken* (Baden-Baden: Nomos, 1999).

Arnim, Hans Herbert von, *Abgeordnetenentschädigung und Grundgesetz* (Landau: Pfälzische Verlagsanstalt, 1975).

Gemeinwohl und Gruppeninteressen (Frankfurt a.M.: Alfred Metzner Verlag, 1977).

Badura, Peter, Fritz Rittner and Bernd Rüthers, *Mitbestimmungsgesetz 1976 und Grundgesetz* (München: C.H. Beck, 1977).

Bailey, Michael A. and Forrest Maltzman, 'Does Legal Doctrine Matter? Unpacking Law and Policy Preferences on the U.S. Supreme Court' (2008) 102 *American Political Science Review* 369–84.

Baldus, Manfred, 'Frühe Machtkämpfe – Ein Versuch über die historischen Gründe der Autorität des Bundesverfassungsgerichts', in Thomas Henne and Arne Riedlinger (eds.), *Das Lüth-Urteil aus (rechts-)historischer Sicht* (Berlin: Berliner Wissenschafts-Verlag, 2005), pp. 237–48.

'Menschenwürde und Absolutheitsthese – Zwischenbericht zu einer zukunftsweisenden Debatte' (2011) 136 *Archiv des öffentlichen Rechts* 529–52.

Baldwin, Robert E. and Christopher S. Magee, 'Is Trade Policy for Sale? Congressional Voting on Recent Trade Bills' (2000) 105 *Public Choice* 79–101.

Barak, Aharon, 'Proportional Effect: The Israeli Experience' (2007) 57 *University of Toronto Law Journal* 369–82.

'Proportionality and Principled Balancing' (2010) 4 *Law & Ethics of Human Rights* 1–18.

Proportionality: Constitutional Rights and their Limitations (Cambridge: Cambridge University Press, 2012).

Baron, Jonathan, *Thinking and Deciding*, 3rd edn (Cambridge: Cambridge University Press, 2000)

Bassok, Or, 'The Two Countermajoritarian Difficulties' (2012) 31 *Saint Louis University Public Law Review* 333–82.

Bateman, Thomas M. J., 'Legal Modesty and Political Boldness: The Supreme Court of Canada's Decision in Chaoulli v. Quebec' (2006) 11 *Review of Constitutional Studies* 317–43.

Beatty, David M., 'Human Rights and the Rules of Law', in David M. Beatty (ed.), *Human Rights and Judicial Review: A Comparative Perspective* (Dordrecht: Martinus Nijhoff, 1994), pp. 1–56.

'The Canadian Charter of Rights: Lessons and Laments' (1997) 60 *Modern Law Review* 481–98.

The Ultimate Rule of Law (Oxford: Oxford University Press, 2004).

Becker, Florian, 'Verhältnismäßigkeit', in Hanno Kube, Rudolf Mellinghoff, Gerd Morgenthaler, Ulrich Palm, Thomas Puhl and Christian Seiler (eds.), *Leitgedanken des Rechts: Paul Kirchhof zum 70. Geburtstag. Band I: Staat und Verfassung* (Heidelberg: C. F. Müller, 2013), pp. 225–36.

Bellamy, Richard, *Political Constitutionalism: A Republican Defense of the Constitutionality of Democracy* (Cambridge: Cambridge University Press, 2007).

Benvenisti, Eyal, 'Reclaiming Democracy: The Strategic Uses of Foreign and International Law by National Courts' (2008) 102 *American Journal of International Law* 241–74.

Benvindo, Juliano Zaiden, *On the Limits of Constitutional Adjudication: Deconstructing Balancing and Judicial Activism* (Berlin: Springer, 2010).

Bernal Pulido, Carlos, 'The Rationality of Balancing' (2006) 92 *Archiv für Rechts- und Sozialphilosophie* 195–208.

'The Migration of Proportionality across Europe' (2013) 11 *New Zealand Journal of Public and International Law* 483–515.

Bernstorff, Jochen von, 'Pflichtenkollision und Menschenwürdegarantie' (2008) 47 *Der Staat* 21–40.

'Die Wesensgehalte der Grundrechte und das Verhältnis von Freiheit und Sicherheit unter dem Grundgesetz', in Felix Arndt et al. (eds.), *Freiheit – Sicherheit – Öffentlichkeit* (Baden-Baden: Nomos, 2009), pp. 40–60.

'Kerngehaltsschutz durch den UN-Menschenrechtsausschuss und den EGMR: Vom Wert kategorialer Argumentationsformen' (2011) 50 *Der Staat* 165–90.

'Der Streit um die Menschenwürde im Grund- und Menschenrechtsschutz: Eine Verteidigung des Absoluten als Grenze und Auftrag' (2013) 68 *Juristenzeitung* 905–15.

'Proportionality without Balancing – Why Judicial *Ad Hoc*-Balancing Is Unnecessary and Potentially Detrimental to the Realization of Individual and Collective Self-determination', in Liora Lazarus, Christopher McCrudden and Nigel Bowles (eds.), *Reasoning Rights: Comparative Judicial Engagement* (Oxford: Hart, 2014), pp. 63–86.

Bethge, Herbert, 'Grundrechtskollisionen', in Detlef Merten and Hans-Jürgen Papier (eds.), *Handbuch der Grundrechte. Band III: Grundrechte in Deutschland: Allgemeine Lehren II* (Heidelberg: C. F. Müller, 2009).

Bettermann, Karl August, *Hypertrophie der Grundrechte* (Hamburg: Hamburgischer Anwaltverein, 1984).

Bickel, Alexander M., *The Least Dangerous Branch: The Supreme Court at the Bar of Politics* (New Haven: Yale University Press, 1962).

Bilchitz, David, 'Does Balancing Adequately Capture the Nature of Rights?' (2011) 25 *SA Public Law* 423–44.

'How Should Rights Be Limited?' (2011) 2011 *Tydskrif vir die suid-afrikaanse Reg* 568–79.

'Necessity and Proportionality: Towards a Balanced Approach?', in Liora Lazarus, Christopher McCrudden and Nigel Bowles (eds.), *Reasoning Rights: Comparative Judicial Engagement* (Oxford: Hart, 2014), pp. 41–62.

Blaauw-Wolf, Loammi, 'The 'Balancing of Interests' with Reference to the Principle of Proportionality and the Doctrine of *Güterabwägung* – a Comparative Analysis' (1999) 14 *SA Public Law* 178–214.

Böckenförde, Ernst-Wolfgang, *Zur Lage der Grundrechtsdogmatik nach 40 Jahren Grundgesetz* (München: Carl Friedrich von Siemens Stiftung, 1989).

'Grundrechte als Grundsatznormen' (1990) 29 *Der Staat* 1–31.

'Menschenwürde als normatives Prinzip' (2003) 58 *Juristenzeitung* 809–15.

'Schutzbereich, Eingriff, verfassungsimmanente Schranken: Zur Kritik gegenwärtiger Grundrechtsdogmatik' (2003) 42 *Der Staat* 165–92.

'Demokratie als Verfassungsprinzip', in Josef Isensee and Paul Kirchhof (eds.), *Handbuch des Staatsrechts der Bundesrepublik Deutschland. Band II: Verfassungsstaat*, 3rd edn (Heidelberg: C. F. Müller, 2004), pp. 429–96.

Bogdandy, Armin von, *Gubernative Rechtsetzung* (Tübingen: Mohr Siebeck, 2000).

Bomhoff, Jacco, 'Lüth's 50th Anniversary: Some Comparative Observations on the German Foundations of Judicial Balancing' (2008) 9 *German Law Journal* 121–4.

Balancing Constitutional Rights: The Origins and Meanings of Postwar Legal Discourse (Cambridge: Cambridge University Press, 2013).

Bork, Robert H., 'Neutral Principles and Some First Amendment Problems' (1971) 47 *Indiana Law Journal* 1–35.

The Tempting of America: The Political Seduction of the Law (New York: Free Press, 1990).

Borowski, Martin, 'Abwehrrechte als grundrechtliche Prinzipien', in Jan-Reinard Sieckmann (ed.), *Die Prinzipientheorie der Grundrechte* (Baden-Baden: Nomos, 2007), pp. 81–104.

Grundrechte als Prinzipien, 2nd edn (Baden-Baden: Nomos, 2007).

'On Apples and Oranges: Comment on Niels Petersen' (2013) 14 *German Law Journal* 1409–18.

Botha, Henk, 'Rights, Limitations, and the (Im)possibility of Self-Government', in Henk Botha, André van der Walt and Johan van der Walt (eds.), *Rights and Democracy in a Transformative Constitution* (Stellenbosch: Sun Press, 2003), pp. 13–31.

Bredt, Christopher D. and Adam M. Dodek, 'The Increasing Irrelevance of Section 1 of the Charter' (2001) 14 *Supreme Court Law Review* 175–88.

Brennan, Thomas, Lee Epstein and Nancy Staudt, 'The Political Economy of Judging' (2009) 93 *Minnesota Law Review* 1503–34.

Brenner, Michael, 'Der Kruzifix-Beschluß des Bundesverfassungsgerichts' (1996) 5 *Thüringer Verwaltungsblätter* 145–52.

Brenner, Saul and Marc Stier, 'Retesting Segal and Spaeth's Stare Decisis Model' (1996) 40 *American Journal of Political Science* 1036–48.

Britz, Gabriele, 'Prozedurale Lösung von Grundrechtskollisionen durch "grundrechtliches Vorverfahren"' (2003) 42 *Der Staat* 35–59.

Brodocz, André, *Die Macht der Judikative* (Wiesbaden: VS Verlag für Sozialwissenschaften, 2009).

Broß, Siegfried, 'Die Würde des Menschen bleibt unantastbar', in Caroline Y. Robertson-von Trotha (ed.), *60 Jahre Grundgesetz: Interdisziplinäre Perspektiven* (Baden-Baden: Nomos, 2009), pp. 41–50.

Brugger, Winfried, 'Menschenwürde im anthropologischen Kreuz der Entscheidung' (2008) 56 *Jahrbuch des öffentlichen Rechts der Gegenwart* 95–124.

Bryde, Brun-Otto, *Verfassungsentwicklung: Stabilität und Dynamik im Verfassungsrecht der Bundesrepublik Deutschland* (Baden-Baden: Nomos, 1982).

'Die Rolle der Verfassungsgerichtsbarkeit in Umbruchsituationen', in Joachim Jens Hesse, Gunnar Folke Schuppert and Katharina Harms (eds.), *Verfassungsrecht und Verfassungspolitik in Umbruchsituationen* (Baden-Baden: Nomos, 1999), pp. 197–210.

'Das Demokratieprinzip des Grundgesetzes als Optimierungsaufgabe', in Thomas Blanke (ed.), *Demokratie und Grundgesetz: Eine Auseinandersetzung mit der verfassungsgerichtlichen Rechtsprechung* (Baden-Baden: Nomos, 2000), pp. 59–70.

'Der Beitrag des Bundesverfassungsgerichts zur Demokratisierung der Bundesrepublik', in Robert Christian van Ooyen and Martin H. W. Möllers (eds.), *Das Bundesverfassungsgericht im politischen System* (Wiesbaden: VS Verlag für Sozialwissenschaften, 2006), pp. 321–31.

Bulla, Simon, 'Das Verfassungsprinzip der Folgerichtigkeit und seine Auswirkungen auf die Grundrechtsdogmatik' (2008) 1 *Zeitschrift für das Juristische Studium* 585–96.

Bumke, Christian, 'Die Pflicht zur konsistenten Gesetzgebung' (2010) 49 *Der Staat* 77–105.

Caldeira, Gregory A., 'Neither the Purse nor the Sword: Dynamics of Public Confidence in the Supreme Court' (1986) 80 *American Political Science Review* 1209–26.

Caldeira, Gregory A. and James L. Gibson, 'The Etiology of Public Support for the Supreme Court' (1992) 36 *American Journal of Political Science* 635–64.

Çali, Basak, 'Balancing Human Rights? Methodological Problems with Weights, Scales and Proportions' (2007) 29 *Human Rights Quarterly* 251–70.

Camilo de Oliveira, Renata, *Zur Kritik der Abwägung in der Grundrechtsdogmatik* (Berlin: Duncker & Humblot, 2013).

Cappelletti, Mauro, *The Judicial Process in Comparative Perspective* (Oxford: Clarendon Press, 1989).

Carrubba, Clifford James, 'A Model of the Endogenous Development of Judicial Institutions in Federal and International Systems' (2009) 71 *Journal of Politics* 55–69.

Chang, Ruth, 'Introduction', in Ruth Chang (ed.), *Incommensurability, Incomparability, and Practical Reason* (Cambridge: Harvard University Press, 1997), pp. 1–34.

Chapman, Pamela A., 'The Politics of Judging: Section 1 of the Charter of Rights and Freedoms' (1986) 24 *Osgoode Hall Law Journal* 867–96.

Charney, Robert E. and S. Zachary Green, 'Auton and Chaoulli: Who Decides the Future of Health Care in Canada?' (2005) 19 *National Journal of Constitutional Law* 263–83.

'Prophets of Doom, Seers of Fortune: 20 Years of Experience under the Oakes Test' (2006) 34 *Supreme Court Law Review* 479–99.

Chemerinsky, Erwin, 'The Vanishing Constitution' (1989) 103 *Harvard Law Review* 43–104.

Constitutional Law: Principles and Policies, 4th edn (New York: Wolters Kluwer, 2011).

Choudhry, Sujit, 'Worse than Lochner?', in Colleen M. Flood, Kent Roach and Lorne Sossin (eds.), *Access to Care, Access to Justice: The Legal Debate Over Private Health Insurance in Canada* (Toronto: University of Toronto Press, 2005), pp. 75–100.

'So what is the real legacy of *Oakes?* Two Decades of Proportionality Analysis under the Canadian *Charter*'s Section 1' (2006) 34 *Supreme Court Law Review* 501–35.

"He had a mandate'; The South African Constitutional Court and the African National Congress in a dominant party democracy' (2009) 2 *Constitutional Court Review* 1–86.

Christensen, Ralph and Andreas Fischer-Lescano, *Das Ganze des Rechts – Vom hierarchischen zum reflexiven Verständnis deutscher und europäischer Grundrechte* (Berlin: Duncker & Humblot, 2007).

Christensen, Ralph and Kent D. Lerch, 'Dass das Ganze das Wahre ist, ist nicht ganz unwahr' (2007) 62 *Juristenzeitung* 438–44.

Classen, Claus Dieter, 'Das Prinzip der Verhältnismäßigkeit im Spiegel europäischer Rechtsentwicklungen', in Michael Sachs and Helmut Siekmann (eds.), *Der grundrechtsgeprägte Verfassungsstaat: Festschrift für Klaus Stern zum 80. Geburtstag* (Berlin: Duncker & Humblot, 2012), pp. 651–67.

Cockrell, Alfred, 'Rainbow Jurisprudence' (1996) 12 *South African Journal on Human Rights* 1–38.

Cohen-Eliya, Moshe and Iddo Porat, 'The hidden foreign law debate in *Heller*: The proportionality approach in American constitutional law' (2009) 46 *San Diego Law Review* 367–413.

'American balancing and German proportionality: The historical origins' (2010) 8 *International Journal of Constitutional Law* 263–86.

'Proportionality and the Culture of Justification' (2011) 59 *American Journal of Comparative Law* 463–90.

Proportionality and Constitutional Culture (Cambridge: Cambridge University Press, 2013).

'Proportionality and Justification' (2014) 64 *University of Toronto Law Journal* 458–77.

Cohen, Joshua and Charles Sabel, 'Direct-Deliberative Polyarchy' (1997) 3 *European Law Journal* 313–42.

Collings, Justin, *Democracy's Guardians: A History of the German Federal Constitutional Court 1951–2001* (Oxford: Oxford University Press, 2015).

Cornils, Matthias, 'Folgerichtiger Nichtraucherschutz: Von Verfassungs wegen keine halben Sachen?' (2008) 1 *Zeitschrift für das Juristische Studium* 660–3.

'Allgemeine Handlungsfreiheit', in Josef Isensee and Paul Kirchhof (eds.), *Handbuch des Staatsrechts der Bundesrepublik Deutschland. Band VII: Freiheitsrechte* 3rd edn(Heidelberg: C. F. Müller, 2009), pp. 1155–224.

'Rationalitätsanforderungen an die parlamentarische Gesetzgebung im demokratischen Rechtsstaat' (2011) 126 *Deutsches Verwaltungsblatt* 1053–61.

Craig, Paul, 'The Nature of Reasonableness Review' (2013) 66 *Current Legal Problems* 131–67.

Cremer, Wolfram, *Freiheitsgrundrechte. Funktionen und Strukturen* (Tübingen: J. C. B. Mohr, 2003).

Currie, Iain and Johan de Waal, *The Bill of Rights Handbook* 6th edn (Lansdowne: Juta, 2013).

Dammann, Ilmer, *Der Kernbereich der privaten Lebensgestaltung: Zum Menschenwürde- und Wesensgehaltsschutz im Bereich der Freiheitsgrundrechte* (Berlin: Duncker & Humblot, 2011).

Dann, Philipp, 'Verfassungsgerichtliche Kontrolle gesetzgeberischer Rationalität' (2010) 49 *Der Staat* 630–46.

Dechsling, Rainer, *Das Verhältnismäßigkeitsgebot* (München: Franz Vahlen, 1989).

Dederer, Hans-Georg, 'Die Garantie der Menschenwürde (Art. 1 Abs. 1 GG)' (2009) 57 *Jahrbuch des öffentlichen Rechts der Gegenwart* 89–124.

Delaney, Erin F., 'Judiciary Rising: Constitutional Change in the United Kingdom' (2014) 108 *Northwestern University Law Review* 543–605.

Denzau, Arthur T. and Michael C. Munger, 'Legislators and Interest Groups: How Unorganized Interests Get Represented' (1986) 80 *American Political Science Review* 89–106.

Detterbeck, Steffen, 'Gelten die Entscheidungen des Bundesverfassungsgerichts auch in Bayern? - Zur prozessualen Bedeutung der Kruzifix-Entscheidung vom 16.5.1996 und zur Deutung von § 31 I BVerfGG' (1996) 49 *Neue Juristische Wochenschrift* 426–32.

Di Fabio, Udo, *Das Recht offener Staaten* (Tübingen: J. C. B. Mohr, 1998).

Dreier, Horst, 'Vorbemerkungen vor Artikel 1 GG', in Horst Dreier (ed.), *Grundgesetz-Kommentar. Band I: Präambel, Artikel 1–19*, 3rd edn (Tübingen: Mohr Siebeck, 2013).

Dworkin, Ronald, *Taking Rights Seriously* (London: Duckworth, 1977).

Freedom's Law: The Moral Reading of the American Constitution (Cambridge, MA: Harvard University Press, 1996).

Easton, David, *A Systems Analysis of Political Life* (New York: John Wiley, 1965).

'A Re-Assessment of the Concept of Political Support' (1975) 5 *British Journal of Political Science* 435–57.

Elhauge, Einer R., 'Does Interest Group Theory Justify More Intensive Judicial Review?' (1991) 101 *Yale Law Journal* 31–110.

Elliott, Mark, 'Proportionality and Deference: The Importance of a Structured Approach', in Christopher Forsyth, Mark Elliott, Swati Jhaveri, Michael Ramsden and Anne Scully-Hill (eds.), *Effective Judicial Review: A Cornerstone of Good Governance* (Oxford: Oxford University Press, 2010), pp. 264–86.

Elsner, Thomas and Klara Schobert, 'Gedanken zur Abwägungsresistenz der Menschenwürde – angestoßen durch das Urteil des Bundesverfassungsgerichts zur Verfassungsmäßigkeit der Sicherheitsverwahrung' (2007) 122 *Deutsches Verwaltungsblatt* 278–87.

Ely, John Hart, 'The Centrality and Limits of Motivation Analysis' (1978) 15 *San Diego Law Review* 1155–61.

Democracy and Distrust: A Theory of Judicial Review (Cambridge: Harvard University Press, 1980).

Endicott, Timothy, 'Proportionality and Incomennsurability', in Grant Huscroft, Bradley W. Miller and Grégoire Webber (eds.), *Proportionality and the Rule of Law: Rights, Justification, Reasoning* (New York: Cambridge University Press, 2014), pp. 311–42.

Engel, Christoph, 'Internationaler Umweltschutz: Systematik der Probleme und der Lösungen', in Jürgen Basedow, Klaus J. Hopt and Hein Kötz (eds.), *Festschrift für Ulrich Drobnig zum siebzigsten Geburtstag* (Tübingen: Mohr Siebeck, 1998), pp. 247–76.

'Rechtswissenschaft als angewandte Sozialwissenschaft: Die Aufgabe der Rechtswissenschaft nach der Öffnung der Rechtsordnung für sozialwissenschaftliche Theorie', in Christoph Engel (ed.), *Methodische Zugänge zu einem Recht der Gemeinschaftsgüter* (Baden-Baden: Nomos, 1998), pp. 11–40.

'Delineating the Proper Scope of Government: A Proper Task for a Constitutional Court?' (2001) 157 *Journal of Institutional and Theoretical Economics* 187–219.

'Offene Gemeinwohldefinitionen' (2001) 32 *Rechtstheorie* 23–52.

'Das legitime Ziel als Element des Übermaßverbots', in Winfried Brugger, Stephan Kirste and Michael Anderheiden (eds.), *Gemeinwohl in Deutschland, Europa und der Welt* (Baden-Baden: Nomos, 2002), pp. 103–72.

'The Constitutional Court – Applying the Proportionality Principle – as a Subsidiary Authority for the Assessment of Political Outcomes', in Christoph Engel and Adrienne Héritier (eds.), *Linking Politics and Law* (Baden-Baden: Nomos, 2003), pp. 285–314.

'Freiheit und Autonomie', in Detlef Merten and Hans-Jürgen Papier (eds.), *Handbuch der Grundrechte. Band II: Grundrechte in Deutschland: Allgemeine Lehren I* (Heidelberg: C. F. Müller, 2006), pp. 389–436.

'Inconsistency in the Law: In Search of a Balanced Norm', in Christoph Engel and Lorraine Daston (eds.), *Is there Value in Inconsistency?* (Baden-Baden: Nomos, 2006), pp. 221–81.

'Öffentliches Wirtschaftsrecht aus Sicht der ökonomischen Theorie', in Dirk Ehlers, Michael Fehling and Hermann Pünder (eds.), *Besonderes Verwaltungsrecht. Band I: Öffentliches Wirtschaftsrecht*, 3rd edn (Heidelberg: C. F. Müller, 2012), pp. 40–62.

'Das legitime Ziel in der Praxis des Bundesverfassungsgerichts: Eine quantitative Analyse der Entscheidungen des Jahres 2011', in Matthias Jestaedt and Oliver

Lepsius (eds.), *Verhältnismäßigkeit: Zur Tragfähigkeit eines verfassungsrechtlichen Schlüsselkonzepts* (Tübingen: Mohr Siebeck, 2015), pp. 97–128.

Englisch, Joachim, 'Folgerichtiges Steuerrecht als Verfassungsgebot', in Klaus Tipke, Roman Seer, Johanna Hey and Joachim Englisch (eds.), *Gestaltung der Steuer rechtsordnung: Festschrift für Joachim Lang zum 70. Geburtstag* (Köln: Verlag Dr. Otto Schmidt, 2010), pp. 167–220.

Epstein, Lee, Jack Knight and Olga Shvetsova, 'The Role of Constitutional Courts in the Establishment and Maintenance of Democratic Systems of Government' (2001) 35 *Law & Society Review* 117–63.

Epstein, Richard A., 'Toward a Revitalization of the Contract Clause' (1984) 51 *The University of Chicago Law Review* 703–51.

Eriksen, Erik Oddvar, 'Deliberation und demokratische Legitimität in der EU: Zwischen Konsens und Kompromiss', in Peter Niesen and Benjamin Herborth (eds.), *Anarchie der kommunikativen Freiheit* (Frankfurt a.M.: Suhrkamp, 2007), pp. 294–320.

Esser, Josef, *Vorverständnis und Methodenwahl in der Rechtsfindung* (Frankfurt a.M.: Athenäum Verlag, 1970).

Fallon, Richard H., 'Strict Judicial Scrutiny' (2007) 54 *UCLA Law Review* 1267–337.

Feinberg, Joel, 'Justice, Fairness and Rationality' (1972) 81 *Yale Law Journal* 1004–31.

Ferejohn, John, 'Instituting Deliberative Democracy', in Ian Shapiro and Stephen Macedo (eds.), *Designing Democratic Institutions* (New York: New York University Press, 2000), pp. 75–104.

'Judicializing Politics, Politicizing Law' (2002) 65 *Law and Contemporary Problems* 41–68.

Fischer-Lescano, Andreas, 'Kritik der praktischen Konkordanz' (2008) 41 *Kritische Justiz* 166–77.

Fishkin, James S., *Democracy and Deliberation: New Directions for Democratic Reform* (New Haven: Yale University Press, 1991).

Flood, Colleen M., 'Chaoulli's Legacy for the Future of Canadian Health Care Policy' (2006) 44 *Osgoode Hall Law Journal* 273–310.

Forst, Rainer, 'The Rule of Reasons: Three Models of Deliberative Democracy' (2001) 14 *Ratio Juris* 345–78.

Forsthoff, Ernst, *Der Staat in der Industriegesellschaft*, 2nd edn (München: C. H. Beck, 1971).

Fowkes, James, *Building the Constitution: The Practice of Constitutional Interpretation in post-apartheid South Africa* (Cambridge: Cambridge University Press, 2016).

Friedman, Barry Evan, 'The Politics of Judicial Review' (2005) 84 *Texas Law Review* 257–337.

The Will of the People: How Public Opinion Has Influenced the Supreme Court and Shaped the Meaning of the Constitution (New York: Farrar, Straus and Giroux, 2009).

Friedman, Barry Evan and Erin F. Delaney, 'Becoming Supreme: The Federal Foundation of Judicial Supremacy' (2011) 111 *Columbia Law Review* 1137–93.

Fudenberg, Drew and Jean Tirole, *Game Theory* (Cambridge: MIT Press, 1991).

García Amado, Juan Antonio, 'Abwägung versus normative Auslegung' (2009) 40 *Rechtstheorie* 1–42.

Gardbaum, Stephen, 'The New Commonwealth Model of Constitutionalism' (2001) 49 *American Journal of Comparative Law* 707–60.

'Limiting Constitutional Rights' (2007) 54 *U.C.L.A. Law Review* 789–854.

'The Myth and the Reality of American Constitutional Exceptionalism' (2008) 107 *Michigan Law Review* 391–466.

'A Democratic Defense of Constitutional Balancing' (2010) 4 *Law & Ethics of Human Rights* 77–106.

The New Commonwealth Model of Constitutionalism (Cambridge: Cambridge University Press, 2013).

'Proportionality and Democratic Constitutionalism', in Grant Huscroft, Bradley W. Miller and Grégoire Webber (eds.), *Proportionality and the Rule of Law: Rights, Justification, Reasoning* (New York: Cambridge University Press, 2014), pp. 259–83.

'Are Strong Constitutional Courts Always a Good Thing for New Democracies?' (2015) 53 *Columbia Journal of Transnational Law* 285–320.

'Positive and Horizontal Rights: Proportionality's Next Frontier or a Bridge Too Far?', in Vicki Jackson and Mark Tushnet (eds.), *Proportionality: New Frontiers, New Challenges* (New York: Cambridge University Press, forthcoming).

Gassner, Ulrich M., 'Gesetzgebung und Bestimmtheitsgrundsatz' (1996) 11 *Zeitschrift für Gesetzgebung* 37–56.

Geis, Max-Emanuel, 'Geheime Offenbarung oder Offenbarungseid? – Anmerkungen zum "Kruzifix-Beschluß" des Bundesverfassungsgerichts' (1995) 43 *Recht der Jugend und des Bildungswesens* 373–86.

Gentz, Manfred, 'Zur Verhältnismäßigkeit von Grundrechtseingriffen' (1968) 21 *Neue Juristische Wochenschrift* 1600–07.

George, Tracey E. and Lee Epstein, 'On the Nature of Supreme Court Decision Making' (1992) 86 *American Political Science Review* 323–37.

Gibson, James L., 'Institutional Legitimacy, Procedural Justice, and Compliance with Supreme Court Decisions: A Question of Causality' (1991) 25 *Law & Society Review* 631–36.

Gibson, James L., Gregory A. Caldeira and Vanessa A. Baird, 'On the Legitimacy of National High Courts' (1998) 92 *American Political Science Review* 343–58.

Gilmour, Joan M., 'Fallout from Chaoulli: Is It Time to Find Cover?' (2006) 44 *Osgoode Hall Law Journal* 327–47.

Ginsburg, Tom, *Judicial Review in New Democracies: Constitutional Courts in Asian Cases* (Cambridge: Cambridge University Press, 2003).

Glaser, Andreas, *Nachhaltige Entwicklung und Demokratie* (Tübingen: Mohr Siebeck, 2006).

Goerg, Sebastian and Niels Petersen, 'Empirical research and statistics', in Emanuel Towfigh and Niels Petersen (eds.), *Economic Methods for Lawyers* (Cheltenham: Edward Elgar, 2015), pp. 146–76.

Goos, Christoph, *Innere Freiheit: Eine Rekonstruktion des grundgesetzlichen Würdebegriffs* (Göttingen: V&R unipress, 2011).

Gottlieb, Stephen E., 'The Paradox of Balancing Significant Interests' (1994) 45 *Hastings Law Journal* 825–66.

Grabitz, Eberhard, 'Der Grundsatz der Verhältnismäßigkeit in der Rechtsprechung des Bundesverfassungsgerichts' (1973) 98 *Archiv des öffentlichen Rechts* 568–616.

Grechenig, Kristoffel and Martin Gelter, 'The Transatlantic Divergence in Legal Thought: American Law and Economics vs. German Doctrinalism' (2008) 31 *Hastings International and Comparative Law Review* 295–360.

Griffin, James, 'Are There Incommensurable Values?' (1977) 7 *Philosophy and Public Affairs* 39–59.

Grimm, Dieter, 'Politische Parteien', in Ernst Benda, Werner Maihofer and Hans-Jochen Vogel (eds.), *Handbuch des Verfassungsrechts der Bundesrepublik Deutschland*, 2nd edn (Berlin: Walter de Gruyter, 1994), pp. 599–656.

'Proportionality in Canadian and German Jurisprudence' (2007) 57 *University of Toronto Law Journal* 383–97.

Gröschner, Rolf, 'Vom Ersatzgesetzgeber zum Ersatzerzieher' (2008) 23 *Zeitschrift für Gesetzgebung* 400–12.

Gröschner, Rolf and Oliver W. Lembcke, 'Dignitas absoluta: Ein kritischer Kommentar zum Absolutheitsanspruch der Würde', in Rolf Gröschner and Oliver W. Lembcke (eds.), *Das Dogma der Unantastbarkeit* (Tübingen: Mohr Siebeck, 2009), pp. 1–24.

Grosskopf, Anke and Jeffery J. Mondak, 'Do Attitudes Toward Specific Supreme Court Decisions Matter? The Impact of Webster and Texas v. Johnson on Public Confidence in the Supreme Court' (1998) 51 *Political Research Quarterly* 633–54.

Gunn, Jeremy T., 'Deconstructing Proportionality in Limitations Analysis' (2005) 19 *Emory International Law Review* 465–98.

Günther, Klaus, 'Ein normativer Begriff der Kohärenz für eine Theorie der juristischen Argumentation' (1989) 20 *Rechtstheorie* 163–90.

Gutman, Amy and Dennis Thompson, *Democracy and Disagreement* (Cambridge: Belknap Press, 1996).

Häberle, Peter, *Die Wesensgehaltsgarantie des Art. 19 Abs. 2 Grundgesetz* (Karlsruhe: Verlag C.F. Müller, 1962).

Habermas, Jürgen, *Between Facts and Norms: Contributions to a Discourse Theory of Law and Democracy* (Cambridge, UK: Polity Press, 1996).

Hailbronner, Michaela, 'Rethinking the rise of the German Constitutional Court: From anti-Nazism to value formalism' (2014) *International Journal of Constitutional Law* 626–49.

Traditions and Transformations: The Rise of German Constitutionalism (Oxford: Oxford University Press, 2015).

Hain, Karl-Eberhard, 'Konkretisierung der Menschenwürde durch Abwägung?' (2006) 45 *Der Staat* 189–214.

Haltern, Ulrich, 'Demokratische Verantwortlichkeit und Verfassungsgerichtsbarkeit' (1996) 35 *Der Staat* 551–80.

'Integration als Mythos. Zur Überforderung des Bundesverfassungsgerichts' (1997) 45 *Jahrbuch des öffentlichen Rechts der Gegenwart* 31–88.

Europarecht: Dogmatik im Kontext, 2nd edn (Tübingen: Mohr Siebeck, 2007).

Hänni, Julia, 'Rechtskonflikte, Wertefolgen und Inkommensurabilität', in Edward Schramm, Wibke Frey, Lorenz Kähler, Sabine Müller-Mall and Friederike Wapler (eds.), *Konflikte im Recht – Recht der Konflikte* (Stuttgart: Franz Steiner Verlag, 2010), pp. 173–85.

Hassemer, Winfried, 'Über den argumentativen Umgang mit der Würde des Menschen', in Gerhard Robbers, Dieter C. Umbach and Klaus-Eckart Gebauer (eds.), *Innere Sicherheit, Menschenwürde, Gentechnologie* (Frankfurt a.M.: Peter Lang, 2005), pp. 65–79.

Häußler, Richard, *Der Konflikt zwischen Bundesverfassungsgericht und politischer Führung* (Berlin: Duncker & Humblot, 1994).

Heckel, Martin, 'Das Kreuz im öffentlichen Raum: Zum "Kruzifix-Beschluß" des Bundesverfassungsgerichts' (1996) 111 *Deutsches Verwaltungsblatt* 453–82.

Heinsohn, Stephanie, 'Der öffentlichrechtliche Grundsatz der Verhältnismäßigkeit', PhD thesis, University of Münster (1997).

Henne, Thomas, '"Von 0 auf Lüth in 6 1/2 Jahren" – Zu den prägenden Faktoren der Grundsatzentscheidung', in Thomas Henne and Arne Riedlinger (eds.), *Das Lüth-Urteil aus (rechts-)historischer Sicht* (Berlin: Berliner Wissenschafts-Verlag, 2005), pp. 197–222.

Herdegen, Matthias, 'Verfassungsinterpretation als methodische Disziplin' (2004) 59 *Juristenzeitung* 873–79.

Herrmann, Dietrich, 'Akte der Selbstautorisierung als Grundstock institutioneller Macht von Verfassungsgerichten', in Hans Vorländer (ed.), *Die Deutungsmacht der Verfassungsgerichtsbarkeit* (Wiesbaden: VS Verlag für Sozialwissenschaften, 2006), pp. 141–73.

Hesse, Konrad, 'Bestand und Bedeutung der Grundrechte in der Bundesrepublik Deutschland' (1978) 5 *Europäische Grundrechte Zeitschrift* 427–38.

Hillgruber, Christian, 'Der Staat des Grundgesetzes – nur "bedingt abwehrbereit"?' (2007) 62 *Juristenzeitung* 209–18.

'Grundrechtsschranken', in Josef Isensee and Paul Kirchhof (eds.), *Handbuch des Staatsrechts der Bundesrepublik Deutschland. Band IX: Allgemeine Grundrechtslehren*, 3rd edn (Heidelberg: C. F. Müller, 2011), pp. 1033–75.

'Ohne rechtes Maß? Eine Kritik der Rechtsprechung des Bundesverfassungsgerichts nach 60 Jahren' (2011) 66 *Juristenzeitung* 861–71.

Hirschberg, Lothar, *Der Grundsatz der Verhältnismäßigkeit* (Göttingen: Verlag Otto Schwartz & Co., 1981).
Hirschl, Ran, *Comparative Matters: The Renaissance of Comparative Constitutional Law* (Oxford: Oxford University Press, 2014).
Hirschman, Albert O., *Exit, Voice, and Loyalty* (Cambridge, Mass.: Harvard University Press, 1970).
Höffe, Otfried, 'Wieviel Politik ist dem Verfassungsgericht erlaubt?' (1999) 38 *Der Staat* 171–93.
Hoffmann-Riem, Wolfgang, 'Grundrechtsanwendung unter Rationalitätsanspruch' (2004) 43 *Der Staat* 203–33.
Höfling, Wolfram, 'Unantastbare Grundrechte: ein normlogischer Widerspruch?', in Rolf Gröschner and Oliver W. Lembcke (eds.), *Das Dogma der Unantastbarkeit* (Tübingen: Mohr Siebeck, 2009), pp. 111–20.
Hofmann, Ekkehard, 'Das Wohl der Allgemeinheit als Enteignungsvoraussetzung: Überlegungen zur Methodik der staatlichen Entscheidungsherstellung und ihrer gerichtlichen Kontrolle im Verwaltungs- und Verfassungsrecht', in Marc Bungenberg *et al.* (eds.), *Recht und Ökonomik* (München: C. H. Beck, 2004), pp. 161–88.
Abwägung im Recht (Tübingen: Mohr Siebeck, 2007)
Hogg, Peter W., 'Section 1 Revisited' (1991) 1 *National Journal of Constitutional Law* 1–24.
Constitutional Law of Canada, vol. 2, 5th edn (Ontario: Thomson Carswell, 2007).
Hubmann, Heinrich, 'Die Methode der Abwägung', in Heinrich Hubmann and Heinz Hübner (eds.), *Festschrift für Ludwig Schnorr von Carolsfeld zum 70. Geburtstag* (Köln: Carl Heymanns Verlag, 1972), pp. 173–97.
Huscroft, Grant, 'Proportionality and Pretense' (2014) 29 *Constitutional Commentary* 229–55.
Huscroft, Grant, Bradley W. Miller and Grégoire C.N. Webber, 'Introduction', in Grant Huscroft, Bradley W. Miller and Grégoire Webber (eds.), *Proportionality and the Rule of Law: Rights, Justification, Reasoning* (New York: Cambridge University Press, 2014), pp. 1–17.
Iacobucci, Frank, 'Judicial Review by the Supreme Court of Canada under the Canadian Charter of Rights and Freedoms: The First Ten Years', in David M. Beatty (ed.), *Human Rights and Judicial Review: A Comparative Perspective* (Dordrecht: Martinus Nijhoff Publishers, 1994), pp. 93–133.
Isensee, Josef, 'Abschied der Demokratie vom Demos: Ausländerwahlrecht als Identitätsfrage für Volk, Demokratie und Verfassung', in Dieter Schwab, Dieter Giesen and Joseph Listl (eds.), *Staat, Kirche, Wissenschaft in einer pluralistischen Gesellschaft: Festschrift für Paul Mikat zum 65. Geburtstag* (Berlin: Duncker & Humblot, 1989), pp. 705–40.
'Bildersturm durch Grundrechtsinterpretation: Der Kruzifix-Beschluss des BVerfG' (1996) 29 *Zeitschrift für Rechtspolitik* 10–5.

'Bundesverfassungsgericht – quo vadis?' (1996) 51 *Juristenzeitung* 1085–93.

'Das Grundrecht als Abwehrrecht und als staatliche Schutzpflicht', in Josef Isensee and Paul Kirchhof (eds.), *Handbuch des Staatsrechts der Bundesrepublik Deutschland. Band IX: Allgemeine Grundrechtslehren,* 3rd edn (Heidelberg: C. F. Müller, 2011), pp. 413–568.

Issacharoff, Samuel, 'Bearing the Costs' (2000) 53 *Stanford Law Review* 519–37

'Gerrymendering and Political Cartels' (2002) 116 *Harvard Law Review* 593–648.

Fragile Democracies: Contested Power in the Era of Constitutional Courts (New York: Cambridge University Press, 2015).

Issacharoff, Samuel and Richard H. Pildes, 'Politics As Markets: Partisan Lockups of the Democratic Process' (1998) 50 *Stanford Law Review* 643–717.

Jackman, Martha, '"The Last Line of Defence for [Which?] Citizens": Accountability, Equality, and the Right to Health in Chaoulli' (2006) 44 *Osgoode Hall Law Journal* 349–75.

Jackson, Vicki C., 'Ambivalent Resistance and Comparative Constitutionalism: Opening up the Conversation on "Proportionality," Rights and Federalism' (1999) 1 *University of Pennsylvania Journal of Constitutional Law* 583–639.

'Constitutional Law in an Age of Proportionality' (2015) 124 *Yale Law Journal* 3094–196.

Jansen, Nils, 'Die normativen Grundlagen rationalen Abwägens im Recht', in Jan-Reinard Sieckmann (ed.), *Die Prinzipientheorie der Grundrechte* (Baden-Baden: Nomos, 2007), pp. 39–57.

Jestaedt, Matthias, *Grundrechtsentfaltung im Gesetz: Studien zur Interdependenz von Grundrechtsdogmatik und Rechtsgewinnungstheorie* (Tübingen: Mohr Siebeck, 1999).

'Die Abwägungslehre – ihre Stärken und ihre Schwächen', in Otto Depenheuer, Markus Heintzen, Matthias Jestaedt and Peter Axer (eds.), *Staat im Wort: Festschrift für Josef Isensee* (Heidelberg: C. F. Müller, 2007), pp. 253–75.

'Phänomen Bundesverfassungsgericht: Was das Gericht zu dem macht, was es ist', in Matthias Jestaedt, Oliver Lepsius, Christoph Möllers and Christoph Schönberger (eds.), *Das entgrenzte Gericht: Eine kritische Bilanz nach sechzig Jahren Bundesverfassungsgericht* (Berlin: Suhrkamp, 2011), pp. 77–157.

Kahl, Wolfgang, 'Vom weiten Schutzbereich zum engen Gewährleistungsgehalt' (2004) 43 *Der Staat* 167–202.

Kahl, Wolfgang and Andreas Glaser, 'Die Nachhaltigkeitsfähigkeit der parlamentarischen Demokratie', in Klaus Lange (ed.), *Nachhaltigkeit im Recht* (Baden-Baden: Nomos, 2003), pp. 9–38.

Kaiser, Anna-Bettina, 'Das Apothekenurteil des BVerfG nach 50 Jahren: Anfang oder Anfang vom Ende der Berufsfreiheit?' (2008) 30 *Juristische Ausbildung* 844–50.

Kant, Immanuel, *The Metaphysics of Morals* (Mary Gregor ed., Cambridge: Cambridge University Press, 1996).

Keck, Thomas M., 'Party, Policy, or Duty: Why Does the Supreme Court Invalidate Federal Statutes?' (2007) 101 *American Political Science Review* 321–38.

Kelly, James Bernard, *Governing with the Charter: Legislative and Judicial Activism and Framers' Intent* (Vancouver: UBC Press, 2005).

Kelman, Mark, *Strategy or Principle? – The Choice between Regulation and Taxation* (Ann Arbor: University of Michigan Press, 1999).

Kennedy, Duncan, 'A Transnational Genealogy of Proportionality in Private Law', in Roger Brownsword, Hans-W. Micklitz, Leone Niglia and Stephen Weatherill (eds.), *The Foundations of European Private Law* (Oxford: Hart, 2011), pp. 185–220.

Kersting, Wolfgang, *Die politische Philosophie des Gesellschaftsvertrags* (Darmstadt: Wissenschaftliche Buchgesellschaft, 1994).

King, Gary, Robert O. Keohane and Sidney Verba, *Designing Social Inquiry: Scientific Inference in Qualitative Research* (Princeton: Princeton University Press, 1994).

Kirchhof, Paul, 'Allgemeiner Gleichheitssatz', in Josef Isensee and Paul Kirchhof (eds.), *Handbuch des Staatsrechts der Bundesrepublik Deutschland. Band VIII: Grundrechte: Wirtschaft, Verfahren, Gleichheit*, 3rd edn (Heidelberg: C. F. Müller, 2010), pp. 697–838.

Klatt, Matthias and Moritz Meister, 'Proportionality – a benefit to human rights? Remarks on the I.CON controversy' (2012) 10 *International Journal of Constitutional Law* 687–708.

The Constitutional Structure of Proportionality (Oxford: Oxford University Press, 2012).

Kleiber, Michael, *Der grundrechtliche Schutz zukünftiger Generationen* (Tübingen: Mohr Siebeck, 2014).

Kloepfer, Michael, 'Leben und Würde des Menschen', in Peter Badura and Horst Dreier (eds.), *Festschrift 50 Jahre Bundesverfassungsgericht. Zweiter Band: Klärung und Fortbildung des Verfassungsrechts* (Tübingen: Mohr Siebeck, 2001), pp. 77–104.

Klug, Heinz, 'Introducing the Devil: An Institutional Analysis of the Power of Constitutional Review' (1997) 13 *South African Journal on Human Rights* 185–208.

The Constitution of South Africa: A Contextual Analysis (Oxford: Hart, 2010).

Kneip, Sascha, *Verfassungsgerichte als politische Akteure* (Baden-Baden: Nomos, 2009).

Knies, Wolfgang, 'Auf dem Weg in den "verfassungsgerichtlichen Jurisdiktionsstaat"?', in Joachim Burmeister (ed.), *Verfassungsstaatlichkeit: Festschrift für Klaus Stern zum 65. Geburtstag* (München: C. H. Beck, 1997), pp. 1155–82.

Knill, Christoph and Florian Becker, 'Divergenz trotz Diffusion? – Rechtsvergleichende Aspekte des Verhältnismäßigkeitsprinzips in Deutschland, Großbritannien und der Europäischen Union' (2003) 36 *Die Verwaltung* 447–81.

Kommers, Donald P., *Judicial Politics in West Germany: A Study of the Federal Constitutional Court* (Beverly Hills: Sage, 1976).

'Germany: Balancing Rights and Duties', in Jeffrey Goldsworthy (ed.), *Interpreting Constitutions* (Oxford: Oxford University Press, 2006), pp. 161–214.

Koskenniemi, Martti, "The Lady Doth Protest Too Much': Kosovo, and the Turn to Ethics in International Law' (2002) 65 *Modern Law Review* 159–75.

From Apology to Utopia: The Structure of the International Legal Argument (Cambridge: Cambridge University Press, 2005).

Koutnatzis, Stylianos-Ioannis G., 'Verfassungsvergleichende Überlegungen zur Rezeption des Grundsatzes der Verhältnismäßigkeit in Übersee' (2011) 44 *Verfassung und Recht in Übersee* 32–59.

Krajewski, Markus, 'Kommunalwahlrechtliche Sperrklauseln im föderativen System' (2008) 61 *Die Öffentliche Verwaltung* 345–53.

Kramer, Larry D., *The People Themselves: Popular Constitutionalism and Judicial Review* (Cambridge: Harvard University Press, 2004)

Kranenpohl, Uwe, 'Die Bedeutung von Interpretationsmethoden und Dogmatik in der Entscheidungspraxis des Bundesverfassungsgerichts' (2009) 49 *Der Staat* 387–409.

Hinter dem Schleier des Beratungsgeheimnisses: Der Willensbildungs- und Entscheidungsprozess des Bundesverfassungsgerichts (Wiesbaden: VS Verlag für Sozialwissenschaften, 2010).

Krauss, Rupprecht von, *Der Grundsatz der Verhältnismäßigkeit* (Hamburg: Kommissionsverlag Ludwig Appel, 1955).

Kumm, Mattias, 'Jenseits des Verhältnismäßigkeitsgrundsatzes: Grundrechtlich er Strukturpluralismus im Verfassungsrecht der Vereinigten Staaten', in Jan-Reinard Sieckmann (ed.), *Die Prinzipientheorie der Grundrechte* (Baden-Baden: Nomos, 2007), pp. 241–62.

'The Idea of Socratic Contestation and the Right to Justification: The Point of Rights-Based Proportionality Review' (2010) 4 *Law & Ethics of Human Rights* 141–75.

'Alexy's Theory of Constitutional Rights and the Problem of Judicial Review', in Matthias Klatt (ed.), *Institutionalized Reason: The Jurisprudence of Robert Alexy* (Oxford: Oxford University Press, 2012), pp. 201–17.

Kumm, Mattias and Alec D. Walen, 'Human Dignity and Proportionality: Deontic Pluralism in Balancing', in Grant Huscroft, Bradley W. Miller and Grégoire Webber (eds.), *Proportionality and the Rule of Law: Rights, Justification, Reasoning* (New York: Cambridge University Press, 2014), pp. 67–89.

Kunig, Philip, 'Zum Dogma der unantastbaren Menschenwürde', in Rolf Gröschner and Oliver W. Lembcke (eds.), *Das Dogma der Unantastbarkeit* (Tübingen: Mohr Siebeck, 2009), pp. 121–32

Kyritsis, Dimitris, 'Representation and Waldron's Objection to Judicial Review' (2006) 26 *Oxford Journal of Legal Studies* 733–51.

'Whatever Works: Proportionality as a Constitutional Doctrine' (2014) 34 *Oxford Journal of Legal Studies* 395–415.

Shared Authority: Courts and Legislatures in Legal Theory (Oxford: Hart, 2015).

Ladeur, Karl-Heinz, *Kritik der Abwägung in der Grundrechtsdogmatik* (Tübingen: Mohr Siebeck, 2004).

Ladeur, Karl-Heinz and Ino Augsberg, *Die Funktion der Menschenwürde im Verfassungsstaat* (Tübingen: Mohr Siebeck, 2008).

Lajoie, Andrée and Henry Quillinan, 'Emerging Constitutional Norms: Continuous Judicial Amendment of the Constitution – The Proportionality Test as a Moving Target' (1992) 55 *Law and Contemporary Problems* 285–302.

Lang, Andrej, 'Wider die Metapher vom letzten Wort: Verfassungsgerichte als Wegweiser', in Dominik Elser *et al.* (eds.), *Das letzte Wort – Rechtsetzung & Rechtskontrolle in der Demokratie* (Baden-Baden: Nomos, 2014), pp. 15–37.

Langbein, Laura I., 'Lobbies and Political Conflict: The Case of Gun Control' (1993) 77 *Public Choice* 551–72.

Laufer, Heinz, *Verfassungsgerichtsbarkeit und politischer Prozeß* (Tübingen: J. C. B. Mohr, 1968).

Leisner-Egensperger, Anna, 'Die Folgerichtigkeit – Systemsuche als Problem für Verfassungsbegriff und Demokratiegebot' (2013) 66 *Die Öffentliche Verwaltung* 533–9.

Leisner, Walter, *Der Abwägungsstaat: Verhältnismäßigkeit als Gerechtigkeit?* (Berlin: Duncker & Humblot, 1997).

Lembcke, Oliver W., 'Das Bundesverfassungsgericht und die Regierung Adenauer – vom Streit um den Status zur Anerkennung der Autorität', in Robert Christian van Ooyen and Martin H.W. Möllers (eds.), *Das Bundesverfassungsgericht im politischen System* (Wiesbaden: VS Verlag für Sozialwissenschaften, 2006), pp. 151–61.

Lenta, Patrick, 'Judicial Restraint and Overreach' (2004) 20 *South African Journal on Human Rights* 544–76.

'Deterrence and capital punishment' (2007) 22 *SA Public Law* 385–404.

Lepsius, Oliver, 'Der Hüter der Verfassung – Demokratietheoretisch betrachtet', in Olivier Beaud and Pasquale Pasquino (eds.), *La controverse sur le "gardien de la constitution" et la justice constitutionnelle. Kelsen contre Schmitt* (Paris: Editions Panthéon-Assas, 2007), pp. 103–26.

'Nachhaltigkeit und Parlament', in Wolfgang Kahl (ed.), *Nachhaltigkeit als Verbundbegriff* (Tübingen: Mohr Siebeck, 2008), pp. 326–50.

'Anmerkung' (2009) 64 *Juristenzeitung* 260–3.

'Die maßstabsetzende Gewalt', in Matthias Jestaedt, Oliver Lepsius, Christoph Möllers and Christoph Schönberger (eds.), *Das entgrenzte Gericht: Eine kritische Bilanz nach sechzig Jahren Bundesverfassungsgericht* (Berlin: Suhrkamp, 2011), pp. 159–279.

'Kritik der Dogmatik', in Gregor Kirchhof, Stefan Magen and Karsten Schneider (eds.), *Was weiß Dogmatik?* (Tübingen: Mohr Siebeck, 2012), pp. 39–62.

'Die Chancen und Grenzen des Grundsatzes der Verhältnismäßigkeit', in Matthias Jestaedt and Oliver Lepsius (eds.), *Verhältnismäßigkeit: Zur Tragfähigkeit eines verfassungsrechtlichen Schlüsselkonzepts* (Tübingen: Mohr Siebeck, 2015), pp. 1–41.

Lerche, Peter, *Übermaß und Verfassungsrecht* (Köln: Carl Heymann, 1961).

Ley, Richard, 'Die Erstbesetzung des Bundesverfassungsgerichtes' (1982) 13 *Zeitschrift für Parlamentsfragen* 521–41.

Lhotta, Roland, 'Das Bundesverfassungsgericht als politischer Akteur: Plädoyer für eine neo-institutionalistische Ergänzung der Forschung' (2003) 9 *Swiss Political Science Review* 142–53.

Lindner, Franz Josef, *Theorie der Grundrechtsdogmatik* (Tübingen: Mohr Siebeck, 2005).

Lindquist, Stefanie A. and David E. Klein, 'The Influence of Jurisprudential Considerations on Supreme Court Decision Making: A Study of Conflict Cases' (2006) 40 *Law & Society Review* 135–61.

Link, Christoph, 'Stat Crux? – Die "Kruzifix"-Entscheidung des Bundesverfassungsgerichts' (1995) 48 *Neue Juristische Wochenschrift* 3353–7.

Lokan, Andrew, 'The Rise and Fall of Doctrine under Section 1 of the Charter' (1992) 24 *Ottawa Law Review* 163–92.

Lübbe-Wolff, Gertrude, 'The Principle of Proportionality in the Case-Law of the German Federal Constitutional Court' (2014) 34 *Human Rights Law Journal* 12–17.

MacCormick, Neil, *Legal Reasoning and Legal Theory* (Oxford: Oxford University Press, 1978).

Manfredi, Christopher P. and Antonia Maioni, 'Judicializing Health Policy: Unexpected Lessons and an Inconvenient Truth', in James B. Kelly and Christopher P. Manfredi (eds.), *Contested Constitutionalism – Reflections on the Canadian Charter of Rights and Freedoms* (Vancouver: UBC Press, 2009), pp. 129–44.

Marmor, Theodore R., 'Canada's Supreme Court and Its National Health Insurance Program: Evaluating the Landmark Chaoulli Decision from a Comparative Perspective' (2006) 44 *Osgoode Hall Law Journal* 311–25.

Mashaw, Jerry L., 'Constitutional Deregulation: Notes Toward a Public, Public Law' (1980) 54 *Tulane Law Review* 849–76.

Massing, Otwin, *Politik als Recht – Recht als Politik* (Baden-Baden: Nomos, 2005)

Mathews, Jud and Alec Stone Sweet, 'All Things in Proportion? American Rights Review and the Problem of Balancing' (2011) 60 *Emory Law Journal* 102–79.

Meister, Moritz, *Das System des Freiheitsschutzes im Grundgesetz* (Berlin: Duncker & Humblot, 2011).

Mendes, Errol P., 'The Crucible of the Charter: Judicial Principles v. Judicial Deference in the Context of Section 1' (2005) 27 *Supreme Court Law Review* 47–104.

Merten, Detlef, 'Der "Kruzifix-Beschluß" des Bundesverfassungsgerichts aus grundrechtsdogmatischer Sicht', in Joachim Burmeister (ed.), *Verfassungsstaatlichkeit – Festschrift für Klaus Stern zum 65. Geburtstag* (München: C. H. Beck, 1997), pp. 987–1009.

'Verhältnismäßigkeitsgrundsatz', in Detlef Merten and Hans-Jürgen Papier (eds.), *Handbuch der Grundrechte. Band III. Grundrechte in Deutschland: Allgemeine Lehren II* (Heidelberg: C. F. Müller, 2009), pp. 517–67.

Meßerschmidt, Klaus, *Gesetzgebungsermessen* (Berlin: Berlin Verlag, 2000).

'The Race to Rationality Review and the Score of the German Federal Constitutional Court' (2012) 6 *Legisprudence* 347–78.

Michael, Lothar, 'Folgerichtigkeit als Wettbewerbsgleichheit: Zur Verwerfung von Rauchverboten in Gaststätten durch das BVerfG' (2008) 63 *Juristenzeitung* 875–82.

Miller, Geoffrey P., 'Public Choice at the Dawn of the Special Interest State: The Story of Butter and Margarine' (1989) 77 *California Law Review* 83–131.

Möller, Kai, 'Proportionality: Challenging the critics' (2012) 10 *International Journal of Constitutional Law* 709–31.

The Global Model of Constitutional Rights (Oxford: Oxford University Press, 2012).

Möllers, Christoph, *Gewaltengliederung: Legitimation und Dogmatik im nationalen und internationalen Rechtsvergleich* (Tübingen: Mohr Siebeck, 2005).

'Legalität, Legitimität und Legitimation des Bundesverfassungsgerichts', in Matthias Jestaedt, Oliver Lepsius, Christoph Möllers and Christoph Schönberger (eds.), *Das entgrenzte Gericht: Eine kritische Bilanz nach sechzig Jahren Bundesverfassungsgericht* (Berlin: Suhrkamp, 2011), pp. 281–422.

Monahan, Patrick and Chanakya Sethi, 'Constitutional Cases 2010: An Overview' (2011) 54 *Supreme Court Law Review* 3–53.

Moreso, José Juan, 'Ways of Solving Conflicts of Constitutional Rights: Proportionalism and Specificationism' (2012) 25 *Ratio Juris* 31–46.

Morgenthaler, Gerd, 'Gleichheit und Rechtssystem: Widerspruchsfreiheit, Folgerichtigkeit', in Rudolf Mellinghoff and Ulrich Palm (eds.), *Gleichheit im Verfassungsstaat: Symposium aus Anlass des 65. Geburtstages von Paul Kirchhof* (Heidelberg: C. F. Müller, 2008), pp. 51–66.

Morlok, Martin, 'Parteienrecht als Wettbewerbsrecht', in Peter Häberle, Martin Morlok and Vassilios Skouris (eds.), *Festschrift für Dimitris Th. Tsatsos* (Baden-Baden: Nomos, 2003), pp. 408–47.

Motala, Ziyad and Cyril Ramaphosa, *Constitutional Law* (Oxford: Oxford University Press, 2002).

Muckel, Stefan, *Kriterien des verfassungsrechtlichen Vertrauensschutzes bei Gesetzesänderungen* (Berlin: Duncker & Humblot, 1989).

Müller-Volbehr, Jörg, 'Positive und negative Religionsfreiheit: Zum Kruzifix-Beschluß des BVerfG' (1995) 50 *Juristenzeitung* 996–1000.

Murphy, Walter F. and Joseph Tanenhaus, 'Publicity, Public Opinion, and the Court' (1990) 84 *Northwestern University Law Review* 985–1023.

Myerson, Roger B., in Steven M. Durlauf and Lawrence E. Blume (eds.), *The New Palgrave Dictionary of Economics, vol. V*, 2nd edn (Basingstoke: Palgrave Macmillan, 2008), pp. 533–42.

Nash, John Forbes, 'The Bargaining Problem' (1950) 18 *Econometrica* 155–62.

Olson, Mancur, *The Logic of Collective Action: Public Goods and the Theory of Groups* (Cambridge: Harvard University Press, 1965).

Ossenbühl, Fritz, 'Verfassungsgerichtsbarkeit und Fachgerichtsbarkeit: Gedanken zur Wahrung der Verfahrensgrundrechte', in Rolf Stödter and Werner Thieme (eds.), *Hamburg – Deutschland – Europa: Festschrift für Hans Peter Ipsen zum siebzigsten Geburtstag* (Tübingen: J. C. B. Mohr, 1977), pp. 129–41.

'Maßhalten mit dem Übermaßverbot', in Peter Badura and Rupert Scholz (eds.), *Wege und Verfahren des Verfassungslebens: Festschrift für Peter Lerche zum 65. Geburtstag* (München: C. H. Beck, 1993), pp. 151–64.

'Abwägung im Verfassungsrecht' (1995) 110 *Deutsches Verwaltungsblatt* 904–12.

Osterloh, Lerke, 'Folgerichtigkeit: Verfassungsgerichtliche Rationalitätsanforderungen in der Demokratie', in Michael Bäuerle, Philipp Dann and Astrid Wallrabenstein (eds.), *Demokratie-Perspektiven: Festschrift für Brun-Otto Bryde zum 70. Geburtstag* (Tübingen: Mohr Siebeck, 2013), pp. 429–42.

Pal, Michael, 'Breakdowns in the Democratic Process and the Law of Canadian Democracy' (2011) 57 *McGill Law Journal* 299–347.

Panaccio, Charles-Maxime, 'In Defence of Two-Step Balancing and Proportionality in Rights Adjudication' (2011) 24 *Canadian Journal of Law and Jurisprudence* 109–28.

Papier, Hans-Jürgen, 'Die Würde des Menschen ist unantastbar', in Rainer Grote *et al.* (eds.), *Die Ordnung der Freiheit: Festschrift für Christian Starck zum siebzigsten Geburtstag* (Tübingen: Mohr Siebeck, 2007), pp. 371–82.

Papier, Hans-Jürgen and Johannes Möller, 'Das Bestimmtheitsgebot und seine Durchsetzung' (1997) 122 *Archiv des öffentlichen Rechts* 177–211.

Payandeh, Mehrdad, 'Das Gebot der Folgerichtigkeit: Rationalitätsgewinn oder Irrweg der Grundrechtsdogmatik?' (2011) 136 *Archiv des öffentlichen Rechts* 578–615.

Perju, Vlad, 'Proportionality and Freedom: An essay on methods in constitutional law' (2012) 1 *Global Constitutionalism* 334–67.

Perry, Michael J., *Constitutional Rights, Moral Controversy, and the Supreme Court* (New York: Cambridge University Press, 2009).

Petersen, Niels, 'Auf dem Weg zur zweckrationalen Relativität des Menschenwürdeschutzes' (2004) 37 *Kritische Justiz* 316–26.

'The Democracy Concept of the European Union: Coherent Constitutional Principle or Prosaic Declaration of Intent?' (2005) 6 *German Law Journal* 1507–25.

'Avoiding the Common Wisdom Fallacy: The Role of Social Sciences in Constitutional Adjudication' (2013) 11 *International Journal of Constitutional Law* 294–318.

'Gesetzgeberische Inkonsistenz als Beweiszeichen: Eine rechtsvergleichende Analyse der Funktion von Konsistenzargumenten in der Rechtsprechung' (2013) 138 *Archiv des öffentlichen Rechts* 108–34.

'How to Compare the Length of Lines to the Weight of Stones: Balancing and the resolution of value conflicts in constitutional law' (2013) 14 *German Law Journal* 1387–408.

'Proportionality and the Incommensurability Challenge in the Jurisprudence of the South African Constitutional Court' (2014) 30 *South African Journal on Human Rights* 405–29.

'The German Constitutional Court and Legislative Capture' (2014) 12 *International Journal of Constitutional Law* 650–69.

'Verfassungsgerichte als Wettbewerbshüter des politischen Prozesses', in Dominik Elser *et al.* (eds.), *Das letzte Wort – Rechtsetzung und Rechtskontrolle in der Demokratie* (Baden-Baden: Nomos, 2014), pp. 59–78.

'Balancing and Judicial Self-Empowerment: A case study on the rise of balancing in the jurisprudence of the German Constitutional Court' (2015) 4 *Global Constitutionalism* 49–80.

Verhältnismäßigkeit als Rationalitätskontrolle: Eine rechtsempirische Studie verfassungsgerichtlicher Rechtsprechung zu den Freiheitsgrundrechten (Tübingen: Mohr Siebeck, 2015).

'Legislative Inconsistency and the "Smoking Out" of Illicit Motives' (2016) 64 *American Journal of Comparative Law* 501–25.

Pildes, Richard H., 'The Theory of Political Competition' (1999) 85 *Virginia Law Review* 1605–26.

'Is the Supreme Court a "Majoritarian" Institution?' (2010) 2010 *The Supreme Court Review* 103–58.

Pohl, Ottmar, 'Ist der Gesetzgeber bei Eingriffen in die Grundrechte an den Grundsatz der Verhältnismäßigkeit gebunden?', PhD thesis, University of Cologne (1959).

Popelier, Patricia, 'Preliminary Comments on the Role of Courts as Regulatory Watchdogs' (2012) 6 *Legisprudence* 257–70.

Porat, Iddo, 'Some Critical Thoughts on Proportionality', in Giorgio Bongiovanni, Giovanni Sartor and Chiara Valentini (eds.), *Reasonableness and Law* (Dordrecht: Springer, 2009), pp. 243–50.

Portuese, Aurelien, 'Principle of Proportionality as Principle of Economic Efficiency' (2013) 19 *European Law Journal* 612–35.

Poscher, Ralf, ' "Die Würde des Menschen ist unantastbar"' (2004) 59 *Juristenzeitung* 756–62.

'Menschenwürde und Kernbereichsschutz' (2009) 64 *Juristenzeitung* 269–77.

Pöße, Jörg, 'Der Einschätzungsspielraum des Gesetzgebers als Gegenstand verfassungsgerichtlicher Kontrollbeschränkung', in Martin Nolte (ed.), *Kontrolle im verfassten Rechtsstaat* (Kiel: Lorenz-von-Stein-Institut, 2002), pp. 33–46.

Prémont, Marie-Claude, 'L'affaire Chaoulli et le système de santé du Québec: cherchez l'erreur, cherchez la raison' (2006) 51 *McGill Law Journal* 167–95.

Priest, George L. and Benjamin Klein, 'The Selection of Disputes for Litigation' (1984) 13 *Journal of Legal Studies* 1–55.

Przeworski, Adam, 'Minimalist conception of democracy: a defense', in Ian Shapiro and Casiano Hacker-Cordón (eds.), *Democracy's Value* (Cambridge: Cambridge University Press, 1999), pp. 23–55.

Putnam, Tonya L., 'Courts without Borders: Domestic Sources of U.S. Extraterritoriality in the Regulatory Sphere' (2009) 63 *International Organization* 459–90.

Raue, Frank, 'Müssen Grundrechtsbeschränkungen wirklich verhältnismäßig sein?' (2006) 131 *Archiv des öffentlichen Rechts* 79–116.

Rawls, John, *A Theory of Justice* (Oxford: Oxford University Press, 1999)

Regan, Donald H., 'Authority and Value: Reflection on Raz's Morality of Freedom' (1989) 62 *Southern Californian Law Review* 995–1095.

Rehnquist, William H., 'The Notion of a Living Constitution' (1976) 54 *Texas Law Review* 693–706.

Reimer, Philipp, 'Verhältnismäßigkeit im Verfassungsrecht, ein heterogenes Konzept', in Matthias Jestaedt and Oliver Lepsius (eds.), *Verhältnismäßigkeit: Zur Tragfähigkeit eines verfassungsrechtlichen Schlüsselkonzepts* (Tübingen: Mohr Siebeck, 2015), pp. 60–76.

Rennert, Dominik, 'Die verdrängte Werttheorie und ihre Historisierung' (2014) 53 *Der Staat* 31–59.

Richards, Mark J. and Herbert M. Kritzer, 'Jurisprudential Regimes in Supreme Court Decision Making' (2002) 96 *American Political Science Review* 305–20.

Rivers, Julian, 'Proportionality and Variable Intensity of Review' (2006) 65 *Cambridge Law Journal* 174–207.

'Constitutional Rights and Statutory Limitations', in Matthias Klatt (ed.), *Institutionalized Reason: The Jurisprudence of Robert Alexy* (Oxford: Oxford University Press, 2012), pp. 248–71.

Roach, Kent, *The Supreme Court on Trial: Judicial Activism or Democratic Dialogue* (Toronto: Irwin Law, 2001).

Robertson, David, *The Judge as Political Theorist: Contemporary Constitutional Review* (Princeton: Princeton University Press, 2010).

Roederer, Christopher J., 'Judicious Engagement: Theory, Attitude and Community' (1999) 15 *South African Journal on Human Rights* 486–506.

Rogers, James R., 'Information and Judicial Review: A Signaling Game of Legislative-Judicial Interaction' (2001) 45 *American Journal of Political Science* 84–99.

Rose-Ackerman, Susan, Stefanie Egidy and James Fowkes, *Due Process of Lawmaking: The United States, South Africa, Germany, and the European Union* (New York: Cambridge University Press, 2015).

Roux, Theunis, 'Principle and Pragmatism on the Constitutional Court of South Africa' (2009) 7 *International Journal of Constitutional Law* 106–38.

The Politics of Principle: The First South African Constitutional Court, 1995–2005 (Cambridge: Cambridge University Press, 2013).

Rusteberg, Benjamin, *Der grundrechtliche Gewährleistungsgehalt* (Tübingen: Mohr Siebeck, 2009).

Rüthers, Bernd, *Die unbegrenzte Auslegung: Zum Wandel der Privatrechtsordnung im Nationalsozialismus* (Tübingen: Mohr Siebeck, 1968).

Sadurski, Wojciech, *Rights before Courts: A Study of Constitutional Courts in Postcommunist States of Central and Eastern Europe* (Dordrecht: Springer, 2005).

'Reasonableness and Value Pluralism in Law and Politics', in Giorgio Bongiovanni, Giovanni Sartor and Chiara Valentini (eds.), *Reasonableness and Law* (Dordrecht: Springer, 2009), pp. 129–46.

Sales, Philip, 'Rationality, Proportionality and the Development of the Law' (2013) 129 *Law Quarterly Review* 223–41.

Sartor, Giovanni, 'The Logic of Proportionality: Reasoning with Non-Numerical Magnitudes' (2013) 14 *German Law Journal* 1419–56.

Sartori, Giovanni, *The Theory of Democracy Revisited. Part I: The Contemporary Debate* (Chatham: Chatham House, 1987).

Saurer, Johannes, 'Die Globalisierung des Verhältnismäßigkeitsgrundsatzes' (2012) 51 *Der Staat* 3–33.

Scalia, Antonin, 'Originalism: The Lesser Evil' (1989) 57 *University of Cincinnati Law Review* 849–65.

Scanlon, T. M., 'Adjusting Rights and Balancing Values' (2004) 72 *Fordham Law Review* 1477–86.

Schaal, Gary S., 'Crisis! What Crisis? Der "Kruzifix-Beschluss" und seine Folgen', in Robert Christian van Ooyen and Martin H.W. Möllers (eds.), *Das Bundesverfassungsgericht im politischen System* (Wiesbaden: VS Verlag für Sozialwissenschaften, 2006), pp. 175–86.

Schachtschneider, Karl Albrecht, 'Das Vertrauensschutzprinzip im Verfassungs- und Verwaltungsrecht', in Max-Emanuel Geis and Dieter C. Umbach (eds.), *Planung – Steuerung – Kontrolle: Festschrift für Richard Bartlsperger zum 70. Geburtstag* (Berlin: Duncker & Humblot, 2006), pp. 133–47.

Schäfer, Hans-Bernd and Claus Ott, *Lehrbuch der ökonomischen Analyse des Zivilrechts,* 5th edn (Berlin: Springer Gabler, 2012).

Scharpf, Fritz W., *Governing in Europe: Effective and Democratic?* (Oxford: Oxford University Press, 1999).

Schauer, Frederick, 'A Comment on the Structure of Rights' (1993) 27 *Georgia Law Review* 415–34.

Playing by the Rules: A Philosophical Examination of Rule Based Decision-Making in Law and Life (Oxford: Clarendon Press, 1993).

'Freedom of Expression Adjudication in Europe and the United States: A Case Study in Comparative Constitutional Architecture', in Georg Nolte (ed.), *European and US Constitutionalism* (Cambridge: Cambridge University Press, 2005), pp. 49–69.

'Balancing, Subsumption, and the Constraining Role of Legal Text', in Matthias Klatt (ed.), *Institutionalized Reason: The Jurisprudence of Robert Alexy* (Oxford: Oxford University Press, 2012), pp. 307–16.

'Proportionality and the Question of Weight', in Grant Huscroft, Bradley W. Miller and Grégoire Webber (eds.), *Proportionality and the Rule of Law: Rights, Justification, Reasoning* (New York: Cambridge University Press, 2014), pp. 173–85.

Schiedermair, Hartmut, 'Das Bundesverfassungsgericht auf der Grenze zwischen Recht und Politik', in Michael Brenner, Peter Michael Huber and Markus Möstl (eds.), *Der Staat des Grundgesetzes – Kontinuität und Wandel: Festschrift für Peter Badura zum siebzigsten Geburtstag* (Tübingen: Mohr Siebeck, 2004), pp. 477–89.

Schlink, Bernhard, *Abwägung im Verfassungsrecht* (Berlin: Duncker & Humblot, 1976).

'Der Grundsatz der Verhältnismäßigkeit', in Peter Badura and Horst Dreier (eds.), *Festschrift 50 Jahre Bundesverfassungsgericht. Zweiter Band: Klärung und Fortbildung des Verfassungsrechts* (Tübingen: Mohr Siebeck, 2001), pp. 445–65.

'Proportionality in Constitutional Law: Why Everywhere But Here?' (2012) 22 *Duke Journal of Comparative and International Law* 291–302.

Schmalz-Bruns, Rainer, *Reflexive Demokratie: Die demokratische Transformation moderner Politik* (Baden-Baden: Nomos, 1995).

Schmidt-Aßmann, Eberhard, 'Der Rechtsstaat', in Josef Isensee and Paul Kirchhof (eds.), *Handbuch des Staatsrechts der Bundesrepublik Deutschland. Band II: Verfassungsstaat*, 3rd edn (Heidelberg: C. F. Müller, 2004), pp. 541–612.

Schmitter, Philippe C. and Terry Lynn Karl, 'What Democracy Is . . . and Is Not' (1991) 2.3 *Journal of Democracy* 75–88.

Scholler, Heinrich, 'Der Grundsatz der Verhältnismäßigkeit im deutschen Verfassungs- und Verwaltungsrecht', in Nikolaos Alivizatos *et al.* (eds.), *Essays in Honour of Georgios I. Kassimatis* (Athens: Ant. N. Sakkoulas Publishers, 2004), pp. 307–21.

Schönberger, Christoph, 'Anmerkungen zu Karlsruhe', in Matthias Jestaedt, Oliver Lepsius, Christoph Möllers and Christoph Schönberger (eds.), *Das entgrenzte Gericht: Eine kritische Bilanz nach sechzig Jahren Bundesverfassungsgericht* (Berlin: Suhrkamp, 2011), pp. 9–76.

Schulze-Fielitz, Helmuth, 'Das Bundesverfassungsgericht in der Krise des Zeitgeists: Zur Metadogmatik der Verfassungsinterpretation' (1997) 122 *Archiv des öffentlichen Rechts* 1–31.

'Das Bundesverfassungsgericht und die öffentliche Meinung', in Gunnar Folke Schuppert and Christian Bumke (eds.), *Bundesverfassungsgericht und gesellschaftlicher Grundkonsens* (Baden-Baden: Nomos, 2000), pp. 111–44.

'Wirkung und Befolgung verfassungsgerichtlicher Entscheidungen', in Peter Badura and Horst Dreier (eds.), *Festschrift 50 Jahre Bundesverfassungsgericht. Erster Band: Verfassungsgerichtsbarkeit, Verfassungsprozeß* (Tübingen: Mohr Siebeck, 2001), pp. 385–420.

Schumpeter, Joseph Alois, *Capitalism, Socialism and Democracy* (Abingdon: Routledge, 2010).

Schwabe, Jürgen, *Probleme der Grundrechtsdogmatik* (Darmstadt 1977).

Schyff, Gerhard van der, *Limitation of Rights: A Study of the European Convention and the South African Bill of Rights* (Nijmegen: Wolf Legal Publishers, 2005)

Segal, Jeffrey A. and Albert D. Cover, 'Ideological Values and the Votes of U.S. Supreme Court Justices' (1989) 83 *American Political Science Review* 557–65.

Segal, Jeffrey A., Lee Epstein, Charles M. Cameron and Harold J. Spaeth, 'Ideological Values and the Votes of U.S. Supreme Court Justices Revisited' (1995) 57 *Journal of Politics* 812–23.

Segal, Jeffrey A. and Harold J. Spaeth, *The Supreme Court and the Attitudinal Model Revisited* (New York: Cambridge University Press, 2002).

Sen, Amartya, *The Idea of Justice* (Cambridge: Harvard University Press, 2009).

Shapiro, Ian, *The State of Democratic Theory* (Princeton: Princeton University Press, 2006).

Shapiro, Martin, *Courts: A comparative and political analysis* (Chicago: University of Chicago Press, 1981).

'The Success of Judicial Review and Democracy', in Martin Shapiro and Alec Stone Sweet (eds.), *On Law, Politics, and Judicialization* (Oxford: Oxford University Press, 2002), pp. 149–83.

Shikano, Susumu and Verena Mack, 'Judges' behaviour and relationship with political parties in a non-common-law country: The Case of the German Federal Constitutional Court', Working Paper, University of Konstanz (2014).

Shinar, Adam, 'Method and Culture in American Constitutional Law: A Critique of *Proportionality and Constitutional Culture*' (2014) 10 *Israel Review of Legal Studies* 137–58.

Sieberer, Ulrich, 'Strategische Zurückhaltung von Verfassungsgerichten: Gewalt enteilungsvorstellungen und die Grenzen der Justizialisierung' (2006) 16 *Zeitschrift für Politikwissenschaft* 1299–323.

Sieckmann, Jan-Reinard, *Regelmodelle und Prinzipienmodelle des Rechtssystems* (Baden-Baden: Nomos, 1990).

'Autonome Abwägung' (2004) 90 *Archiv für Rechts- und Sozialphilosophie* 66–85.

Siegel, Stephen A., 'The Origin of the Compelling State Interest Test and Strict Scrutiny' (2006) 48 *American Journal of Legal History* 355–407.

Smith, Jean Edward, *John Marshall: Definer of a Nation* (New York: Henry Holt, 1996).

Sobota, Katharina, *Das Prinzip Rechtsstaat* (Tübingen: Mohr Siebeck, 1997).

Spiecker gen. Döhmann, Indra, *Staatliche Entscheidungen unter Unsicherheit* (Tübingen: Mohr Siebeck, forthcoming).

Spitz, Richard and Matthew Chaskalson, *The Politics of Transition: A Hidden History of South Africa's Negotiated Settlement* (Oxford: Hart, 2000).

Starck, Christian, 'Staatliche Organisation und staatliche Finanzierung als Hilfen zu Grundrechtsverwirklichungen?', in Christian Starck (ed.), *Bundesverfassungsgericht und Grundgesetz: Festgabe aus Anlaß des 25jährigen Bestehens des Bundesverfassungsgerichts. Zweiter Band: Verfassungsauslegung* (Tübingen: J. C. B. Mohr, 1976), pp. 480–526.

Steinsdorff, Silvia von, 'Verfassungsgerichte als Demokratie-Versicherung? Ursachen und Grenzen der wachsenden Bedeutung juristischer Politikkontrolle', in Klemens H. Schrenk and Markus Soldner (eds.), *Analyse demokratischer Regierungssysteme: Festschrift für Wolfgang Ismayr zum 65. Geburtstag* (Wiesbaden: VS Verlag für Sozialwissenschaften, 2010), pp. 479–98.

Stern, Klaus, 'Zur Entstehung und Ableitung des Übermaßverbots', in Peter Badura and Rupert Scholz (eds.), *Wege und Verfahren des Verfassungslebens* (München: C. H. Beck, 1993), pp. 165–75.

Verfassungsgerichtsbarkeit und Gesetzgeber (Opladen: Westdeutscher Verlag, 1997).

Stolleis, Michael, 'Parteienstaatlichkeit: Krisensymptome des demokratischen Verfassungsstaats' (1986) 44 *Veröffentlichungen der Vereinigung der Deutschen Staatsrechtslehrer* 7–45.

'Überkreuz: Anmerkungen zum Kruzifix-Beschluß (BVerfGE 93, 1–37) und seiner Rezeption' (2000) 83 *Kritische Vierteljahresschrift für Gesetzgebung und Rechtswissenschaft* 376–87.

Geschichte des öffentlichen Rechts in Deutschland. Vierter Band: Staats- und Verwaltungsrechtswissenschaft in West und Ost 1945–1990 (München: C. H. Beck, 2012).

Stone Sweet, Alec, *Governing with Judges: Constitutional Politics in Europe* (Oxford: Oxford University Press, 2000).

Stone Sweet, Alec and Jud Mathews, 'Proportionality Balancing and Global Constitutionalism' (2008) 47 *Columbia Journal of Transnational Law* 73–165.

Stratman, Thomas, 'What Do Campaign Contributions Buy? Deciphering Causal Effects of Money and Votes' (1991) 57 *Southern Economic Journal* 606–20.

Sullivan, E. Thomas and Richard S. Frase, *Proportionality Principles in American Law: Controlling Excessive Government Actions* (New York: Oxford University Press, 2009).

Sullivan, Kathleen M., 'Post-Liberal Judging: The Roles of Categorization and Balancing' (1992) 63 *University of Colorado Law Review* 293–317.

Sunstein, Cass R., 'Public Values, Private Interests, and the Equal Protection Clause' (1982) 1982 *The Supreme Court Review* 127–66.

'Naked Preferences and the Constitution' (1984) 84 *Columbia Law Review* 1689–732.

'Interest Groups in American Public Law' (1985) 38 *Stanford Law Review* 29–87.

'Incommensurability and Valuation in Law' (1994) 92 *Michigan Law Review* 779–861.

'Incommensurability and Kinds of Valuation: Some Applications in Law', in Ruth Chang (ed.), *Incommensurability, Incomparability, and Practical Reason* (Cambridge: Harvard University Press, 1997), pp. 234–54.

Designing Democracy: What Constitutions Do (Oxford: Oxford University Press, 2001).

Susnjar, Davor, *Proportionality, Fundamental Rights, and Balance of Powers* (Leiden: Martinus Nijhoff, 2010).

Sweeney, JoAnne, 'Creating a More Dangerous Branch: How the United Kingdom's Human Rights Act has Empowered the Judiciary and Changed the Way the British Government Creates Law' (2013) 21 *Michigan State International Law Review* 301–35.

Teifke, Nils, *Das Prinzip Menschenwürde: Zur Abwägungsfähigkeit des Höchstrangigen* (Tübingen: Mohr Siebeck, 2011).

Tiedemann, Paul, 'Vom inflationären Gebrauch der Menschenwürde in der Rechtsprechung des Bundesverfassungsgerichts' (2009) 62 *Die Öffentliche Verwaltung* 606–15.

Tocqueville, Alexis de, *De la démocratie en Amérique* (Paris: Pagnerre, 1835).

Towfigh, Emanuel, 'Komplexität und Normenklarheit – oder: Gesetze sind für Juristen gemacht' (2009) 48 *Der Staat* 29–73.

'Demokratische Repräsentation im Parteienstaat', in Ulrich Jan Schröder and Antje von Ungern-Sternberg (eds.), *Aktualität der Weimarer Staatsrechtslehre* (Tübingen: Mohr Siebeck, 2011), pp. 211–34.

Das Parteien-Paradox: Ein Beitrag zur Bestimmung des Verhältnisses von Demokratie und Parteiem (Tübingen: Mohr Siebeck, 2015).

'The economic paradigm', in Emanuel Towfigh and Niels Petersen (eds.), *Economic Methods for Lawyers* (Cheltenham: Edward Elgar, 2015), pp. 18–31.

Towfigh, Emanuel and Niels Petersen, 'Public and social choice theory', in Emanuel Towfigh and Niels Petersen (eds.), *Economic Methods for Lawyers* (Cheltenham: Edward Elgar, 2015), pp. 121–45.

Trakman, Leon E., William Cole-Hamilton and Sean Gatien, 'R. v. Oakes 1986–1997: Back to the Drawing Board' (1998) 36 *Osgoode Hall Law Journal* 83–149.

Tremblay McCaig, Geneviève, 'L'affaire Chaoulli c. Procureur général du Québec: appartient-il aux tribunaux de remettre en question les objectifs politiques qui modèlent le système de santé?' (2007) 41 *Revue juridique Thémis* 157–204.

Tsakyrakis, Stavros, 'Proportionality: An assault on human rights?' (2009) 7 *International Journal of Constitutional Law* 468–93.

Tschentscher, Axel, *Prozedurale Theorien der Gerechtigkeit* (Baden-Baden: Nomos, 2000).

Tushnet, Mark, *Taking the Constitution Away from the Courts* (Princeton: Princeton University Press, 1999).

Weak Courts, Strong Rights: Judicial Review and Social Welfare Rights in Comparative Constitutional Law (Princeton: Princeton University Press, 2008).

Uerpmann, Robert, *Das öffentliche Interesse: Seine Bedeutung als Tatbestandsmerkmal und als dogmatischer Begriff* (Tübingen: Mohr Siebeck, 1999).

Urbina, Francisco J., 'Is it Really That Easy? A Critique of Proportionality and 'Balancing as Reasoning'' (2014) 27 *Canadian Journal of Law and Jurisprudence* 167–92.

'Incommensurability and Balancing' (2015) 35 *Oxford Journal of Legal Studies* 575–605.

Vanberg, Georg, *The Politics of Constitutional Review in Germany* (Cambridge: Cambridge University Press, 2005).

'Verfassungsgerichtsbarkeit und Gesetzgebung: Zum politischen Spielraum des Bundesverfassungsgerichts', in Steffen Ganghof and Philip Manow (eds.), *Mechanismen der Politik – Strategische Interaktion im deutschen Regierungssystem* (Frankfurt a.M.: Campus Verlag, 2005), pp. 183–213.

'The Will of the People: A Comparative Perspective on Friedman' (2010) 2010 *Michigan State Law Review* 717–28.

'Constitutional Courts in Comparative Perspective: A Theoretical Assessment' (2015) 2015.18 *Annual Review of Law and Social Science* 167–85.

Veel, Paul-Erik N., 'Incommensurability, Proportionality, and Rational Legal Decision-Making' (2010) 4 *Law & Ethics of Human Rights* 177–228.

Vermeule, Adrian, *The Constitution of Risk* (New York: Cambridge University Press, 2014).

Vesting, Thomas, 'Gegenstandsadäquate Rechtsgewinnungstheorie – eine Alternative zum Abwägungspragmatismus des bundesdeutschen Verfassungsrechts?' (2002) 41 *Der Staat* 73–90.

Vorländer, Hans, 'Deutungsmacht – Die Macht der Verfassungsgerichtsbarkeit', in Hans Vorländer (ed.), *Die Deutungsmacht der Verfassungsgerichtsbarkeit* (Wiesbaden: VS Verlag für Sozialwissenschaften, 2006), pp. 9–33.

'Die Deutungsmacht des Bundesverfassungsgerichts', in Robert Christian van Ooyen and Martin H.W. Möllers (eds.), *Das Bundesverfassungsgericht im politischen System* (Wiesbaden: VS Verlag für Sozialwissenschaften, 2006), pp. 189–99.

Vos, Pierre de and Warren Freedman, *South African Constitutional Law in Context* (Cape Town: Oxford University Press, 2014)

Wahl, Rainer, 'Lüth und die Folgen: Ein Urteil als Weichenstellung für die Rechtsentwicklung', in Thomas Henne and Arne Riedlinger (eds.), *Das Lüth-Urteil aus (rechts-)historischer Sicht* (Berlin: Berliner Wissenschafts-Verlag, 2005), pp. 371–97.

Waldron, Jeremy, 'A Right-Based Critique of Constitutional Rights' (1993) 13 *Oxford Journal of Legal Studies* 18–51.

Law and Disagreement (New York: Oxford University Press, 1999).

'The Core of the Case Against Judicial Review' (2006) 115 *Yale Law Journal* 1346–406.

Webb, Hoyt, 'The Constitutional Court of South Africa: Rights Interpretation and Comparative Constitutional Law' (1998) 1 *University of Pennsylvania Journal of Constitutional Law* 205–83.

Webber, Grégoire C. N., *The Negotiable Constitution* (Cambridge: Cambridge University Press, 2009).

'Proportionality, Balancing, and the Cult of Constitutional Rights Scholarship' (2010) 23 *Canadian Journal of Law and Jurisprudence* 179–202.

Weiler, Joseph H.H., *The Constitution of Europe* (Cambridge: Cambridge University Press, 1999).

'Epilogue: Towards a Common Law of International Trade', in Joseph H.H. Weiler (ed.), *The EU, the WTO, and the NAFTA: Towards a Common Law of International Trade?* (Oxford: Oxford University Press, 2000), pp. 201–32.

Weinrib, Lorraine Eisenstat, 'Canada's Charter of Rights: Paradigm Lost?' (2002) 6 *Review of Constitutional Studies* 119–78.

Weinrib, Sara, 'The Emergence of the Third Step of the Oakes Test in Alberta v. Hutterian Brethren of Wilson Colony' (2010) 68 *University of Toronto Faculty of Law Review* 77–97.

Wendt, Rudolf, 'Der Garantiegehalt der Grundrechte und das Übermaßverbot' (1979) 104 *Archiv des öffentlichen Rechts* 414–74.

Winkler, Adam, 'Fatal in Theory and Strict in Fact: An Empirical Analysis of Strict Scrutiny in the Federal Courts' (2006) 59 *Vanderbilt Law Review* 793–871.

Wittig, Peter, 'Zum Standort des Verhältnismäßigkeitsgrundsatzes im System des Grundgesetzes' (1968) 21 *Die Öffentliche Verwaltung* 817–25.

Wolfrum, Rüdiger and Volker Röben, *Legitimacy in International Law* (Berlin: Springer, 2008).

Woolman, Stuart, 'Out of Order? Out of Balance? The Limitation Clause of the Final Constitution' (1997) 13 *South African Journal on Human Rights* 102–34.

Woolman, Stuart and Henk Botha, 'Limitations', in Stuart Woolman, Michael Bishop and Jason Brickhill (eds.), *Constitutional Law of South Africa*, 2nd edn (Cape Town: Juta, 2006), ch. 34.

'Limitations: Shared Constitutional Interpretation, an Appropriate Normative Framework & Hard Choices', in Stu Woolman and Michael Bishop (eds.),

Constitutional Conversations (Pretoria: Pretoria University Law Press, 2008), pp. 149–86.

Young, Alison L., 'Proportionality is Dead: Long Live Proportionality!', in Grant Huscroft, Bradley W. Miller and Grégoire Webber (eds.), *Proportionality and the Rule of Law: Rights, Justification, Reasoning* (New York: Cambridge University Press, 2014), pp. 43–66.

Zimmer, Karl-Otto, 'Nochmals: Zur verfassungsnäheren Gestaltung der 5-%-Klausel' (1985) 38 *Die Öffentliche Verwaltung* 101–2

Zweigert, Konrad and Hein Kötz, *An Introduction to Comparative Law*, 3rd edn (Oxford: Oxford University Press, 1998).

INDEX